B
528
.L334
2012

$25⁰⁰

STOIC PRAGMATISM

D1127719

WITHDRAWN

LIBRARY
ELIZABETHTOWN COMMUNITY
& TECHNICAL COLLEGE
600 COLLEGE STREET RD
ELIZABETHTOWN, KY 42701

AMERICAN PHILOSOPHY

John J. Stuhr, *editor*

Editorial Board

Susan Bordo

Vincent Colapietro

John Lachs

Noëlle McAfee

José Medina

Cheyney Ryan

Richard Shusterman

LIBRARY
ELIZABETHTOWN COMMUNITY
& TECHNICAL COLLEGE
600 COLLEGE STREET RD
ELIZABETHTOWN, KY 42701

STOIC PRAGMATISM
JOHN LACHS

Indiana University Press
Bloomington and Indianapolis

This book is a publication of

Indiana University Press
601 North Morton Street
Bloomington, Indiana 47404-3797 USA

iupress.indiana.edu

Telephone orders   800-842-6796
Fax orders   812-855-7931

© 2012 by John Lachs

All rights reserved

No part of this book may be reproduced or utilized in any form or by any means, electronic or mechanical, including photocopying and recording, or by any information storage and retrieval system, without permission in writing from the publisher. The Association of American University Presses' Resolution on Permissions constitutes the only exception to this prohibition.

☉ The paper used in this publication meets the minimum requirements of the American National Standard for Information Sciences— Permanence of Paper for Printed Library Materials, ANSI Z39.48–1992.

Manufactured in the United States of America

Library of Congress Cataloging-in-Publication Data

Lachs, John.
    Stoic pragmatism / John Lachs.
        p. cm. — (American philosophy)
    ISBN 978-0-253-35718-2 (cloth : alk. paper) —
ISBN 978-0-253-22376-0 (pbk. : alk. paper) —
ISBN 978-0-253-00721-6 (electronic book) 1. Stoics.
2. Ethics. I. Title.
    B528.L334 2012
    171'.2—dc23

                            2011048732

1 2 3 4 5   17 16 15 14 13 12

CONTENTS

STOIC PRAGMATISM

INTRODUCTION

Age clarifies. In the course of a life of reflection, one's attitude to the weightiest questions emerges only slowly. Given the demands of the academic world, professional philosophers are likely to start their careers writing about technical problems. The dialectic and the swirl of footnotes this requires obstruct self-discovery, so that they may think of the positions they take as capturing their deepest beliefs. That this is not so comes into view only late in life or not at all. If it does, it takes the form of writing something that one suddenly recognizes as expressing an idea one has always thought.

There is no easy answer to why self-knowledge eludes us for so long. Perhaps we need the varied experiences of life to determine where we stand. We may have to turn from the problems of philosophy to the issues that confront us in daily life. Possibly we need to live awhile with our favorite ideas to realize that they really do not matter. Whatever the reason for slow development, the arrival of self-recognition warrants celebration.

This book had its origin in such quiet personal joy. I take delight in thinking that I have now discovered my beliefs about some of the deepest problems, beliefs I think I have acted upon all my life. In my writing, I have come closer and closer to expressing these ideas, but I have not formulated them explicitly until a few years ago.

Concerns about materialist theories of mind occasioned me to start my career studying German idealists and defending epiphenomenalism. Work on mediation uncovered my devotion to the significance of individuals and the wholesome effects of immediacy. My exploration of human natures called attention to socially harmless but personally vivifying variety among us and the consequent need for toleration. It was, however, only recently that I managed to characterize my attitude to life as that of a stoic pragmatist. Once I did, it was easy to find traces of the position in earlier writings and in my decisions at crucial points in life.

Stoic pragmatists are committed to making life better until their powers are overwhelmed. When circumstances render aggressive affirmation no longer possible, however, they surrender to the inevitable gracefully and without complaint. As pragmatists, they insist on the centrality of intelligence in the conduct of life, but they extend the reach of good sense to the acknowledgment of failure or futility. Intelligence must guide not only our efforts, but also our surrenders both in daily endeavors and in decisions about the end of life.

The great question we face again and again is how long to pursue our goals with all our energy and when to pack it in. This is a matter of practical wisdom, and therefore it is easy to get it wrong. We may give up just at the stage where perseverance begins to reap results, or we may keep trying in the teeth of overwhelming odds. Cancer patients requiring painful treatment must make such decisions under adverse conditions, but even under the best circumstances we must often choose without adequate information. Consequently, we tend to follow our cognitive habits: pragmatists are unlikely ever to give up, while stoics may acquiesce too soon. If each belief-tendency modifies the other, we may enjoy more graceful and satisfactory lives.

Embrace of stoic pragmatism explains my acknowledgment of the significance of human finitude. There is nothing infinite about us, except perhaps our pretensions. Those who would assign us unending moral duties, striving, or desires are romantics of the ilk of Faust, maintaining that for humans nothing is enough and good enough. I feel sorry that they have not had any of the thoroughly satisfying experiences of life and that they cannot take pleasure in their nature and in the celebration of its limits. Stoic pragmatism does not keep us from aspiring; on the contrary, it invites us to live long and well. It also reminds us, however, of the great lesson of Ozymandias and of sound religion that even our greatest achievements return to dust.

The stoic side of my view explains also my conviction that many things riling people greatly really do not matter at all. This is the foundation of my desire to leave people alone to conduct their lives as they see fit, that is, of my respect for autonomy and also of the tolerant attitude I take to the harmless varieties of human nature. The pragmatist side of the position leads me to appreciate ordinary experience, immediacy, and the qualitative element in life. Santayana was my first love in philosophy, and there is no doubt that his attitude of distant assessment was that of a stoic. But he never allowed himself to become a part of the exertions of a community, and so he never felt the pull and charm, the full satisfaction of pragmatism. James and Dewey, on the other hand, saw only the surrender of stoicism and not its grace.

Stoic pragmatism would be of little interest to me if it were only a theory. I mean for it to guide practices and express attitudes that shape life and that can meet the pragmatic test of making it better.

CHAPTER 1

WHAT CAN PHILOSOPHY DO TO MAKE LIFE BETTER?

Philosophy: A Primer

Aristotle was right when he said that philosophy begins in wonder. To primitive cave dwellers, everything was in need of explanation and humans had very little of life in their control. The world must have seemed a magical and frightening place, full of mysteries and surprises. Reflection was an intermittent response wrung from the soul by circumstances; neither systematic nor persistent, it amounted to little more than puzzlement about the workings of the world.

Sustained inquiry tends to yield results, sometimes even a practical advantage. Thales, the first philosopher in the West, is reputed to have learned so much about weather and growing cycles that he managed to corner the olive market in Greece. Such coincidences of knowledge and practicality have been relatively rare in the history of thought, and Thales himself showed the other side of philosophy by clumsily falling into a well and drowning in the act of speculation.

Thales thought that in the last analysis everything is made of water. The Ionian philosophers who followed him continued to look for one or a few principles that would explain the movement of everything. In line with the tendency of philosophers, they exhausted or nearly exhausted the available alternatives. Some thought the hot, the cold, the wet, and the dry constituted adequate principles of explanation. Others gave pride of place to love and strife, to fire, or to an elemental continuum called "the boundless." Heraclitus maintained that everything changes; Parmenides was certain nothing does. Again, as is frequently the case in philosophy, there was overgeneralization without the benefit of a procedure for selecting the best of a multitude of theories.

Plato

Plato's Socrates found mechanical explanations, that is, explanations by reference to the automatic operations of nature, inadequate. He called attention to the significance of purposes, and through them of knowledge and mind, for understanding what happens in the world. Plato was the first great systematic thinker of the West. His influence on subsequent generations has been so great that Alfred North Whitehead, an important twentieth-century philosopher, averred that all of philosophy may well be a series of footnotes to Plato.

Through the work of Plato, philosophy acquired a primary interest in human affairs. The earlier Ionian thinkers focused their reflections on the operations of nature; Plato, by contrast, viewed nature as but the backdrop to the drama of life in society. He attempted to develop a precise notion of justice and other virtues, drew a sharp distinction between knowledge and mere belief, and spent great effort at describing the political order that best promotes human flourishing. Most important, perhaps, Plato directed the attention of philosophers to the initially useful but ultimately futile search for the essence or inner nature of things.

Plato's so-called theory of forms amounts to the idea that everything has a nature that it shares with other beings of the same kind. Some form or structure makes humans humans and rats rats, and this is displayed by every member of the species and no one or nothing besides. Plato depicts the search for essences as difficult and not always successful; in spite of his extraordinary dialectical skills, Socrates is shown in the dialogue *Euthyphro* unable to develop a precise definition of piety. Once the search succeeds, however, grasp of the form or species-essence provides amazing benefits. It enables us to understand the nature of things and, because nature grounds perfection, also to judge their performance.

Nature is normative in that it sets the standard to which all beings of the same kind are to approximate. Nevertheless, nothing quite lives up to its ideal; no human is totally wise, brave, self-controlled, and just. So instead of being perfect, we seek perfection through our actions. What Plato calls "eros," or love of the good, motivates us to reach for the higher, for what would truly fulfill us. What is good, Plato argues, is also true and beautiful, though ultimately it is the form of the good alone that gives intelligible structure to the world.

Plato spent considerable effort describing and defending his notion of the ideal community. The small state he has in mind is based on knowledge of the good and is, accordingly, ruled by wise men or philosopher-kings. In such a community, careful education and strategic lies assure compliance with the laws. Division of labor makes it possible for everyone to gain satisfaction by developing their special talents. Artists and other potential troublemakers are banned and everyone can flourish under the benevolent gaze of unselfish rulers. To Plato's credit, he had the courage to try to convert his ideas into reality. When the tyrant of Syracuse invited him to serve as his advisor, he eagerly accepted and traveled to Sicily. As one could have predicted, things did not work out and his employer sold Plato into slavery.

Knowledge of the Eternal

The grand system of ideas Plato developed set the tone, the terms, and the method of one major form of philosophy. This type of thought presents philosophical reflection as a source of superior knowledge we cannot gain by ordinary experience. It sees the world as fostering perfection and professes to reveal realities inaccessible without its services. Philosophy of this type often allies itself with religion and offers proofs of the existence of God, the unreality of time, and the purposes of the universe. In this mood, philosophy claims to be the ultimate science, giving its practitioners certain knowledge of the eternal.

In the case of Plato, as in many other cases in philosophy, it didn't take long for someone holding radically different views to emerge. Aristotle, Plato's student, rejected many of his teacher's opinions in the process of inventing such concepts as potentiality and actuality and thereby establishing what we now consider the worldview of common sense. In his great *Nicomachean Ethics*—meant as instruction for his son, Nicomachus—Aristotle made it clear that in such vital fields as ethics and politics, certainty is impossible to attain and the work of philosophy consists of the analysis and improvement of our ordinary practices. Accordingly, he proceeded to develop the principles of logic, for example, not from some imaginary ideal, but with careful reference to what people do when they actually reason. The disagreement between Plato and Aristotle on the method of philosophy is still with us today, inviting thinkers to characterize themselves as rationalists, stressing the possibility of insight into the hidden, timeless nature of things, or empiricists, emphasizing experience and successful practice as the only valid sources of knowledge.

Rationalism vs. Empiricism

This conflict played itself out in the seventeenth and eighteenth centuries in the clash of the monumental figures now called "Continental rationalists" and "British empiricists." The great rationalists Descartes, Spinoza, and

Leibniz were from the continent of Europe; the empiricists Locke, Berkeley, and Hume were subjects of the British crown. The rationalists recommended intuitively evident premises and logical reasoning as the method of philosophy. The empiricists, by contrast, maintained that philosophical knowledge must have its foundation in sense experience. Descartes' starting point was the famous "I think, therefore I am," which indicated immediate and certain acquaintance with oneself. He proposed to deduce the entire system of our beliefs from this, to him unquestionable, truth. Spinoza preferred to commence reasoning from the idea of a God that is the impersonal totality of the universe. Leibniz rejected the ideas of his predecessors and built his system on the notion that the world consists of an infinite number of independently existing sentient beings called "monads."

How are we to decide which starting point is the correct one or the best? And how can we tell which system comes closer to being a true and defensible account of how things are? Should we think of God as the benevolent creator of the world or the impersonal sum of all beings? Should we believe that the mind is an independently existing, indestructible entity or that it is but a fragment of one of the infinite manifestations of the Deity? Each philosopher's view has a certain plausibility, yet each system is brought into question by the plausibility of the others. The problem rationalists face is their inability to supply a basis for deciding among the profusion of their visions of reality. Without such a decision procedure, no system is more than a collection of imaginative ideas.

Empiricists are committed to considering nothing as legitimately in the mind that was not first in the senses. This requires an exceptionally sharp-sighted and honest account of the content of sensation. What is present to the senses when we seem to see a table? Does the actual table make an appearance in consciousness or do we sense only some colors and shapes that we merely *believe* to be an external object? If the latter is true, is the entire world made up of our sense experiences? Moreover, what are we to make of important ideas that can never be supported by sensations, such as the notions of infinity and God? The awful consequences of restricting knowledge to what we can sense dawned slowly on Locke and Berkeley; only Hume realized the skeptical bite of the position. In this way, empiricism undercuts its commitment to keep faith with ordinary life, for our daily operations suggest that we know a great deal even if we cannot provide a flawless account of how or why.

Kant

Kant recognized the bankruptcy of all previous philosophy and attributed it, correctly, to a failure of method. He challenged the shared assumption of rationalists and empiricists, namely that there is an external world independent of the cognitive efforts of human beings. He proposed a "Copernican revolution," placing the human mind at the center of the world we inhabit. He was prepared to pay the price of calling this world one of appearances for the benefit of being able to say that it is knowable. The reason we can know it, he thought, was because we make it. The human mind provides space, time, quantity, quality, and causation —in brief, all significant features and relationships—to reality. The transcendental method of proof he developed proceeds from the fact of shared human knowledge to the necessary conditions of its possibility. This amounts to asking what else must be true if it is true that there is knowledge. Kant was ready with an answer, but the system he constructed on that basis is generally acknowledged to be arcane and implausible.

Kant's problem is the unwarranted assumption of a human mind that is not the mind of any person and yet serves as the dynamic agency constructing the world. To be sure, something like what Kant located on the transcendental level actually goes on empirically; especially since the Industrial Revolution, humans have been recreating the world to suit their purposes. This has been taken seriously by such American pragmatists as John Dewey, but the reconstruction they address is concrete and piecemeal, and it presupposes a structured environment amenable to human effort. Kant's translation of mundane facts into the transcendental operations of mind or reason confers plausibility on the claim that instead of revealing secret realities, philosophy only converts observable social developments into the medium of thought.

Philosophy and Progress

Something close to this idea was embraced by Kant's successor, Hegel, who thought that philosophy constitutes the self-consciousness of the age. Such German idealists as Fichte, Hegel, and Schelling adopted totality as the central concept of their thought yet found it difficult to escape the pull of nationalist sentiments and to avoid the glorification of war. The traditional view is that philosophy offers eternal truths. Yet philosophers have been notably time-bound in their positions. Aristotle was undisturbed by the practice of slavery, and one can read hundreds of thinkers without suspecting that half the human race is constituted by women. Earlier missteps in thought would be easier to accept if philosophy progressed in line with the improving moral climate of human life. And, indeed, the sentiments of at least some philosophers have become markedly better. There is, however, no discernible progress in the quality of philosophy or in the quantity of truths it uncovers. In this respect, it is not at all like science, which amazes with continuous series of new discoveries. Philosophy is more like music and literature: just as there is no match today for Mozart and Shakespeare, so we have no one who can approximate the accomplishments of Plato or Hegel.

This does not mean that philosophy is in decline or, as some even suggest, dead. Many a thinker has made a name for himself and earned a comfortable living by announcing the death of his field of endeavor. The fact that philosophy is in this respect unlike science, however, is no reason to declare it useless. It deals with the most difficult problems of human existence, ranging from the nature of happiness to our proper relations to others and from the meaning of life to the possibility of personal immortality. These are not questions that can be settled once and for all. We may never know the answers to them with any level of certainty. But they are not, as the logical positivists of the first half of the twentieth century maintained, meaningless queries that we had best forget. They are important and formative of our lives; we begin asking them in the teenage years and continue pondering them until we go to the grave. Philosophy is not something we outgrow. It travels with us through life and its problems acquire special urgency in times of crisis.

Ethics

Examples of the importance and frustrations of philosophy abound in the realm of ethics. In order to improve our understanding and increase the amount of good in the world, we must learn what makes some actions right and others wrong. Unfortunately, philosophers seem unable to agree on an answer. There are three plausible but incompatible possibilities, and ethicists have held every one of them. John Stuart Mill and other utilitarians maintain that the rightness of actions depends on their consequences; the right action is the one that creates the greatest amount of good over the long term. Kant and so-called deontologists believe that the key factor is the intention with which the action is performed. Joseph Butler and other intuitionists assert that some actions are just right in and of themselves, independently of intention and consequence.

Each of the positions has a recommended procedure for identifying right actions. Mill suggests that we add up all the reasonably expectable good and deduct from it the reasonably expectable harm for each alternative action; the right action is the one with the greatest net sum of good. Kant proposes that we test our intention to see if the principle on which we propose to act would remain intact and operable even if everyone adopted it. Butler feels certain that if we distanced ourselves from the heat of passion and thought about things in "the cool of the afternoon," the true moral features of the action would become clearly visible.

How are we to decide among these theories and procedures? We see here once again the recurrent problem of philosophy: each view and method has something to be said for it, none can be established conclusively, and they are incompatible with each other. The same standoff presents itself in accounts of the nature of happiness. Some thinkers maintain that it is impossible to be happy without getting what we like. Others argue that happiness consists of liking what we get. Which of the two views is nearer the truth? At certain points in life, one view will seem stronger; at others, the other. It may be tempting to combine the two, but the attitudes and efforts required by one are incompatible with those demanded by the other.

Disagreement

What are we to make of the fact that philosophers do not agree on any idea and cannot present a single truth as authenticated by their methods? This is a conclusive objection to philosophy for those who prize unanimity. The leading faculty in philosophy, however, is the imagination, not reason. Philosophical thinking spreads a feast of alternatives. It opens the mind to the values of other people and enriches our sympathies for what may seem alien forms of life. It also presents different sorts of belief, placing what we have been taught from childhood in a context of rival conceptions and thereby liberating us from the rule of unexamined faith. There is no certainty in philosophy, but then there is no certainty anywhere else either, and being able to choose what we want to believe should be at least a partial compensation for never being able to let our guard down by feeling sure.

Such American pragmatists as William James and John Dewey remind us that life is but a series of experiments. We face problems at every turn, try out possible solutions, and build habits out of successful operations. We revise the habits reluctantly and only when they no longer yield results. Our ideas are tools by means of which we accomplish what we want, so we can change them to suit the occasion and the demands of circumstances. Evidence for our beliefs is obviously important, but only because it is an indication of prior operational success. When evidence is lacking, James points out, as in the case of God and immortality, we can believe whatever works best for us. The scope of this liberty may be astounding or disquieting, but we find that that in fact is what people tend to do. They dedicate their lives to God or else defiantly embrace the atheist creed, and abandon their positions only when they no longer make sense of their lives.

Philosophy as Critique

The role of philosophy for Dewey is to serve as critic of beliefs and practices. When we are reluctant to leave old ideas behind or fail to detect contradictions among our convictions, a hard jolt from an external rational source may prove productive. Social and political life are especially likely to harbor the vestiges of old commitments and conceptual survivals of an earlier age. A philosophical examination of our culture may well identify the outgrown, the nonfunctional, and the perhaps even pernicious among our values and practices and, exposing them, contribute to their elimination. This gives philosophers a vital social task and an important political function. Although many thinkers are too timid to exercise this role, at least a few have been willing to stand up and assume the mantle of the public intellectual. John Stuart Mill ran for Parliament and served a term, Emerson and James took on some of the sacred cows of their communities, and Dewey himself was constantly engaged in the controversies of his age.

The opportunities for relatively disinterested philosophical observation and criticism have greatly increased of late. The need for ethical reflection in a rapidly changing world has thrust philosophers into hospitals, businesses, and government agencies. Finding them as members of health care teams or preparing "ethical impact statements" for proposed actions or policies would have been unthinkable a scant forty years ago. Today, presidential bioethics commissions, hospital ethics committees, and ethics experts in newspapers provide the dispassionate analysis and broad-gauged empathy necessary for responsible action under conditions of stress and uncertainty. Philosophers are, of course, not the only people capable of fulfilling this function, but their conceptual sophistication, sensitivity to language, and reasoning skills equip them particularly well for such activities.

Current trends in philosophy have reversed the Platonic fascination with the essence or inner nature of things. The Darwinian continuity of species, along with the frustrations of a futile search, have turned both American pragmatists and postmodern Continentalists away from an interest in determining what things "really" are toward tracing their functions and interrelations. The way we group things is seen more and more as a free exercise governed by our purposes or prevailing power relations. We tend to conceive of species or classes as collections of individuals displaying certain resemblances, but not as sharing a single essence that makes them what they are. This is a wholesome development, redirecting the efforts of philosophers toward understanding the variability and indeterminacy of all things and away from the idea that the world is defined by rigid categories.

Philosophy and Science

This raises the question of the relations of philosophy to science. The most important consideration here is to see their continuities along with their differences. In one way or another, philosophy is the parent of all the sciences, having launched their inquiries and having subsequently separated itself from them. Physics was once called "natural philosophy" and was initially conducted as a philosophical enterprise. When Plato spoke of the soul as animating the body, he meant this idea to be taken, among other things, as a biological hypothesis. There were no research findings in those days to operationalize the theory, but there can be no doubt that Plato and Aristotle were doing biology when they spoke of the physical functions of the soul and psychology when they discussed thought and memory. Psychology itself was not launched on its separate career until a little more than a hundred years ago when experimental procedures took the place of introspection and speculation. Even sociology had its origin in the philosophical work of such thinkers as J. S. Mill and Emile Durkheim.

As a research enterprise focused on empirical detail, science today is clearly different from philosophy. In its theory construction, however, science invites both the conceptual imagination and the critical acumen of philosophers. The complementary nature of science and philosophy can also be seen in the way they collaborate in creating a coherent picture of reality. The material provided by the sciences is often so detailed that its significance gets obscured or even lost. Although philosophers have no additional facts to contribute, their synthesizing powers provide order and context for new discoveries. The creation of a meaningful view of the world out of materials obtained from other sources has always been an important function of philosophy. The vast increase of our knowledge of the details of reality has made this task more difficult today than it has ever been. Nevertheless, the job of making sense of our knowledge requires exceptional skills of vision and generalization, which are the routine possessions of philosophers.

Philosophy and Religion

The relations of philosophy to religion present special problems. Historically, many thinkers have turned to philosophy to establish credible defenses of their favorite religious dogmas. The American philosopher Josiah Royce, for example, set himself the task of making Christianity acceptable to the modern mind. Much of his effort was focused on providing imaginative reinterpretations of the central doctrines of his faith. In other cases, such as that of St. Thomas Aquinas, it is difficult to separate his religious beliefs and his theology from his philosophy. There is no denying that in much of the history of Western thought, God occupied a central place. Even John Locke, who fought the intolerance often associated with religion, felt compelled to try to demonstrate the existence of God. Some philosophers considered these proofs routine piety and of no great significance, but others, such as Descartes, assigned the central functions of continuously recreating the world and guaranteeing our knowledge of it to the Deity.

The presence of religion in philosophical writings might suggest that the two are inseparable partners. It would, however, be wrong to come to this conclusion. The reason is that although philosophy is receptive to religious considerations, it is neutral with respect to religious commitments. This is amply demonstrated by the work of the large numbers of thinkers who are professed atheists. The German philosopher Arthur Schopenhauer maintained that the cheerful message of religion is a cruel hoax and that if anyone created this miserable world, it must have been the devil. The ultimate difference between the philosophical and the theological approaches to religious questions is that the latter starts with pre-existing aims or premises while the former permits the argument to go wherever it will.

The Future of Philosophy

Today, philosophy continues to deal with the same problems it has tackled for more than two thousand years. In ethics, it examines the relation of pleasure to the good life, the obligations we must meet, and the rights we have on account of being humans. In epistemology, it inquires into how we know what we claim to know and what counts as sufficient evidence for belief. Metaphysicians continue to try to catalogue the furniture of the universe and to understand the intricacies of the world-process. Political philosophers engage in spirited debates about the best form of government and the vexed relations of individuals to their communities. Those interested in aesthetics ponder what makes for beauty, for good taste, and for art. Philosophers of mind attempt to accommodate their views to the latest findings of brain scientists. The multitude of professional thinkers devoted to exploring "philosophy of ___" topics, such as philosophy of religion, philosophy of literature, and philosophy of sport, labor to master the field they want to examine, and then develop a deeper grasp of it by means of critical philosophical scrutiny.

What is the function of philosophy in a busy world that does not reward quiet reflection? Will the entire field wither away once it becomes clear that it has no final answers? Will it be thought a childish indiscretion once the childlike insistence of its questioning turns tiresome?

We all die, but the oft-announced death of philosophy is not a likely event. The phenomenon of conscious life in a vast unconscious world generates permanent bafflement. We ask what human decency requires in our relations with others multiple times a day. Social and political life invite skeptical reflection and then a knowing smile. How we are to live our lives and raise our children are not theoretical questions but concrete problems that burn with urgency. The questions of philosophy are questions that matter and will continue to haunt us so long as humans remain finite, baffled animals. The fact that philosophy offers no final answers is not an impediment but a lesson. That first great lesson of philosophy is that we must learn to live with uncertainty.

Labor and Hope:
The Condition of American Philosophy Today

Over the past hundred years, philosophy has isolated itself in universities. It has focused on narrow, and often technical, topics of little interest to the ordinary person. In this process, it has abandoned its traditional tasks of providing moral guidance to individuals and assuming a critical stance toward questionable social practices.

The conversion of universities into knowledge factories renders this development not at all surprising. But it is particularly lamentable in America, where the tradition of the public intellectual and social critic goes back at least to Emerson and Thoreau. By the first decade of the twentieth century, pragmatists such as William James and John Dewey had set the standard for the effective involvement of philosophers in their communities. Seventy-five years later, all this seemed lost, as philosophers turned inward to focus their attention on their language and concepts.

The reason for this turn was the desire of philosophers to imitate science and carve out for themselves a small area of inquiry of which they and they alone could offer knowledge. This science envy, along with uncertainty about how philosophy could adjust itself to the prevailing scientific world-view, came to dominate the work of the best practitioners in the field. To this day, philosophers have not faced up to the fact that their *philosophical* efforts have failed to contribute even a small fragment to the sum of human knowledge. Worse, there is not a single philosophical proposition that commands universal assent in the field.

This does not mean, as some have feared, that philosophy is worthless. On the contrary, it can make vital contributions to human life, even if not in the form of uncovering new bits of information. As if to demonstrate this, the past thirty years have seen the emergence of critical thinking, bioethics, and business ethics as primary areas of instruction embraced by philosophers. These and other "applied" fields within the discipline bring to bear the sensitivity and exquisitely careful thought that constitute the primary outcomes of philosophical education. Philosophy teaches skills, habits, and attitudes; its products are not verified propositions but sophisticated inquirers and humanized activities.

Philosophy in America today is guided by three distinct sorts of paradigms. Analytic philosophers prize clarity and tend to focus their efforts on achieving a precise grasp of relatively isolated issues. Continental thinkers paint with a much broader brush, relying on significant historical texts and attempting to capture the structure of human practices. Philosophers working in the American tradition aim to deal not with technical professional issues but with social and personal problems as they arise in the process of living.

These characterizations are rough and can be misleading. There are many ways of doing analytic philosophy, and—among Continentalists—the aims and methods of phenomenologists are very different from the investigative techniques of Foucault. Moreover, we find significant overlaps among the views of the three groups: there are pragmatic strands in Wittgenstein, and reductive materialism is shunned by many in each camp. Nevertheless, the politics of philosophy has created the impression that every practitioner belongs to one and only one group and that the work and commitments of the groups are incompatible.

The artificial separations have been given teeth by scurrilous charges. Some analytic philosophers think of Continentalists as incompetent, while more than a few Continentalists maintain that their analytically minded colleagues spend their efforts on logic-chopping irrelevance. Members of the older generation who have fought these battles for decades overlook the fact that young people tend not to respect political boundaries and read whichever authors promise to advance their work. Even some established thinkers have managed to overcome easy categorization: Rorty, Rescher, and Putnam are analytic philosophers with distinct pragmatic commitments, while Sallis and Charles Scott are Continentalists with a penchant for clarity.

As always in its history, philosophy stands at a crossroads without adequate guidance. Its advances have typically been hagiographic, with crowds of lesser thinkers clustering around a revered personage. Quine, Sellars, and Rawls were such figures, but their deaths quickly took them out of the limelight. On the Continental side, Derrida and Foucault commanded unqualified admiration, but the deep pronouncements of the former seem no longer so fascinating, and concerning the latter nearly everything possible has already been said.

There is a flutter of interest in philosophers touched by pragmatism. Rorty, Habermas, and a few others get attention in philosophy journals and seem for the moment appealing also to professionals in other fields. This interest, however, is unlikely to last and is in any case not very productive. It is, of course, impossible to predict when the next major philosopher will emerge. But even if a dozen outstanding thinkers published important books next year, the future of philosophy would not be secure. For that, we have to gain a better understanding of what philosophy is good for and how the more than ten thousand members of the American Philosophical Association can contribute to its flourishing.

In some ways, the most heartening development of the past thirty years is the recovery of classical American philosophy. Peirce, James, Dewey, Mead, Royce, and Santayana provide rich resources for reflecting on the personal value and social usefulness of philosophy. Completed editions of the writings of James and Dewey, continuing work on editions of Peirce and Santayana, and a contemplated critical edition of Royce suggest intense interest in resuscitating the sort of public philosophy they championed and continue to represent. They maintained that philosophy must address the concerns of ordinary people and that it must start from the acknowledged facts of experience. Their insistence on the importance of context and relations, their attention to the interests that direct inquiry, and their commitment to life-enhancing consequences make their ways of doing philosophy relevant to the concerns of all of us.

The Public Philosophy Committee recently established by the American Philosophical Association may well serve as a supporting mechanism for the re-engagement of philosophy with the community that supports it. The recently published *Encyclopedia of American Philosophy* promises additional resources for leaving what has been called "the linguistic turn" behind and facing at last the multitude of real-life problems that beset us.

Many philosophers have already turned in this new direction. In hospitals, well-educated philosophers deal with issues of life and death; in corporations, they introduce moral considerations into financial decision making; at newspapers, they explore what counts as objectivity in reporting the news; in government service, they examine issues of fairness in the administration of the laws. Although philosophers of science have not succeeded in teaching scientists much about the scientific method, some ethicists have now become vital sources of help in dealing with problems in research ethics. These thinkers have left the abstractions of the ivory tower and dirtied their hands with resolving the urgent problems of life. We see more and more lawyers with advanced degrees in philosophy, and even some physicians seek the training in careful and critical thought that only philosophy provides. The United States would be a better nation if, in addition to a Council of Economic Advisors, it also had a Council of Ethics staffed by philosophers.

Philosophers are among the cleverest people on earth, so we can look forward to the new methods, new angles of vision, and new theories they will develop in the course of their work. The methods will be inventive and the angles of vision fascinating, but we must not expect the theories to be true. Uncovering new truths is not what philosophy is best at doing. Its task is to educate people by expanding their imaginations and honing their critical skills so they may become courageous members of their communities.

This educational mission leaves plenty of room for advanced research in the field. Nothing incites critical thought more intensely and immediately than the wealth of divergent ideas of which the history of philosophy consists. It cannot come as a surprise to thoughtful professionals that even their best ideas will not survive the assaults of their critics and that, at best, they will amount to mere wrinkles in the history of thought. This suspicion has never stopped philosophers from thinking. Even if it rises to the level of conviction, they will continue to spin a web of concepts to explore their consistency and usefulness and bearing.

A central element of philosophy focused on the problems of life is rejection of its self-contained status. Generations of graduate students were taught that philosophy had a sovereign subject matter and unique method: all they needed to know was how to think. The fiction that any field of knowledge is independent of others fractures inquiry and fragments our picture of the world. The departmental structure of universities is only a convenience and does not reveal the nature of reality. To understand anything is to understand its relations to all manner of other things.

As a result, truly productive philosophy will always be in debt to a variety of other fields in the humanities and the sciences. Philosophical problems shade into problems of sociology and psychology; anthropology offers a host of insights into human nature; novels expand the imagination; astronomy reveals our relation to the vastness of nature. Most important perhaps, philosophy uninformed by history and economics yields only the most rudimentary and naïve perspectives on the world.

To the question "What is the current state of American philosophy?" there are multiple answers. It is moribund if we measure its condition by the emergence of great new ideas. It is vigorous if we look at the number of people engaged in teaching in the field. It is exciting if we view it from the perspective of how many good thinkers are undertaking how many different sorts of inquiries. It is promising if we focus on its budding efforts to find a new public and a voice in which to address it. But it is, lamentably, in a rudimentary stage of self-understanding if we examine it from the vantage point of what philosophy can contribute to the world and what it cannot.

This is obviously a mixed report. But American philosophers have always had a love affair with the future. And with regard to the future, there is reason for labor and for hope.

Can Philosophy Produce Public Intellectuals Today?

Plato accepted the invitation to serve as advisor to the ruler of Syracuse. John Stuart Mill ran for Parliament and served a term. Bertrand Russell got involved in nearly every public policy debate of his time, championing trial marriage and promoting a view that was expressed in the infamous phrase "better red than dead." Why is it that philosophers today, when rational discourse is in terribly short supply and ethics is known mainly for its absence, have disappeared as influential factors from the national scene?

To be sure, a few philosophers make halting efforts to become voices in the conversation of the nation. Between bouts of excessive gambling, William Bennett took time out to wage war on drug abuse and to edit a popular book on virtue. In the process, however, he became a politician rather than a public intellectual. On the other side of the political spectrum, Cornel West endorsed candidates for election and attempted to use the art of rap to get a hearing for philosophical ideas. But the predictability of his themes and the repetitiousness of his public performances have made it difficult for him to retain credibility.

Why has philosophy retreated to the ivory tower and abandoned its traditional role as the critic of our beliefs and practices? And why has it moved in the opposite direction from other professions when economists, historians, and even physicians are taking an ever more visible role in public life?

The explanation lies in a peculiar ambivalence at the heart of philosophy today. The field is infected with the quiet fear that it has nothing useful to offer the community sustaining it. Its methods beyond the common rules of logic are not reliable guides to truth, and hence it contributes no settled results to inquiry. Much as they love the exhilaration of conceptual play, in the depths of their souls many philosophers suspect that there is something unserious about what they do. After all is said and done, it makes little or no difference in the world.

As is often the case, insecurity breeds excessive claims of excellence. Some of our colleagues aggressively declare that philosophy is the queen of the sciences, that psychologists and the like suffer from conceptual confusions, and that our field of study can make genuine headway without a thorough examination of its limits and foundations. The arrogance goes so far as to justify, in the view of these deep thinkers, knowing glances at each other when colleagues from other fields present their theories. The message appears to be that only philosophers know what they are talking about.

The ambivalence pulls philosophers in opposite directions. Yet in relation to taking a role in public affairs, the two incompatible beliefs issue in the same result. Insecurity leads to the conviction that philosophers have nothing to say about the urgent problems of the day; commitment to the transcendent virtue of philosophy begets the idea that it is futile to engage an ignorant public. Either philosophers have nothing to offer or what they offer is so arcane that only professionals can grasp it. Both beliefs present a convenient excuse for staying out of the struggles for the soul of our society and for being satisfied with a comfortable life within the university.

I am not suggesting, of course, that philosophers shirk the duties of citizenship. They pay taxes, vote, and do their best to obey the laws. Some of them join movements working for social justice; others opt to be vegans. These, however, are personal choices largely unconnected to philosophical reasoning. They may even fly in the face of good sense and critical acumen, as when during the 1960s, Hilary Putnam, a leading epistemologist, started spewing mindless Leninism. Such sharp divorces between personal conviction and philosophical critique remain strikingly common, and we find distressingly many philosophers whose everyday lives are radically out of sync with their official opinions. As I argued elsewhere, inner divisions are relatively harmless in the case of chemists, whose professional views may have little bearing on their lives. But lawyers who violate the laws, atheist priests, bankrupt financial advisors, and obese physicians, along with irrational philosophers, rightly arouse suspicion.

The desire to steer clear of public affairs receives reinforcement from three features of professional philosophy as it exists today. With the exception of some of those who write on science, philosophers tend to be averse to facts. In their graduate education, young professionals are taught that argument is king, and for that knowledge of facts is superfluous. Even some phenomenologists, who have no love for argument, maintain that experience suffices for philosophy, leaving out of account vital and complex political realities. Engagement in public affairs requires significant familiarity with current events and social and economic processes, so it is not surprising that philosophers feel ignorant or overwhelmed. This nescience is justified even today by many on the basis of pursuing grander truths than transitory realities can offer. When I was much younger, I refused to spend time reading newspapers because, I believed, they held little relevance for the timeless truths I was seeking.

The second feature of our profession discouraging engagement with a broader public is its perverse incentive structure. From the first year of graduate school, students are taught to prize complexity presented in technical language. Approval and rewards accrue to those who invent new wrinkles or those who resuscitate old, implausible positions in new raiment. The technically cleverest among them get jobs in graduate schools, where they replicate the pattern that made them famous. Department chairs and deans fall in line with the judgment of the profession, offering endowed chairs and eye-popping salaries as rewards for obscurity. No one seems to notice that all technical innovations are soon found wanting and no philosophically significant proposition is ever established beyond controversy. Nevertheless, good teaching and engagement with the community remain inadequate for tenure and are held in contempt by leading thinkers.

The third feature of the profession that keeps philosophers inside the university takes the form of a flawed conception of the field. The departmental structure of the university places philosophy in misleading parity with physics and anthropology. The sciences enjoy the benefits of reliable methods and bodies of confirmed conclusions. Nothing like this is available in philosophy. To expect that it will contribute to the sum of human knowledge the way the sciences do is to misunderstand its nature and value. Yet the ideas of research and discovery dominate the field of philosophy in the same manner as they structure and define such areas of endeavor as microbiology. This wrongheaded ideal focuses the efforts of our colleagues on reading, conversation, reflection, and writing, all of which are best done within the safe precincts of the university.

And then there is courage. Academics are inherently fearful, easily intimidated by deans and presidents, and rarely ready to put themselves on the line. Public intellectuals must be willing to formulate judgments and stand by them in the face of resistance and ridicule. When I was gathering signatures for a petition to remove an incompetent chancellor, many colleagues agreed that the man should go but would nevertheless not sign. As tenured full professors, without the need for another raise for the rest of their lives, what made them afraid? Safe invisibility is the preferred condition of academics. They may have bold things to say in the classroom, but when it comes to putting their complaints into action, they often fail to show.

So far, I have been talking about what might be called "mainline" philosophy, that is, roughly what goes on in college and university departments of that name. My account would be incomplete, however, if I left out an important positive development that occurred in the past thirty years. The growth of applied ethics has turned the attention of at least a portion of the profession toward sites beyond the university where people struggle with difficult personal and social problems. Medical ethics, business ethics, engineering ethics, journalistic ethics, even accounting ethics have undergone significant development both in the number of practitioners and in the quality of their contributions.

This single factor should have been enough to turn philosophy in a more productive direction than it followed in the first seven decades of the twentieth century. That it did not is the result mainly of the insecurity of applied ethicists and the ambivalence of their institutional positions. Many of them were refugees from metaethics and epistemology who continued to believe that those fields constitute the heart of philosophy, even though they could not make them their home. They viewed applied ethics as an ersatz philosophy instead of as the perfection of the field, that is, as something you do if you cannot excel at austere conceptuality. Even worse, they saw themselves as interlopers in medicine and the other professions, people who did not earn the right to have a say. This impression was reinforced by doctors and trained members of the professions, who viewed philosophers as fifth wheels and refused to treat them with much respect. This is beginning to change now, but progress comes slowly because it requires that philosophers attain competence in the fields they critique.

Is it not odd that the president has a Council of Economic Advisors and the separate office of the National Economic Council, while he has not a single official to advise him on matters of morality? To be sure, presidential bioethics commissions offer special reports on issues relating to health and life, but they are heavily politicized and their purview and efficacy are limited. We cannot suppose that economic life is more significant than fairness and moral decency, because those virtues are indispensable conditions of commercial exchange. Astonishingly, politicians seem to think that the solution of moral problems can be left to good upbringing and religious feeling. If these fail, as they often do, leaders of all sorts naturally turn to lawyers, who find it notoriously difficult to distinguish moral from legal obligation.

The recent apparent attempt by the governor of Illinois to sell a Senate seat demonstrates the desperate need for ethicists at the highest levels of government. Detentions at Guantanamo, outrageous lying in political races, and the inability to distinguish local from national interests demand serious attention from people sensitive to moral issues and trained in reasoning. How can we motivate philosophers to fill this need and how can we help the leaders of our society see that private decency and civic virtue constitute prime conditions of good lives?

We cannot expect spontaneous insight and immediately changed behavior. If you take a bird out of its cage, it will resist. If you open the door to the cage, on the other hand, it will find its way out and try its wings. The door of the university needs to open toward the community and there must be sufficient incentives for philosophers to embrace the freedom to practice their art. They are, after all, natural critics. At least a few of them have enough of a spirit of adventure to employ their sensitivity, dialectical skill, and imagination in the service of the critical examination of our practices.

Such birds emerging from the cage of the university will, however, be relatively rare exceptions, and even Aristotle knew that one swallow does not make spring. In order to interest a significant number of philosophers in the problems of their communities, they must be shown that engagement beyond the classroom is valued and appropriate. This can be done only by philosophy department chairpersons and university administrators, and they will do it only once *they* are convinced that the research/discovery paradigm of philosophy is wrongheaded and unproductive. Who will take the first steps necessary to convince them?

Chairpersons view themselves as champions of their departments who compete for support essentially with all the other units of the university. It would be odd indeed if they visited the dean with the news that philosophers will never discover any new facts, but since they are pretty good at criticizing other people, their department needs three more positions. Deans, in turn, are in a fierce competitive struggle with other schools within the university and with other universities. They have little interest and not much understanding of the subtly different things diverse departments accomplish. They want new discoveries, a distinguished faculty (even if they have to heap distinctions on them themselves), and a flood of publications. To them, philosophy as a critical agent sounds vaguely corrosive, and their conversation with department chairs does not go on long before they ask, "Why can't you be like everybody else?"

Who will educate the educators? I see only one possibility and that, alas, is not likely to be actualized. The American Philosophical Association is the pre-eminent society in our field; it falls to it to promote the profession in all its disorganized pluralism. Instead of celebrating technical competence and name recognition in the election of its presidents, it needs to spend its energy studying the growing edges of philosophy. So far, it has clearly failed to do so. For decades, the official program of the Eastern Division gave no hint of the existence of the burgeoning field of medical ethics. Even today, Kant gets far more attention than medical futility, in spite of the fact that millions of people face wrenching decisions concerning continued treatment near the end of life and no one agonizes about the transcendental deduction.

The APA needs to establish a commission to study the full range and effectiveness of philosophy. The results of that examination will largely depend on the commission's membership, so it should contain representatives of a broad range of constituencies within the profession and it must not have a majority of traditionalists. Report of the deliberations of such a commission is likely to be of significant general interest; at any rate, it could be disseminated to the deans and presidents of universities across the country. If it affirmed the legitimacy of public engagement, it will have opened the door to a revision of incentives and expectations in philosophy. The point of this revision is not to drain support from traditional fields or to deny the value of controversies concerning long-established problems. The hope, instead, is that the profession may be expanded in the direction of what it once proudly recognized as its purpose and perfection.

Is the APA likely to undertake such a task? Not at all, if we judge by its past performance. And that means that those of us interested in the public role of philosophy have nowhere to look for help. We'll just have to convince our colleagues, if necessary one by one, of the importance of addressing the real problems of real people. In this endeavor, there is reason for cautious optimism. We are surrounded by moral problems public and private. People search blindly for a worthy life. Few see reason for life-giving self-control. It is simply intolerable that a profession with the potential to help in such matters should stand idly by in the academy.

What Can Philosophy Contribute?

I owe a debt of gratitude to Professor Weber for pointing out what has escaped me over decades of philosophical work. I did not explicitly recognize that the view I articulated in "Stoic Pragmatism" has been for a long time, and perhaps from the first, a defining feature of my thought. As early as "To Have and To Be" and in retrospect very visibly in *Intermediate Man,* I maintained that the human lot can be improved and that our efforts should be focused on improving it. At the same time, I always thought that there are sharp limits to what we can achieve in life and that some of the things that happen to us must in the end be accepted as beyond change or redemption.

In "Stoic Pragmatism," these dual tendencies attained explicit expression in arguing that stoics give up too soon and pragmatists make the mistake of never wanting to give up. If the two views were suitably combined, we could acknowledge the legitimacy of both struggle and surrender and embrace both human power and our finitude. I continue to believe that some such attitude is by far the best for a satisfying life and a peaceful death. The difficulty, as always, is with knowing when to be resolute in struggle and when to yield to the inevitable with a gracious smile.

The question of what can and what cannot be accomplished raises its head everywhere, but especially where genuine achievements are hard to come by. It is an enduring problem for thoughtful philosophers who look at the outrageous claims of their colleagues with amazement and dismay. Understandably perhaps, graduate students are given the impression that when they become professionals, they will be able to offer contributions of the first order to human knowledge. They are made to believe that they will be able to outthink physicists and psychologists, that they will correct everyone else's mistakes, and that, if they work hard enough, they will discover some striking (and perhaps eternal) truths about the world.

As a result, young philosophers enter the classroom and controversies in the journals with a sense of preternatural confidence. They know they will clean out the Aegean stables of fuzzy thinking and they are convinced that the side they take in any argument is demonstrably right. Strikingly, professionals who pride themselves on knowing how to be skeptical seem never to have any doubts about their own abilities and ideas. If anything, letting loose the fireworks of skepticism becomes for them an instrument of self-assurance.

All but a few philosophers lose this self-certainty over time, and the ones who don't become insufferable boors. The decline in self-confidence goes hand in hand, unfortunately, with a loss of interest in philosophical problems, and especially in the problem of what philosophy is good for. They come to believe that it is good, primarily, for earning a modest but comfortable living and for shaking up unsuspecting undergraduates. These chastened souls, unable to gain the respect of people in other fields and no longer believing that they will ever add much to the sum of knowledge, flash their wares to impress students and consider it a victory when they convince one or another of them to enter the profession.

The cynics in the field, on the other hand, believe in the depth of their souls that philosophy is worthless and will soon be interred. The death of philosophical reflection is announced regularly by people who make their living, and fame, by its continued vitality. The living contradiction makes no impression on these fine professionals, who seem not to realize that they are in the business of putting themselves out of business.

So we have in philosophy the excess and deficiency Aristotle identified with vice: some thinkers maintain that philosophy can do everything, while others insist it can do nothing. Some look for an endless series of achievements, while others quickly reconcile themselves to failure. There is a happy medium between these views, but uncovering it is impossible without a clear understanding of the nature and limits of philosophy. So long as we fail to take a dispassionate and critical look at our field of endeavor, we will not be able to assess its value and potentialities.

We must begin by recognizing that the administrative structure of colleges and universities places philosophy in a misleading position. The fact that there are *departments* of philosophy suggests a parity with fields such as physics and sociology. This invites the idea that, like other inquiries, philosophy has a unique subject matter, an established method, and the bright prospect of making new discoveries. In reality, none of this is true. Philosophy is at its best when dealing with the investigations and results of other fields, it has no accepted fertile method, and it has not uncovered a single true proposition on which its practitioners agree.

As I have argued above, the impotence of philosophy in exploring the world is more than made up for by its skill in educating inquirers. Philosophers can lavish exquisite critical attention on the assumptions and methods of other fields and produce a morally and politically sophisticated citizenry. They have already established indispensable roles for themselves in hospitals, in the formulation of public policies, and in corporations. Their influence would be greatly enhanced if they were dispersed all over the university and the community instead of being isolated in their own departments.

This leaves the roles of philosophical research and writing in question. Professor Weber seems to think that "academic philosophical scholarship should not be taken too seriously."[1] By contrast, I see no problem in according it room and respect, so long as it is done not naïvely with a view to establishing truths, but as exercises of dialectical skill, clarity of vision, and imaginative conceptual construction. The study of good philosophical writing and the effort to express difficult ideas with clarity are vital tools in the education of philosophers. The key is to realize that teaching critical skills must not be viewed as the cash cow that pays for research but as the ultimate justification of arcane philosophical controversies.

I agree with Weber that the educative function of philosophy must not be confined to colleges and universities. Philosophers, because of their training in critical thought, can have interesting and vitally important things to say about the moral and political problems facing our communities. Such public intellectuals as Emerson, Thoreau, James, and Dewey have had a profound influence on the tone of American culture. Even less-accomplished minds can offer their ideas in books, op-ed articles, and public lectures, so long as the topic is relevant, the presentation engaging, and the language accessible.

To encourage involvement in issues of interest to the general public, a few years ago the Centennial Committee of the American Philosophical Association offered a prize for the best op-ed article written by a professional philosopher and published in the immediately prior twelve-month period. The number and quality of the submissions came as a surprise to all concerned. The interest of philosophers in the problems of their communities proved to be much greater than anticipated. It became clear that professors were writing voluminously for their local papers on issues that ranged from the timely to the eternal.

Strikingly absent from the many submissions, however, were high-impact statements from well-known philosophers in elite institutions. People who had made a name for themselves in the profession seemed satisfied to be dealing with abstract problems and writing for a minuscule audience of specialists. Many academic disciplines create public intellectuals of significant visibility; philosophy has done little of it in the past fifty years. At least

1. Eric Weber, "The Responsibilities and Dangers of Pragmatism," *Transactions of the C. S. Peirce Society,* vol. 43, pp. 390–94.

a part of the cause for this failure is the desire of professionals not to look unsophisticated. Technical complexity commands respect, while "populariz-ers" are treated with contempt. Even though many of the great philosophers wrote in a way thoroughly accessible to persons of ordinary intelligence, a certain amount of obscurity guised in a flood of strange words is considered necessary in the field today.

Professor Weber is correct to point to the difficulty of evaluating the work of philosophers who focus their efforts on addressing the community. But this problem, he rightly insists, must be placed in the context of the obstacles standing in the way of the sound assessment of research and espe-cially of teaching. The quality of teaching is a function not primarily of what students recall by exam time, but what they remember and act on twenty-five years later. Student evaluations of teaching performance are an indicator of this, though not a particularly accurate one. The assessment of research suf-fers from the self-aggrandizement of the in-group. Tenure evaluators must be in one's narrow area of specialization, and all such individuals have a vested interest in seeing colleagues in their field succeed. So it is obvious that evalu-ation of every academic activity is problematic, and especially problematic when we deal with its long-term effects.

Nevertheless, appraising the contributions of what Weber calls "engaged philosophers" is by no means beyond our capacity. If we listen to undergradu-ates about in-house teaching, we can listen to the people in the community who are addressed and affected by the public philosopher. Editors of news-papers can offer valuable information about op-ed writers, physicians can estimate the usefulness of medical ethicists, and the public at large can assign a value to the ideas it is offered. In relation to philosophy, both administrators and philosophers must give up the expectation of important research break-throughs. Once this expectation is surrendered, ample evaluative standards can be developed for appraising the value of every type of philosophical contribution.

Weber hits the right note once again in thinking of teachers as examples for their students. No greater compliment can be paid to an idea than acting on it, and there is no better way to undermine the value of a belief than to endorse it only verbally. Even in adulthood, the best learning is by imitation. This imposes a momentous responsibility on teachers: they must enact their beliefs or else be fraudulent. Philosophers are particularly burdened by this requirement, because the precepts and principles they teach bear directly on how people lead their lives. The ideal of unifying action and belief is difficult to achieve, but it sets the standard for those who understand that teaching is offering oneself as a living exemplar of what one's ideas can accomplish.

Pragmatists are not the only philosophers to outgrow the narrow confines of their departments in the academy. Professionals who work in applied ethics, along with others who understand that the primary role of philosophy is to aid people in living well, naturally seek help from other fields and aim their efforts at improving the community. This need not result in the eventual disappearance of philosophy departments; they will no doubt continue to be necessary for educating young professionals. But more and more philosophers will become attached to other departments, and double appointments and secondary appointments may open the minds of others to the areas of the university and of community life where they can make lasting contributions. The future lies in regaining for philosophy the power it once enjoyed and making it again a central player in the drama of gradual human self-improvement.

CHAPTER 2

STOIC PRAGMATISM

The Past, the Future, and the Immediate

It is unseemly to question one's heritage. What prior generations gave us is best accepted with gratitude or at least accommodated within the compass of who we are. Whether we find a use for what went before or quarantine it in a private closet of the mind, examining it too closely or raising objections to it is of little value. Our inheritance is the gift of a past, and that means, among other things, that as past it must be left behind.

We can, of course, reflect on the past, try to understand it, and occasionally even learn from it. But what can we learn from, or do with, the past of pragmatism? What, in particular, can we do with, or learn from, the fact that Hegel, like a silent volcano, casts his shadow over some of the greatest pragmatists? Peirce declared himself to be a Hegelian[1] and Dewey grew to philosophical maturity embracing much of what Hegel championed. Hegel figures prominently in the work of James and in the voluminous writings of the proto-pragmatist, Santayana. And in the end, only Fichte comes near to matching the influence of Hegel on the idealistic pragmatism of Josiah Royce.

The importance of Hegel for all these thinkers is undeniable, but it is easily overstated. For Peirce insisted on the irreducibility, and the unsublatability, of firsts and seconds to thirds. Dewey embraced context, but emphatically rejected the Absolute that made unilinear development and a nonempirical totality essential parts of Hegel's system. James and Santayana experienced Hegel in what he would call the mode of determinate negation: they targeted his ideas for extermination. Even Royce found Hegel fundamentally wanting, substituting the idea of community for that of the state, and moral striving for historical development.

---

1. C. S. Peirce, *The Collected Papers of Charles Sanders Peirce*, vol. 6, ed. C. Hartshorne and P. Weiss (Cambridge, Mass.: Harvard University Press, 1931–35), p. 305. Hereafter *CP*.

These and other similarities and differences between Hegel and sundry pragmatists are well known even if they have not received canonical treatment in the secondary literature. They are instructive and may be philosophically interesting, but they are unlikely to help us answer the living questions we face. Philosophy is wise to begin with what others have thought and with comparisons of the ideas of great thinkers. But this can be no more than a beginning. Soon, learning must be brought to bear upon the pressing problems of the day.

The issues we need to tackle are not puzzles of professional philosophy, but problems that arise in the process of everyday living. Such problems sometimes involve the past: we must learn to deal with yesterday's disappointments and to get beyond old achievements when they become obstacles to growth. But the point of looking to the past is to improve the future. Since what happened is past changing, the only profit we can derive from history is avoidance of old mistakes. That is something we desperately need, yet our record in this regard is not at all impressive.

Remarkably, Hegel shows no interest in learning from history. He is, of course, keen to understand what happened by rehearsing the stages in the development of spirit. But he maintains that philosophical activity is exhausted in tracing the teleology of the past. Philosophers offer the idea of rational spirit to those wishing to understand history.[2] The resulting vision displays a single line of development—that of the growth of freedom—accomplished by what Hegel calls "the cunning of reason."[3] By a powerful inversion of the traditional idea, Hegel wrenches purposiveness out of any relation to the future and restricts it to past events and their culmination in the present moment.

Since philosophy deals with reason alone, it is silent about the future. What is yet to come cannot now be known—spirit has not yet determined the shape it will take tomorrow. Humans act impulsively or by passion,[4] and this irrationality provides the ragged material out of which spirit constructs its seamless edifice. Hegel appears to despair of introducing good sense into life; he seems to think that humans are unlikely to follow rational advice, and even if they did, their purposes would be systematically subverted. But what if we persist in seeking to learn how to avoid the mistakes of the past? Even

2. G. W. F. Hegel, *Reason in History,* ed. and trans. Robert S. Hartman (Indianapolis, Ind.: Bobbs-Merrill, 1953), p. 11.

3. Ibid., p. 44.

4. Ibid., p. 28.

then, philosophy is the wrong place to turn, for it recognizes no mistakes and therefore has no helpful advice to dispense.

The idea that there are no mistakes in history may appear absurd, but that, in the end, is Hegel's position. There are, of course, personal missteps, some of which can cost individuals their lives. Yet from the standpoint of historical development, everything works out just fine. The gratuitous cruelties, the stupidities, miscalculations, misdirected ambitions, and grandiose posturings that dot the landscape of history are all useful, even necessary, to make reason grow. What may appear as a series of devastating errors is, in fact, only the labor of the negative essential for progress and the emergence of a rational whole.

Hegel displays his profound ambivalence toward philosophy in his belief that nothing escapes the reach of reason, yet philosophical insight offers no help with the affairs of life. The ambivalence may be dialectically proper, reminding us that philosophy is both everything and nothing, both a potent force and an impotent shadow, but it is ungrounded and unsatisfying. There is little reason to believe in the truth of any grand historical narrative, and it is simply false that we cannot learn from the mistakes of the past. Moreover, human beings tend not to be content with seeing the complex ways in which the past issues in the present; they seek to learn lessons for controlling the future. Marx captured this attitude when he said that philosophers typically want to understand the world, but "the point is to change it."[5]

The sort of large-scale and abrupt change Marx aimed at is not what most people have in mind when they look to the past in order to make the future better. They want gradual improvement along multiple avenues of growth. Hegel was surely right that we know the meaning, and thus the nature, of our actions only by their consequences—in his language, when they move from their certainty to their truth. But historical events are not radical particulars. They display sufficient similarities for us to recognize old follies in what we are tempted to do today. So if we attend to what did not work before, we should be able to draw sensible conclusions about what not to try again in our personal and in our national lives.

Even on the most charitable interpretation, there is something peculiar about Hegel's refusal to deal with the future. What has gone before and what is yet to come are connected by a host of dialectical relations. That the future is indeterminate or nonexistent should be no obstacle to its philosophical treatment. Being lacks determinacy and Nothing is bereft of existence, yet

5. Karl Marx, "Theses on Feuerbach," in *Selected Writings,* ed. David McLellan (Oxford: Oxford University Press, 1977), p. 158.

Hegel shows no reluctance to discuss them at length. Moreover, if actions acquire their nature through their consequences, only the future can offer an understanding of the past. The continuous unrest of the womb of time structures and restructures what, because it is past, we wrongly suppose settled and therefore dead.

Peirce understood the oddness of Hegel's neglect of the future and took steps to remedy it. The meaning of any concept or event, for him, is the set of consequences to which it gives rise. Only these eventual outcomes enable us to grasp what exists today, and they do so by giving it nature. Things and thoughts are not fully structured realities enclosed in a moment; they are dynamic processes developing over time. Peirce seems to think that the present is a seed whose conversion into plant and flower is a teleological task left to the future.

This view is a mirror image of what Hegel had in mind. For Hegel, the present is the culmination of the purposive development of the past; for Peirce, it is the germ of growth that is yet to come. The difference between the two cannot be overstated. Hegel's stance is essentially spectatorial, examining history for the purpose of understanding it. Peirce, by contrast, focuses on the future, maintaining that it must be created by intelligent human action.

Peirce attaches two hallmark views to this recognition of the role humans play in shaping the future. The first is a reversion to Fichte in embracing the idea that future development, and the struggle that is a central part of it, must be infinite. Knowledge and reality emerge, in his view, only at the end of endless inquiry. Until then, we face a labor of love[6] in pursuing inquiry and in interpreting and reinterpreting the world.

Peirce's second claim about the future is that it involves the growth of "concrete reasonableness." This process is characterized by the gradual disappearance of force and chance; thirds or laws and regularities take the place of dynamic seconds and the immediacies he calls firsts. Peirce thus converts the covert rationality of the cunning of reason into the public and palpable victory of purposive mind over brute power and uncontrolled happenstance. One of the central elements of progress toward the final emergence of a fully ordered world is control by humans of their passions and commitment to enacting what reason demands.

Dewey contributed no novel idea to this train of thought; he satisfied himself with taking the metaphysics out of what Peirce had said. Progress, for Dewey, becomes local and piecemeal, and hence lacking a single end.

---

6. Literally. Peirce believes in what he calls "agapasm," the idea that love governs the evolution of the universe. See *CP*, vol. 6, p. 302ff.

Instead of focusing on supposed cosmic trends that favor growth, Dewey was captivated by the tools that enable us to enlarge the range of local intelligence. He paid particular attention to three distinct but related instruments of human improvement: education, the reconstruction of social institutions, and philosophical critique.

All three of these instruments focus on the future. The central issues of education are determining which habits to foster in young people and constructing conditions that tend to establish and strengthen those habits. Even today, many people suppose that the reconstruction of social institutions should aim at the rectification of past injustices. Dewey takes a far more progressive and sensible position: he thinks the point is to avoid injustices and irrationalities in the future and thereby to improve lives in the years to come. Even social critique, a prime function of philosophy, must target questionable elements of our shared life with a view to their amelioration.

This love of the future is a natural consequence of the pragmatic stress on action. As long as we seek only understanding, we are restricted to reflections on the past. Hegel was certainly right that the owl of Minerva appears only at dusk;[7] the dust must settle before we can sort out what happened. Action, by contrast, neither permits nor requires such clarity. Its aim may be obscure and its outcome unpredictable because it falls in the realm of the turbulent will, not the calm intellect. Yet, Dewey claims, we can introduce a modicum of intelligence into what we desire, plan, and do. That is the job of philosophy and, more broadly, of education. If we permit our activities to express uneducated passion and remain satisfied with teaching the young to replicate the patterns of their parents, we crush all hope of progress toward our chosen goals.

The shift of emphasis from past to future makes for a sea change in philosophy. It legitimates a critical stance toward the practices of one's society. It replaces the ethics of blame and condemnation with an ethics that guides ameliorative action. It thrusts the philosophy of education to the center of attention. It converts the philosophy of history from the search for a singular pattern of development to a study of repeated errors, which hold lessons for the future. Most important perhaps, it trades dubious knowledge for sustained hope and holds out the possibility of improvement as a result of intelligent human striving. These are the reasons pragmatism takes the place of lame versions of Marxism and religious thought as the philosophy of hope and effort.

7. G. W. F. Hegel, *Philosophy of Right,* trans. T. M. Knox (Oxford: Oxford University Press, 1952), p. 13.

Hegel believes that the world system as a whole is rational and that this rationality arises from the irrationality of its elements. Reason deviously subverts the intentions of individuals and converts their blind self-seeking into the building blocks of a higher reality. Rationality seems restricted, therefore, to the realm of means; the end emerges without anyone deliberately and intelligently taking aim at it. But actually no one chooses the means rationally either, for that would require awareness of the end to be attained. For a philosopher of consciousness, Hegel certainly acknowledges a great deal of unconsciousness in the way history proceeds. Reason, for him, is an impersonal process rather than the drive for harmony and self-improvement that operates in individuals.

The contrast with Dewey could not be more stark. What reason there is in the world, Dewey maintains, is intelligence embodied in concrete individuals. This intelligence shapes our choice of ends no less than it structures our selection of the means to achieve them. We suit our instruments to our purposes, but we also revise our aims on the basis of their cost and of the availability of tools for their attainment. With immense, one might say Hegelian, sophistication, Dewey refuses to draw an ultimate line between means and ends. In a view typically overlooked by those who take pleasure in accusing him of crude instrumentalism, he maintains that when we view things in their relations within the sequential order, they are means, but when we approach them to enjoy their intrinsic qualities, they are ends.

Both means and ends are, therefore, revisable in accordance with the dictates of intelligence. We can learn from our mistakes, rein in our passions, and by changing what we want and what we do make the future better than the past has been. Even if people are irrational today, experience and education can turn them around. To be sure, we are not going to become paradigms of rationality or perfect exemplars of self-control and intelligence. But under favorable circumstances and with enough effort, we can do and be a little better than we did and were yesterday. Our goals must not be cosmic and the improvements we craft may not last, but here and there we can break the hold of bad habits and resist our propensity to act before we think.

Hegel's idea that humans have attained freedom, and spirit self-consciousness, in the Prussian state appears grotesque today. The belief that history displays a single line of development is a discarded element of discredited ideologies. The notion that progress is an impersonal and irresistible force has lost any plausibility it may once have possessed. Thoughtful people cannot seriously believe that nothing in the main line of history is marred by tragic errors. The very hope that the past can be understood in the teleological terms Hegel favored has been abandoned long ago. So we see that in spite of the remarkable Hegel revival we are witnessing, many of his substantive positions enjoy little support in the philosophical community.

Of greater concern is surrender of belief in the possibility of progress of the modest sort Dewey advocates. One of the striking processes of the past fifty years has been the growth of sensitivity in Western industrialized countries. People whose liberal sentiments make them sensitive to the sensitivities of others have greatly increased in number and have taken charge of the conscience and the public opinion of nations. This is an altogether positive development, making life in those countries better for many powerless and disadvantaged individuals. In spite of the discrimination and misery that still remain, women, racial minorities, adherents of out-of-favor religions, the poor, and the disabled have made astonishing and appropriate headway in having their claims acknowledged.

The paradoxical downside of these developments is that people whose humaneness and organized generosity far exceed anything the world has ever seen refuse to affirm their goodness. Moral leaders in Western countries cannot get themselves to say that their tolerant values are better than those embodied in the bestial rule of tyrants. They embrace the absurd notion that there is nothing about liberal regimes that makes them preferable to traditional societies. Masters at self-abnegation, they justify those who, by force of arms, resist the spread of toleration and universal human rights. Madly, they honor as a moral authority anyone who belongs to or speaks on behalf of an oppressed minority.

The growth of decency goes, in this way, hand in hand with uncertainty about its own value. The result is that morally sensitive people must not even breathe that we might have made some progress in how we treat others. Words such as "civilized" are banned from public discourse, and the mark of enlightenment is the ability to see the excellence of societies that, if we had to live in them, we would find unbearably oppressive. The claim of progress so easily made in the nineteenth century cannot be asserted now that we have actually forged ahead. Our values of universal appreciation seem to make it impossible for us to render a just account of how far we have come.

Pragmatists preach amelioration, and improvement of our condition is just what progress means. If we do not permit ourselves to suppose that we progress, we ban pragmatism as a mode of thought and a way of life. Dewey certainly believed that societies mastered their physical circumstances more or less successfully and that they promoted more or less satisfactory relations among their members. He was clear that freedom, self-determined growth, control over the consequences of action, and rich and multifaceted experience were values of which more is better and less worse. There is no way of avoiding the conclusion that democratic, technologically sophisticated, and humanely organized societies constitute an advance over hierarchical, oppressive, and technically incompetent nations.

To avoid misunderstanding, let me add at once that no pragmatist thinks progress is inevitable or likely to be indefinitely sustained. As a possibility hard work may actualize, it is a local and perhaps temporary achievement. Moreover, the fact that one nation may be ahead of another in moral growth does not entitle it to take over the other's life. Contrary to what aggressive colonial powers supposed, no civilized state has a right or an obligation to civilize the world. Open communication, a shared life, and setting a good example suffice to make the ways of liberal democracies attractive to many nations.

To say that we have progressed does not mean that we are beyond further improvement. The solution of every problem creates new ones. Establishing control over the material conditions of life in this country required relentless drive and the expenditure of vast human effort. Once we attained a significant measure of control, the drive did not subside; like a sorcerer's apprentice that found its way into our hearts, it keeps operating us at a frantic pace. We believe that success demands devotion to labor, that the good life consists of accumulating goods, and that satisfaction is guaranteed when we buy and consume.

Those who think that our culture is given to hedonistic enjoyment of the present have not examined it carefully enough. The truth is that we are in love with the future, worshipping its promise and answering all its demands. Students in universities match their curriculum to their career plans, and when they apply for a job they ask about the retirement plan. Everyone looks for a promotion, for when the children will be grown, for when income will at last match expenses. The lunch hour, the weekend, the annual vacation, and eventual retirement fill the mind with longing. In the meantime, we move in an irredeemably busy world, performing activities whose point is always past them, forever trying to catch up so we are not left behind.

An unfriendly interpreter of pragmatism might maintain that it captures the American psyche, and more generally the modern industrial psyche, because of its love of the future and its efforts to make the world safe for retirement and death soon thereafter. But this is an unfair depiction. Dewey's pragmatism does not support the sort of hurried and fragmented existence many lead in the world today. On the contrary, he laments the "narrowed, embittered, and crippled life, ... congested, hurried, confused and extravagant life"[8] that consumer societies invite us to enjoy. Yet the love of business that Santayana thought was the ruling passion of America[9] is a love of what is to come as a result of our efforts. This passion makes it difficult under current circumstances to separate the comfort we enjoy from the endless labor that makes it possible.

Hegel points to the importance of understanding the past. Pragmatists propose to give this knowledge a practical bent by using it to guide our actions, that is, to make the future better. But once the future gets its hook into them, people want to wiggle free. We see this in the vast pull of entertainment and the growing interest in spirituality. Many people care little for the past and do all they can to forget, even if only for a moment, the plans and worries that relate us to the future. They seek release, in most cases only temporary, from hurry, pressure, concern, and irrelevance, and especially from the rounds of compulsory activities that constitute jobs and that are required to sustain life.

Philosophical articulation of these inchoate desires suggests that what people want is something valuable for its own sake, something that does not point to a beyond. They feel the need to empty their minds of the world of means so they may fill them with unhurried enjoyment of beauty or a moment's union with something higher. They desire peace, rest, and the sort of satisfaction that meeting deadlines and chasing after things can never give. Even success as the world measures it fails to provide the respite that leaves the soul, for a moment, without desires. "Will you never have a pause, as for a Sabbath, and turn a speculative eye upon regions distant and serene?" Santayana asks.[10] There are very few of us who don't want to and even fewer who feel happy when we don't try.

There is a deep tradition that understands and can answer this need, although it is not the tradition of pragmatism or of Hegel. The present, when it is detached from its relations to the future and the past, holds a permanent promise of momentary satisfaction. The delightful absorption doesn't last—nothing does. But so long as it fills the mind, it feels free of the temptations and the disappointments of the world. This is the *nunc stans* or eternal present of which Schopenhauer speaks[11] and which is a living part of the

8. John Dewey, *Experience and Nature, The Later Works, 1925–1953,* vol. I, ed. Jo Ann Boydston (Carbondale and Edwardsville: Southern Illinois University Press, 1988), p. 272.

9. George Santayana, "Tradition and Practice," in *Animal Faith and Spiritual Life,* ed. John Lachs (New York: Appleton-Century-Crofts, 1967), p. 457.

10. Ibid., p. 458.

11. Arthur Schopenhauer, *The World as Will and Representation,* vol. I, trans. E. F. J. Payne (New York: Dover Publications, 1969), pp. 175, 279. Hereafter *WW.*

sacred traditions of both East and West. It may be the only spirituality open to nonreligious people, though it is probably the same spiritual experience religious people interpret in religious terms.

Throwing oneself into the relationless moment is not taking possession of the present as Hegel claims we do when knowledge reaches the Absolute.[12] That present is fully mediated; the web of its relations individuates it and connects knowers to the world rather than distancing them from it. The immediacy is also not exclusive concern with present circumstances, expressed by the cry of "carpe diem," uttered in drunk self-absorption. Both Hegel and the sensualist speak of presents situated in their temporal and causal contexts, not of a present that appears severed from time and presents a momentary glimpse of the eternal.

The splendor of such absorption in the moment is its universal availability. The sunset is as beautiful from the dungeon as it is from the palace, Schopenhauer remarks.[13] What he does not say, but should, is that it doesn't take a conventionally lovely object to induce absorption; virtually any object will do. Taking time to pay heed to the details of the world is particularly likely to yield suitable features or relations for rapt attention. The pattern of rings on a piece of wood, the feel of a baby's skin, or the sound of a distant violin, along with countless other marvels of immediate consciousness, is sufficient to immobilize the mind and reduce (or elevate) it to a stance of speechless appreciation.

The object that evokes grateful delight need not, of course, be sensory. For decades, I have enjoyed thinking Spinoza's grand system of eternity without supposing for a moment that it describes anything real. Mathematicians, we are told, can be absorbed in the intricate relations of numbers or variables, and many children live in the imaginary world of witches and sorcerers. All that matters is that ulterior significance be detached from whatever occupies the center of consciousness. This focuses attention on whatever is present in the present; being unable to do anything with the momentary vision, the mind devotes itself to its quiet contemplation. Since time involves the relation of the present to the future and the past, and since all relations have for the moment been dropped, the object of attention appears timeless or at least removed from the history of the world. This is where the present meets the eternal and our souls find momentary rest.

For a full appreciation of the value of the present, we need to look at the beginning and the end of life as well as its busy middle. The ability of children

12. G. W. F. Hegel, *Phenomenology of Spirit,* trans. A. V. Miller (Oxford: Oxford University Press, 1977), p. 488.
13. *WW,* p. 197.

to lose themselves in their activities is probably unmatched. This carefree absence of self is what makes childhood so attractive, and so unreachable, for adults. At the other edge of life, there are times when death no longer knocks at the door but has knocked it down. People who suffer from painful terminal diseases have little hope of amelioration or even Deweyan growth. For them, embrace of a happy moment is all the "quality" life can offer. Abstracted from regrets for the past and worry about the bleakness of the future, their present can shine with the joy of fading light. Finally, those of us still in the fray need time away from action simply *to be*. Not only meaning in life but even sanity requires that from time to time the rush recede and permit the inner voice to sing. These are the moments when everything feels right, when silence flowers and the wounded soul is healed.

Stress on the importance of the present is not unprecedented in the history of philosophy. "Only the present is our happiness," Goethe says, echoing both epicurean and stoic philosophy.[14] What Goethe has in mind is a little murky, but the ideas of the stoics and the epicureans are clear enough, and it is important to distinguish their ideas from mine. The central difference is this: both stoics and epicureans want to use the present to bring to light and focus on their favored values.

The epicureans aver that the present is the only sure locus of pleasure. The past is dead, the future uncontrollable; if we wish to get anything out of our brief lives, we must seize the moment and squeeze it for its honey. This is a strategy to maximize the timid satisfactions of the animal in us, offering safety, companionship, and modest success. Such pleasures busy the mind instead of clearing it. They tether us to the concerns of the world, for we must control at least our neighborhood for the immediately next present to bring us pleasure rather than pain.

The same concern remains in the stoic absorption in what is directly before us. The present, for the stoic, is a task; it presents the difficult job of establishing control over our desires. The rational self-contentment Kant correctly identifies as the stoic's reward[15] is in complex interaction with the

14. Johann Wolfgang von Goethe, *Faust,* 9381. Pierre Hadot offers an interpretation of Goethe's relation to the stoics and epicureans in "'Only the Present is Our Happiness': The Value of the Present Instant in Goethe and in Ancient Philosophy," in *Philosophy as a Way of Life* (Oxford and Cambridge: Blackwell Publishers, 2001), pp. 217–37. Hadot captures the epicurean view but misses the connection of stoics to the present and, surprisingly, does not relate enjoyment of the moment to Aristotle's idea of activity (*energeia*).

15. Immanuel Kant, *Critique of Practical Reason,* trans. Lewis White Beck (Chicago: University of Chicago Press, 1949), pp. 221–22. Hereafter *CPR*.

efforts that must be expended to achieve the self-control that yields it. The result is concern at least with the immediate future that presents the perpetual danger of weakness of will or rebellion of our desires.

The only presents stoics and epicureans acknowledge are immediacies with second thoughts. Neither is prepared to let go and surrender caring even for a short time. Understanding the past and controlling the future have taken over Western life to such an extent that even enjoyment of the present depends on one or both of them. Shelving the two concerns for the moment liberates the present to display the sheer joy of conscious existence independently of what happened and what may come. This is transcendence of this care-laden life—an embrace of whatever there is that, though imprisoned in the moment, touches eternity.

Hegel attacks such immediacies with a vigor that suggests personal animus. They are, of course, beyond the realm of language, but nevertheless living realities in the mind of anyone who stops to attend. Much of what is interesting and truly important in life cannot be put in words—try describing a scent, the joy of a vague childhood memory, or your relationship to God. For sensitive nonverbal people, and perhaps for some animals, life consists of such immediacies, with overlooked transitions among them. For the rest of us, they are moments of self-surrender and joy and celebration, raisins in the bread of life.

Pragmatists are better phenomenologists of human experience than is Hegel; they acknowledge the reality and significance of the immediate. Peirce makes room for these luminous moments in the form of what he calls firsts. In a passage that clearly takes aim at Hegel, he says, "[T]he Immediate (and therefore in itself unsusceptible of mediation—the Unanalyzable, the Inexplicable, the Unintellectual) runs in a continuous stream through our lives."[16] When James speaks of our inability to penetrate the minds and feelings of others,[17] he is thinking of the unspeakable inner immediacies of which conscious life consists. Even Dewey accommodates moments of self-contained delight in his discussions of the consummatory. He believes that if we look at any item in our experience for its connections to other things, we

16. Charles Sanders Peirce, "Some Consequences of Four Incapacities," *CP,* vol. 5, pp. 264–317.
17. William James, "On a Certain Blindness in Human Beings," in *Talks to Teachers on Psychology and to Students on Some of Life's Ideals,* ed. Frederick H. Burkhardt, Fredson Bowers, and Ignas K. Skrupskelis (Cambridge, Mass.: Harvard University Press, 1983), p. 132.

view it as instrumental. But if we enjoy it for its intrinsic quality, the world stops while we savor it as a passing unique and final end.

Although pragmatists are well aware of the possibilities of absorption, celebration of the present does not come easily to them. If one's ultimate concern is with amelioration, glorying in the moment can seem compensatory. Peirce acknowledges firsts, but proceeds immediately to thirds and the growth of reason. One can hardly read Dewey on consummations without feeling that though he knows they are important, he wants to get on with his study of instrumentalities. He is far more interested in how to reach the consummatory than in how to linger and enjoy it. James comes closest to embracing the immediate, but even he moves on to consider how to get one's psychic life in order.

Even when we combine Hegel's attempt to understand the past with the pragmatic commitment to improve the future, the middle where all of life occurs remains curiously empty. This center, the present where reality reveals itself, is the source of energy and the home of a love that knows no longing. In exploring it, we trace the geography of joy and receive the lesson that the incommunicable doesn't need to be communicated because it is shared. Enjoyment of the present does not take the place of understanding the past and planning for the future. It completes the circle of human life by offering something that can stand on its own and whose value, though not whose existence, escapes the grave.

Stoic Pragmatism

Whatever specific beliefs pragmatists share concerning experience, knowledge, value, and meaning, they generally agree that a central part of the business of life is to make life better. James speaks of the ideal of meeting all needs, Royce of defeating evil, and Dewey of making experience richer and more secure. They are at one in thinking that human intelligence can make a vast difference in how well we live, and they extol the possibility of improving our circumstances. They tend to be dissatisfied with the status quo and see indefinitely sustained amelioration as the solution to our problems.

Stoics, in sharp contrast, are quick to call attention to the limits of our powers and recommend accepting them without complaint. They tend to think that only our beliefs and attitudes fall securely in our control. Epictetus, Seneca, and Marcus Aurelius agree that anything we would consider an improvement of the human condition is temporary and that, in any case, fulfilling our desires accomplishes little. The key to living well, they maintain, is control over self, not over circumstance, and they embrace inner calm in the face of whatever misfortune befalls us.

Even such a brief characterization of these two great philosophical traditions makes it clear that pragmatic ambition and stoic equanimity appear to be incompatible values. Pragmatists and stoics seem to occupy opposite ends of the spectrum, with the former busy trying to improve the conditions of life and the latter adjusting their desires to the course of nature. Much as Dewey's language is grating to contemporary ears, he comes close to capturing the apparent difference between the two sets of beliefs and practices in his famous contrast of the civilized and the "savage" attitudes to life. He writes:

> A savage tribe manages to live on a desert plain. It adapts itself. But its adaptation involves a maximum of accepting, tolerating, putting up with things as they are, a maximum of passive acquiescence, and a minimum of active control, of subjection to use. A civilized people enters upon the scene. It also adapts itself. It introduces irrigation; it searches the world for plants and animals that will flourish under such conditions; it improves, by careful selection, those which are growing there. As a consequence, the wilderness blossoms as a rose.[18]

I think that this radical distinction between the stoic and the pragmatist is misleading and inaccurate. My argument is designed to bring the two views closer together than it has been supposed possible. First, I will try to show that there are times when the pragmatic attitude is inappropriate and good sense requires that pragmatists believe and act like stoics. If intelligent pragmatists have to be stoics from time to time, then pragmatism and stoicism are not incompatible after all.

The second stage of my argument aims to connect pragmatic and stoic attitudes more closely by showing that the usual distinction between them as active and passive is ill-conceived. In fact, if we pay careful attention to the writings and practices of stoics, we recognize that they are disposed to undertake action and improvement no less than are pragmatists. The difference between them is not primarily in what they do, but in their motivation for doing it.

18. John Dewey, *Democracy and Education, The Middle Works, 1899–1924, Vol. 9*, ed. Jo Ann Boydston (Carbondale and Edwardsville: Southern Illinois University Press, 1985), p. 52.

Finally, I will proceed to connect stoic and pragmatic ideas even more intimately. I want to show that in every case in which we wish to improve something, we have to accept the conditions that make amelioration possible. We must be satisfied, among other things, with the tools at hand, the skills with which we handle them, the circumambient situation, and the range of our prospects. In this way, every improvement relies on what cannot at the time, or perhaps ever, be improved but must be embraced without complaint.

None of this means, of course, that there are no differences between what pragmatists and stoics believe. On the contrary, there are important disagreements, but they are of a sort whose presence does not make the constructive combination of the two views impossible. I want to show that a view we might call "stoic pragmatism" is not only possible, but also desirable, and that it provides a better attitude to life than either of the two views alone.

I

Pragmatists tend to maintain that the good is some process rather than an end state, however desirable. Dewey, for example, argues that the ultimate value is growth, by which he means progressive enrichment of experience and improved control over circumstances. This is a brilliant move, eliminating such narrow or final-state values as pleasure, happiness, self-realization, and doing one's duty as contenders for the top spot. Their place is taken by a unitary value with variable content; what counts as growth depends on where we are in life, what we need, and what is possible.

Growth is an appropriate value for children and for adults ready to tackle new challenges. Even older people continue to grow in some respects: they can learn to drive an RV after retirement and increase their knowledge of highways that lead to Florida. In the twilight years, however, the modalities of growth become restricted. Increasing forgetfulness and other disabilities impoverish experience and so have negative value. The areas in which positive development can occur slowly recede until the old find themselves bed-ridden, dependent on others, and barely conscious. At that point or before, all opportunities for growth disappear, and life offers only exhausted ineptitude made bitter by the memory of better days. At such times, seeking growth is unintelligent. We are better advised to accept what cannot be changed and thereby reduce frustration and pain.

The wisdom of seeking acceptance rather than growth is by no means restricted to extreme old age. Quadriplegics undergo a period of growth after their accidents; they learn to cope with their grievous physical condition. But soon, they master the meager repertoire of actions possible for them, and, at least in that important respect, acceptance of limits must take the place of trying to do more. The same is true in innumerable other contexts in which people or circumstances restrict our operational range. Children who want to be adults have no choice but to wait. Unrequited love, unattainable ideals, the permanent absence of means, and hopes out of season, among many other conditions, leave room only for acquiescence and make continued attempts at amelioration futile and thus irrational.

People who think growth is always possible could object here that, if all else fails, we can at least increase our ability to accept circumstances without complaint. But acceptance does not work that way. Some activities and features of activities admit of degree: one may, for example, make one's responses in dating people more and more intelligent. Other doings are of the all-or-none variety, and that is clearly where acquiescence falls. We can accept one thing and not another, and some people accept fewer things while others accept more. But in the case of any event or circumstance, we either accept it or we don't. Growth in acceptance is possible only by adding to the things to which we accede, and not by increasing the degree of our acquiescence.

Moreover, exploration of the condition in which we find ourselves is typically followed by acceptance of its limits as a totality. Quadriplegics can wish for improvement and hope that the harsh restrictions on what they can do will one day melt away. But intelligence demands that they resign themselves to the confines of their ability completely and as a whole. In this, all humans are like quadriplegics: we must accept the operational constraints imposed on us by who we are. We cannot lift ourselves out of three-dimensional space or deposit ourselves in a different epoch of history. More specifically, we cannot fly by flapping our arms, cannot become prosperous by thinking we are, and cannot avoid the damage wrought by age. We can of course try to sidestep some of these inabilities by finding alternative means to accomplish what we want. If our arms will not fly us home, there is always an airline willing to sell tickets. But the very attempt to employ other instruments presupposes that we recognize and bow to what we cannot do.

If we turn to James now, we see a closely similar situation. He thinks that desires and needs are demands for satisfaction; the ideal is to leave no such demand unmet. Ameliorative work consists, therefore, of doing everything we can to fulfill our desires and to help others fulfill theirs. But James recognizes at once that desires—a "howling mob"[19]—are tragically disorderly

19. William James, "The Moral Philosopher and the Moral Life," in *The Will to Believe and Other Essays in Popular Philosophy*, ed. Frederick H. Burkhardt, Fredson Bowers, and Ignas K. Skrupskelis (Cambridge, Mass.: Harvard University Press, 1979), p. 154.

and miscellaneous: the satisfaction of some of them is incompatible with the satisfaction of others. Whatever desires we favor, some others will remain out in the cold. They will have to be, as James says, "butchered" in the name of constructing the most inclusive set of satisfactions possible. The best world we can create in this way, the best world *possible,* is not the *best* world. We have to make choices, and the exclusion of otherwise legitimate desires makes the choice tragic no matter which way we proceed.

James does not say in so many words that this awful and unavoidable loss is to be endured with stoic equanimity. But clearly, our actions must be directed at bringing about the most inclusive order, that is, the largest compossible set of satisfactions. This is as far as amelioration can go. For the rest, we must learn to accept the price of such achievements as inescapable. What we have to give up is rather more than opportunity costs, for those include things we cannot do but may well not desire. The price of satisfying some desires is to surrender others equally or more fervently sought, and therefore to yield to the sad inevitable. Throwing our support to other wants changes only the desires to be crushed; the "pinch between the ideal and the actual" requires that we always leave "a part of the ideal behind."[20] The proper attitude to this feature of the world is to accept it and to learn to live with it. Acquiescence measures the distance between the best we can do and the truly best.

There are two significant differences between Dewey and James concerning the need for acceptance rather than ameliorative action. The first is that Dewey says little about circumstances in which growth is impossible and must therefore be supplanted by a less activist value.[21] James, by contrast, clearly announces that loss is unavoidable, and points in this way to the limits of amelioration. Further, given Dewey's structuring value of growth, the need for acceptance is not ubiquitous and tends to surface especially in the aftermath of tragic events and in circumstances near the end of life. James, on the other hand, detects tragic loss all around and sees no way in which it can be stemmed.

II

The most notable feature of pragmatists is their commitment to bring life under intelligent and effective human control. This activism contrasts

20. Ibid., p. 153.
21. Larry Hickman reminds me that in *A Common Faith* Dewey shows awareness of the need for acceptance. Just as in some places (see below) Seneca comes near to being a pragmatist, so there, Dewey embraces an important element of stoicism. At these times, they approximate being stoic pragmatists.

neatly with the supposedly passive attitude of stoics to anything outside the self. Epictetus epitomizes this frame of mind when he says, "Do not seek to have events happen as you want them to, but instead want them to happen as they do happen, and your life will go well."[22] One way to draw this contrast is by noting that pragmatists look for technologies that help them change the world, while stoics want to develop technologies to change the self. If the primary aim is to achieve equanimity, it is best to desire nothing and to learn to live with failure and misfortune. The attempt to bring the world in line with one's wishes is, for the stoic, a fool's errand, offering only distorted values and perpetual disappointment.

Pragmatists, on the other hand, view the diversion from energetic engagement with the world to inward-turning manipulation of one's wants as compensatory. Surrender of the task of mastering circumstances in times of social upheaval is a natural and understandable response, but it leaves individuals vulnerable and societies without hope. Since control is necessary for life, stoics restrict the field of their endeavor to what they can surely command: their attitudes, desires, and values. But pragmatists can charge that this bargain is both illusory and unwise. All control over the external world cannot be relinquished: life demands that we breathe, find food, and sleep in safe places. Moreover, stoics underestimate the intimacy of the connection between the physical and the mental. In abandoning the struggle for control of at least some parts of the external world, we leave ourselves powerless to defend even our internal autonomy.

Depicting pragmatists and stoics as in sharp opposition, the former active in the attempt to transform the world while the latter passively accept whatever comes along, plays well until we look more deeply at stoic texts and practices. Even Epictetus declares, "Appropriate actions are in general measured by relationships."[23] "Appropriate actions," Cicero's *officia* or duties, are roughly the obligations we incur as a result of the natural relations in which we find ourselves. Epictetus explains the idea by reference to having a father: the son's relation to the father "entails taking care of him, yielding to him in everything, putting up with him."[24] This demands not only self-control, but also a variety of physical activities. Taking care of a father may well involve paying for his support, feeding and clothing him, and making sure that he gets medical help.

22. Epictetus, *The Handbook,* trans. Nicholas White (Indianapolis, Ind.: Hackett, 1983), p. 13. Hereafter *The Handbook.*
23. Ibid., p. 20.
24. Ibid.

Such natural relations extend well beyond biology. On account of his heritage, Marcus Aurelius found himself in line to be emperor. He did not seek the job and, when his turn came, he did not spurn it. Pursuing it would have committed him to valuing power and riches, which are unworthy goods. But given his family background and the long-standing customs that governed the selection of Rome's rulers, rejecting it would have meant denying who he was. Stoic indifference in the deepest sense suggested that whether he did or did not become emperor mattered little in the cosmic scheme of things and should therefore have been of no consequence to him at all. Shirking obligations, however, would have mattered intensely, as it still matters to stoics today, because it touches on internal control the absence of which denies us self-respect. Freedom from concern over external, contingent events is thus not at odds with shouldering responsibility; on the contrary, the inability to master the world turns stoics to the task of mastering themselves, the heart of which consists of accepting what comes their way, *including obligations.*

Meeting one's responsibilities and keeping one's promises, especially in the teeth of contrary inclinations, is a source of quiet satisfaction. This "rational self-contentment," as Kant called it,[25] arises not from *achieving* what is expected of one, but from *choosing* the right course of action and doing one's best to carry it out. The central issue is the integrity of the person, that is, the unity of the agent as it exerts control over its desires. This normative structure of the self serves as the foundation of stoic virtue, which consists of living in accordance with nature. The invocation of nature, however, does not justify doing whatever comes naturally: right action is restricted to what meets the demands of reason, our highest faculty. Reason does not normally counsel inactivity; on the contrary, it requires that we bring our actions, no less than our attitudes, in line with its commands.

The active political lives of Seneca, Cicero, and countless other Roman stoics do not violate their philosophical commitments. They embrace action as a necessary part of the full life. They believe it important to be engaged members of their communities, to criticize irrational habits, and to educate both the public and its leaders about what is of permanent value. Seneca's essay "On Clemency" is addressed to the emperor Nero. Elsewhere, he writes that "your first task is to judge a thing's value, your second to assume a controlled and tempered impulse with reference to it, and your third to harmonize your action with your impulse."[26] Intelligence can make a difference in

25. *CPR*, p. 221.
26. *The Stoic Philosophy of Seneca,* ed. and trans. Moses Hadas (Garden City, N.Y.: Doubleday, 1958), pp. 222–23.

STOIC PRAGMATISM

our lives. Seneca advises us to "apply good sense to your problems; the hard can be softened, the narrow widened, and the heavy made lighter."[27] In places, he is indistinguishable from a pragmatist. He remarks that "the man who laughs at the human race deserves more gratitude than the man who mourns over it, for he allows the hope of amelioration, whereas the foolish weeper despairs of the possibility of improvement."[28]

These considerations make it obvious that the contrast between active pragmatists and passive stoics is simplistic and will not stand scrutiny. Pragmatists are just as vitally interested in habits of self-control as stoics are committed to appropriate social ameliorative action. The similarity is so close that if we observe only their nonlinguistic behavior, we may find it difficult to tell the two groups apart. This does not mean that their likely reactions to every event and circumstance would be identical, only that systematic differences between them are hard to find. But even though stoics may well do what pragmatists advise, their motivations for closely similar or identical actions are sharply different. Stoics seek nobility of mind and tranquility of soul, and they view actions as either indifferent or merely means to internal self-transformation. Dewey, by contrast, values the consequences of our acts both as means and as ends, never shying away from satisfying desires and enriching the material aspects of life. Perhaps oddly, therefore, the difference between those who stress the significance of external achievements and those who focus on the internal life is internal or motivational.

III

Perhaps we should not be surprised at the similarities between such apparently different philosophies as stoicism and pragmatism. Both are, after all, comprehensive views of how to live well and both extol the value of intelligence and control. Here is yet another important resemblance between these systems of ideas: each captures only about half the truth about the human condition. Pragmatists stress the alterable elements of our situation, stoics the features of life that cannot be changed. In focusing on its central insight, each overlooks the valid points of the other and exaggerates the scope of its own. Pragmatists are so taken with all we can do to make life better that they tend to say little about our circumambient impotence. Some stoics, on the other hand, are so impressed with the uncontrollability of external events that they declare all attempts at amelioration futile. Only by correcting these

27. Ibid., pp. 93–94.
28. Ibid., p. 102.

oversights and overstatements can we hope to develop a philosophy that adequately reflects our situation and our prospects.

Epictetus draws a sharp distinction between matters that are within our power and those that are not. The former include only "internal" conditions, such as belief, attitude, and desire.[29] Everything else falls in the other category: reputation, money, social standing, physical health, and the very actions of our bodies that are beyond our ability to affect. This is an extraordinarily bold claim that flies in the face of everyday experience. For most of us, attitudes and desires are much more difficult to control than the movements of our hands. Moreover, it is simply false that defrauding people does not harm one's reputation even as it helps one's finances, that smoking does not tend to impair one's health, and that we are unable to walk, drive cars, and chatter endlessly about all the things we cannot do.

Epictetus hints at but does not develop a distinction between what is essentially and what is only accidentally in our power. This way of presenting the matter avoids the foolish suggestion that we never have control of our bodies and affirms only that we can readily lose it. Desires and attitudes, by contrast, even though we may choose not to rein them in, are presumably always within our orbit of influence. The essential/accidental conceptual frame helps to make clear what Epictetus has in mind, but in the end it is not defensible. For starters, as all references to essence, it has its foundation in values embraced rather than in facts observed; in this case, it serves as testimony of the stoic commitment to view self-control as a permanently accessible good. In reality, however, our power to think and feel as we wish is more tenuous than our ability to move about and see, and it is sometimes largely dependent on it. Rule over the internal environment is a rare and difficult achievement; physical control, by comparison, is often effortlessly easy. Further, integrity of bodily action persists through much of life, but many people are haunted by ugly thoughts and quickly lose their temper. The sharp contrast between what we can and what we cannot control is a fiction designed to bolster stoic resolve to be high-minded and steel-willed.

In any case, why should the impermanence or fragility of social and physical goods militate against their value? If anything, short-lived and rare satisfactions are especially desirable on account of their scarcity, and there is nothing ignoble about social pleasures. Much of what is uniquely admirable and distinctively human derives from the way we cherish and support each other. The stoic injunction to be as independent and invulnerable as

29. *The Handbook*, p. 11.

the gods may speak to us in times of abandonment, but as a plan of life it is grievously truncated. To give up on creating a full human existence out of the contingencies that swamp us amounts to a sad, if not cowardly, escape. The rich life of which Dewey rightly speaks includes satisfactions appropriate to circumstances and sufficiently diversified to touch every element of our being. Though control may slip out of our hands at any moment, there is no reason to believe that a strategy of minimizing commitments and retreating to the citadel too soon makes for a nobler or better life.

Just as stoics overlook the positive contributions of pragmatism, pragmatists underrate important stoic insights. The reason is understandable: humans have acquired awesome power over nature and their circumstances since the beginning of the Industrial Revolution. Improvements in health care, travel, communication, and the production of food have changed life dramatically. Growing respect for rights and increased concern for the welfare of all have rendered existence generally safer, longer, and richer in worthwhile experiences. Those who extrapolate from these developments now speak of gaining control of human nature itself so that we may cure all its diseases and eliminate its flaws. Pragmatism is the consciousness of this burgeoning power, the happy conviction that things never thought possible will soon be achieved with ease. At their best, pragmatists do not forget the counsels of finitude. They know there are limits to what we can do. But it is difficult to preach fall in the summer of achievement and not be blinded by love for the grand technologies of change. Without a sober assessment of what is possible, we tend to forget how situated, local, limited, and perhaps even passing our accomplishments remain. This is the point where stoic reminders may help.

Consider what we cannot change, no matter what we do. The inexorable passage of time is beyond our ability to affect: youth comes but once, loss is irreversible, every action excludes a hundred alternatives, and each inaction exacts a toll. The unforgiving properties of space are no less past change: absence and distance haunt us, presence makes us vulnerable. The physical features of things must be reckoned with: that gravity tethers, weight crushes, and steel penetrates must be accepted. We do not control where we were born and in what century, even though such facts set the parameters of life and opportunity. How can we reverse the damage of being born without bowels, with a failing immune system, or lacking a supple brain? Who can counteract the influences of poor upbringing, awful teachers, and cruel events? The failures and misfortunes of which some lives consist cannot be undone.

In some of these cases, someone at some point might have made a difference; in others, nothing ever could be done. But even where there is room for intervention, the opportunity soon passes and it is too late for a remedy. That is how all of us live, bearing the wounds of the undying past. Why is it that people, drowning in impotence, do not despair of their condition? A few do, of course, and live in quiet grief. But for most, limits and disabilities recede into background conditions of existence: they become things we cannot help and must maneuver around. And finesse and maneuver we do, declaring that what we cannot change must not matter much, that we are fortunate to be as well off as we are, and that disabilities are really opportunities. These may be effective strategies for coping with what fortune casts our way, but they disguise our true condition, as shopping takes one's mind off bankruptcy.

The scope of things beyond control and thus inviting acceptance is even broader than this. When I want to have my car fixed, I have to operate with what knowledge I have of its problems and with the mechanics available. I could, of course, seek additional knowledge of the combustion engine, but the growth of my understanding would then be dependent on my intelligence and on the information that can be obtained. Or I could search out better mechanics in a distant town; but then my success would turn on useful contacts, access to transportation, and my ability to judge people who are in the business of fixing cars by the promises they make. The same situation would replay itself if I wanted to increase my information, enhance my contacts, obtain transportation, or improve my ability to judge. Amelioration has definite conditions the existence of which must be presupposed unchanged; each time we improve something, something else closely connected with it must remain unimproved. The ambition to make the world better in some particular requires that we accept it in many others.

This shows the intimate connection between the need for acquiescence and the possibility of amelioration. The two are indissolubly wedded; we simply cannot have one without the other. I must accept the hammer as it is if I want to drive a nail and the razor available when I need to shave. We do not improve tools when we use them,[30] and even the general properties of space and time that serve as conditions of action are embraced unchanged, eagerly though perhaps unconsciously, as we avail ourselves of them. If acceptance is the price of improvement, we readily see that stoics and pragmatists call attention to different sides of the same coin. The former stress all we must take for granted, the latter the useful changes we can make.

---

30. Vincent Colapietro remarks that according to pragmatism, tools are transformed in the act of using them. This may well be true in exceptional cases, such as when I use a knife to turn screws, but it is clearly not the norm. No such transformation occurs when I board my scheduled flight or don a hat.

IV

The last consideration points to the appropriateness of a new stoic pragmatism. This view combines the accepting modesty of the former with the search for improvement championed by the latter. The theory reflects the attitude of human beings who seek a better life but feel ready to face reality when all else fails. It reduces the boundless ambition encouraged by the success of science and offers a sensible account of our prospects as individuals and as a species. It neglects neither sound counsels of finitude nor the vigorous assault on life essential to making it better, supplementing guarded optimism about the future with a realistic sense of the limits of achievement and the possibilities of failure.[31]

Stoicism and pragmatism enrich and complete each other. In combination they can serve as a valuable guide to social planning and individual life. On the social side, we face the temptation of supposing that existence can be rendered not only richly enjoyable, but also safe and free of accident. Heady advances in controlling nature and overcoming injustice have made us believe that our power can be extended without limits. Human cooperation in science, engineering, and global commerce promises a golden age of happiness for all. New discoveries in genetics and neuroscience hold out hope for a world without disease; eternal youth, with coquettish smile, seems to beckon to us from just around the corner. Huge government investments in research by armies of scientific investigators create expectations of daily progress and frequent breakthroughs. The growing repudiation of exclusionary practices and enhanced commitment to the good of all enables us to say that never before in the history of humankind have things looked so good for so many.

These perceptions and hopes are not illusory. The values of the Enlightenment are alive and well in pragmatism and in our daily practices. Sustained effort guided by intelligence has made the world a vastly better place for us than it has ever been. The key to improving things further is not to abandon the faith that energy and smarts can advance us. But important as it is not to lose momentum, it is even more vital to guard against crushing disappointment. The probability of frustration and consequent disenchantment is directly proportional to the immensity of our expectations; the more we want to accomplish, the greater the chance that we will fail. Accordingly,

---

31. Jose Medina rightly argues that both the pragmatist and the stoic are stringent critics of values and practices. In stoic pragmatism, each adds an important critical principle to the work of the other: the former insists on gauging the efficacy of actions, the latter on assessing their futility.

stoic pragmatists tend to scale down their hopes even as they increase their efforts to make life better. The attitude with which people approach their tasks is a central part of the welfare of the community. If they feel amazed and grateful that we have come so far, they are not likely to ask for the sky or cease their efforts in the face of difficulty.

The stoic in stoic pragmatists reminds them of the contingency of life, the vastness of the universe, the finitude of everything human, the tragic cost of whatever we do, and the possibility that our efforts will be of no avail. Stoics whisper "memento mori," as religion used to but perhaps no longer does, calling the attention of communities to the larger, historical cycles over which they exercise no control. Without a cosmic perspective, we cannot present a just assessment of our situation. With this prospect clearly in mind, we can never place ourselves at the center of the universe. Stoic detachment is a powerful antidote to the hype that elevates science to the level of savior and social effort above natural limits.

On the personal side, pragmatism teaches drive, stoicism surrender. Both are necessary for living well; the former so that we may develop what is latent in us, the latter so we do not become slaves to our success. The Protestant ethic puts many people in overdrive and makes it difficult for them to abandon effort and let go. We may become fixated on an activity or fall so deeply in love with life that we never reach the moment of equanimity that enables us to quit. How long should we pursue people we adore but who show no interest in us, or a profession for which we have no aptitude? Too often we tend to persist, believing that continued work will win the day. Although we cannot succeed without effort, there is no assurance that effort always pays. Wisdom consists of knowing how far to push and when to hang it up.[32]

This is perhaps the most valuable contribution of the stoic. Consider decisions about the end of life. Sooner or later, almost everyone must join the battle with old age or disease. The pragmatist advises all-out war: let the fur fly if the prize is more or better life. Initially, or so long as there is something of substance to gain, this surely is the right attitude. But at some point, combat becomes futile. Another operation and yet another round of untested chemotherapy amount to torture and gain no result. Nature checkmates us in the end, and when that becomes plain, it is unbecoming to knock over the

32. Richard Shusterman reminds me that sometimes only acceptance can improve one's situation, viz. that in some cases only by being a stoic can one achieve pragmatic amelioration. The widespread phenomenon of aging people throwing themselves into youthful activities and failing at them comes immediately to mind.

board in anger and pointless to play out every move. At that stage, the stoic teaches us to smile, to say it was a good game, and now goodnight.

Pragmatism and Death

The ameliorative strategy to life that is the hallmark of pragmatism fails, critics say, because it cannot deal with the ultimate fact of death. It is not altogether clear what "dealing with death" means, that is, what critics expect pragmatists to do about the termination of life. Stoics supposedly know what to do about death, namely accept it without complaint. Deeply believing Christians also know what to do when it comes time to die: they make a last confession, commend their souls to God, and pass away in the faith that they will meet their maker face to face.

Neither one of these strategies is open to pragmatists because they are committed to the improvement of life here and now. Their theory requires completion in practice, and this suggests that critics expect pragmatists to attain a decisive victory over the end of life, a victory to establish once and for all that "death shall have no dominion." Short of such a mighty achievement, pragmatism seems to offer only Band-Aids for the wound of life that permit us to bleed to death.

It is understandable that critics should hold pragmatism accountable for what it says about death. Its central interest is in the improvement of life or, in Dewey's version, in the growth of what is precious. The upward trajectory this celebrates suffers abrupt interruption in death; from the subjective standpoint, the termination of one's existence counts at once as the loss of everything. To be sure, individuals may make some contribution to the flow of life or introduce some changes to the culture of their day. But these achievements tend to be small to the point of insignificance, leaving what is of genuine value unpreserved: in death, the record and distillate of a lifetime of experience disappear without a trace. The termination of life leaves nothing of the skills, memories, judgments, perspectives, and unique ways of savoring the world that constitute a person.

Some philosophers have attempted to address this momentous loss by reassuring us that it is either not final or not real. Religious thinkers call upon God not to permit any created value to lapse by guarantying our immortality or by letting his memory serve as the guardian of everything good. If, as St. Thomas, Kant, Royce, and innumerable others suggest, our subjectivity will never perish or, as Whitehead and other process thinkers insist, it will at least be remembered by God, we can go about developing our personalities in the sure knowledge that what we create represents a permanent addition to the total value of the world.

Such answers to our anxieties are clear and, even if untrue, count as significant suggestions. The argument that the loss of personal life is of no significance, on the other hand, lacks plausibility. Hegel, for example, maintains that an inner life that is inexpressible amounts to nothing and that its supposed extinction—normally viewed as utter personal ruin—is therefore of little moment. This explains Hegel's cavalier attitude to the death of individuals, but it is of little value to people in immediate contact with their private values and feelings. Hegel may be satisfied with whatever small contribution persons can make to their cultures, but such objective immortality is cold comfort to those whose intense personal lives convince them that they are more than wavelets in the stream of life.

Pragmatism is primarily a secular view, so it cannot offer assurances that we are immortal or that nothing of real value is ever lost. One could imagine pragmatists agreeing with Lucretius that though death is final, it is nothing to fear because we will never experience it. But this is an attempt to deal with the dread surrounding the end of life rather than taking aim at death directly. It counsels calm acceptance of the inevitable instead of offering a strategy to sidestep or delay it. As such, it is insufficiently proactive for the pragmatist, who seeks concrete measures to stem the tide of death that forever surrounds us.

That death can and must be defeated is a view embraced by a growing number of scientists and physicians today. Some maintain that death is a disease of which we can be cured. Others, more modestly, believe that the human lifespan can be extended to 150 years soon, and indefinitely beyond that if we are inventive and make the right investments. One might suppose that these thinkers are the true pragmatists, setting their sights on the endless improvement of the human condition and foreseeing a time at which we will be essentially immortal. Yet I find it difficult not to view such ideas as a parody of pragmatism. There is, of course, nothing wrong with extending human life by a year or a decade. That, in fact, is what has occurred in a spectacular way in the past hundred years. Life expectancy in the United States increased from 47.3 years in 1900 to 78.4 years in 2008. We can reasonably expect further modest increases unless pandemics, natural catastrophes, or large-scale armed conflicts intervene. To suppose, however, that we can extrapolate and look for such explosive growth to continue is baseless.

There are natural though relatively indeterminate limits to growth of every sort. If we extrapolated from children's first five years of life and supposed that they will grow an equal number of inches in each five-year period, we would expect to see thirty-foot giants at retirement. The limits are difficult to gauge but they are nevertheless real. Plenty of protein and some growth hormone can make individuals grow taller than they would otherwise, but good food and chemical enhancements can do only so much, and people who grow too tall tend to suffer, in any case, from poor coordination and unpredictable organ failures.

The situation is likely to be similar with those who live for a very long time. We already see that the gradual deterioration of body and mind leaves the elderly shipwrecked in nursing homes. Hitherto rare diseases beset them and, like everything else in the world, parts of their bodies wear out. The dream of indestructible physical objects must have had its source in our frustration at seeing everything decay, and it gains support from the apparent imperishability of the hills and the buildings we raise to crown them. But the permanence is illusory: neither hills nor magnificent structures survive the ravages of nature. Is it not odd that all of us know this and yet serious people declare that of all the physical objects in the world, human beings can be made the most durable?

The ambition verges on madness when scientists announce that aging is a disease. Because what is debilitating illness in one society may be viewed as the touch of the divine by another, no one has yet succeeded in developing a satisfactory account of the notion of disease. If illness is simply an undesirable biological process, some pregnancies could be seen as diseases, as could instances of hunger. This conceptual weakness aside, the belief that aging is a sickness confuses the basic processes of life with their impediments, condemning everything we do and everything that happens to us as noxious and in need of change. This is the latest scientific version of what used to be called original sin, with biological researchers taking the role of Jesus Christ, our advocate who relieves us of our rottenness.

There is a totalizing impulse behind this drive for everlasting life, propelling us to believe that if an extra year of life is good, an infinite number of them must be vastly better. Our Faustian love of infinity makes us want it all: youthful vigor when we are a thousand years old, a supple mind at age five thousand, and love in the afternoon on our ten thousandth birthday. The social changes necessary to accommodate this crazed vision of life cannot even be imagined. The endless existence of the first generation to achieve immortality would leave no room for the young. The wholesome decline of the weary would be replaced by hoary men and women bubbling with the energy of Shangri-La. The subjective consequences of guaranteed survival would be equally devastating. Without finite compass, lives could have no trajectory, leading to the growth of boredom and the desire to die. How long would it take to explore the possibilities of life if our development were arrested to keep us forever eighteen years of age? Beyond that, we would face only repetition and the weariness that comes of enacting the same script day by day.

Finitude is a condition of the architecture of life. We can build ourselves into striking structures in a limited time, but would lack motivation to do much in an endless life. The lesson is constraint, leading to effort and achievement. The wholesome message of finitude is that we don't have all day, that time will run out, and that we just can't do everything we want. Endless life eliminates the regimen of choice and labor and makes us habitual procrastinators. Rejecting the desirability of an endless noon does not mean, of course, that adding a year or two to how long we live is a trivial advancement. To the contrary, that way lie good sense and the foundation of a satisfying life. It is emphatically not the case that the shorter the life the more it is to be valued. As with salt and sex, more is good up to a point but loses its attractiveness when we face a glut. Aristotle was right that there is a natural range of optimal performance for many behaviors. The range falls between what is too much and what is too little, as determined by enlightened experience. Something like this also holds for length of life. The appropriate range may be broad (say, from sixty to one hundred), and with the improvement of medicine, health, and nutrition, it may creep up over time. But we know that some deaths are premature and others, fervently hoped for, are too slow to arrive.

Pragmatists do not have to deny that there are limits to what humans can accomplish and to the number of their days. Accepting the fact that our lives and powers are finite is consistent with their gradual expansion. This is the belief of a pragmatism chastened by ultimate acquiescence, a pragmatism with a stoic correction for the times when intelligence and effort fail. Such times arrive in everyone's life, and when they do, quiet surrender is appropriate. But pragmatists will not yield without a fight, to test if there might not be a way to avoid checkmate. They know that we need two sorts of wisdom in leading a good life. The first enables us to invent ways to attain our ends; the second helps us recognize dead ends. The trouble is that the success of the first obstructs the operation of the second: a lifetime of getting our way creates the conviction that we can extricate ourselves from any situation. This is why we do battle to see if there is an escape. At a certain point, however, intelligent people stop the fight and acknowledge futility.

What, then, is it that the critics of pragmatism want it to do in "dealing" with death? I can see two possible and sensible demands. The first is to provide a way of integrating the fact of death into meaningful and satisfying lives. The second takes the form of making useful suggestions for how to live in the shadow of death, diminishing its power by delaying the inevitable. The first is a conceptual task; the second focuses on practical strategies. What I mean by "conceptual task" is the demand to develop forms of thinking to help us understand the complex relations between the process of living well and its termination. Valuable guidance in how to avoid dying is particularly important for pragmatism because of its interest in practical outcomes. Concrete moral problems can serve only as illustrations in Kant's system of ethics, but their resolution functions as the ultimate test of the value of pragmatism.

There are ample conceptual resources in the history of philosophy to help pragmatists think about the end of life. The most useful idea may well be that of the life cycle, depicting birth and death as natural termini of individual existence. Birth as bursting on the scene and death as abrupt disappearance balance one another in the process of life. The balance is further supported by the symmetry of growth and decline every organism undergoes. Focusing on this image enables us to view death as a natural and not extraordinary event, something that holds neither terror nor mystery.

The notion of the life cycle also reinforces our connection to nature. Our cats and dogs die, as do the squirrels in the yard. We may live longer and perhaps better than they, but we unite with them in our fate. The notion to combat is what Santayana characterized as the conviction that we are "too good for extinction," that what happens to "mere" animals cannot happen to us. A colossal sense of egotism hides behind such beliefs, reinforced by our refusal to be satisfied with however much life offers. Seventy or eighty years of existence should be enough to accomplish what we want, particularly since prior generations were lucky to have forty or fifty. Satisfactions are seasonal: a normal lifespan enables us to enjoy the exhilaration of childhood, the achievements of maturity, and the peace of old age. If we consider that the mayfly manages to do all of this in a day, the time available to us appears nearly endless.

The naturalness of death is further emphasized by the cycle of human vigor. As we age, the energy runs out and peace takes the place of striving. The very old witness a striking transformation: having been an enemy, death comes to be a friend. People in the flower of life find it difficult to understand how anyone could welcome dying. But that is the energy speaking in them and the plans still hoping to be embodied. Only as one ages can one appreciate that there is something deeply appropriate in dying when our purposes are fulfilled, the work is done, and there is no power left to start anew.

Knowledge of the social value of clearing the field for the next generation also enhances the private peace of dying at the right time. The gradual transfer of power and responsibility to the young is a fitting response to aging; at death, control of life and free decision making are completely ceded to those who come after us. Since others stepped aside so we could have our day in the sun, this is as it should be. It serves as the foundation of intergenerational justice, securing the continuity and the integrity of communal life. On one reading, this transfer is the ultimate purpose of education, which is preparation for carrying forward the values and traditions of a society. As one nears death, there is something immensely satisfying in the thought that the affairs of the world are in good hands and that the young will carry on the projects we left behind.

Critics of pragmatism may well argue that this is too rosy a picture of life and death. Isn't the reality far more bleak? Walt Whitman once confessed that he could not live another day if he believed he was not immortal. He said:

> If all came but to ashes of dung,
>
> If maggots and rats ended us, then Alarum! for we are betray'd,
>
> Then indeed suspicion of death.
>
> Do you suspect death? if I were to suspect death I should die now,
>
> Do you think I could walk pleasantly and well-suited toward
>
> annihilation?

The dark underside of the desire never to die is a sense of the meaninglessness of striving in the face of extinction. The counterpart to Whitman's "To Think of Time" is Shelley's "Ozymandias," king of kings, whose greatest achievements get covered by the sands of time. Shelley's point is that in the end nothing remains: the generations that come after us forget our names, destroy our monuments, and lay waste to our plans. Strange and unintelligible customs take the place of our comfortable ways until, were we to return, we would no longer know our home. And then a catastrophe is likely to wipe out the human race, some event tragically self-wrought or else brought on by the dying of the sun. Imagine a world in which there is no one to appreciate the music of Mozart, the joy of laughter, the camaraderie of the corner pub. That is what we face. What is the point of doing anything if it is all undone and the death of everything precious leaves only a world of atoms moving in the dark?

This criticism represents a severe abuse of the power of foresight. Although the Rockies are hundreds of miles down the road, it is too soon to shift into low gear when driving through Missouri. We *know* that the Rockies are ahead with far greater assurance than anyone knows the death of our sun or of the universe. So what looks like foresight is really only forecast, and we are familiar with the fact that far more often than not, forecasts are erroneous. Even if we disregard this significant consideration, however, the possibility of distant disaster is an inadequate reason for ceasing our efforts and failing to enjoy the moment. Athletic teams work hard to win the championship, undaunted by the prospect that their achievement will not carry through to the next season. Couples beget children and lovingly raise them, undisturbed by the knowledge that eventually they will die. People sit in the sun and tan themselves, unmindful of the day when our middling star will no longer keep us warm.

It is sensible to concern ourselves with the near consequences of our acts, but not with what might flow from them in the unforeseeably distant future. Experience of what comes next teaches us what to do and what to abstain from, but only the power of language enables us to waste our energy wondering what might happen a million years from now. This is genuinely useless activity; it does not contribute to handling our problems now and its horror may immobilize us. It may sound harsh but is in fact the heart of sanity to say that what may happen in the hazy future has no relevance to our lives today. Moreover, the idea that events in the remote reaches of time can undo the value of what we love today amounts to the claim that nothing is intrinsically good, that everything is always at risk of having its value revoked. The kiss that leads to an unwanted child may be unfortunate in its consequences but nevertheless sweet at the time it is enjoyed. What is valuable in itself is insulated even from the immediate misfortunes of time. It is completely immune to what may come much later.

The optimistic pragmatist account of death is open also to another, much more serious, objection. We find young children dying of cancer, high school graduates killing themselves as they crash their cars, and individuals cut down by heart attacks and strokes in the prime of life. Their deaths are not good and valuable; they serve no purpose and cause mainly grief. Any glowing account of the appropriateness of death in its season must be balanced by a gloomy inventory of the sorts of death that occur out of season, at times and in ways that undercut human ambition and effort. In some circumstances, death *is* the enemy because it is poorly integrated into the stream of life.

The facts on which this objection is based are incontestable. Death may come at inappropriate times and take cruel advantage of unsuspecting people. But pragmatists do not operate with the "feeble grasp of reality" of which William James accused Leibniz. They know that things do not always go well, that untoward circumstances or uncooperative processes can disrupt even the best-directed existence. The expectation that nothing will trump our purposes is thoroughly unreasonable and the thought that we will always prevail is downright naïve. But lest we become too impressed with the frequency of untimely death, we need to distinguish the termination of life due to human desire or error from its end caused by uncontrolled natural events. A significant proportion of early deaths results from suicide, calculational mistake, carelessness, failing to act on what everybody knows, and luxuriant stupidity. Smokers, drunk drivers, drug addicts, daredevils, soldiers of fortune, and people who win Darwin Awards create their own ends. Absent their folly, many of them could reach a ripe old age and die in peace among their grandchildren.

The rest of early departures are caused by natural catastrophes, genetic construction errors, uncontrolled disease processes, and unpredictable accidents. People who dispose of themselves in slow or violent ways die because they have control over their fate; those who lose their lives in accidents or sickness leave us because they don't have adequate mastery of their lives. And that leads me to the practical advice pragmatists can give us concerning death. Their recommendation is that if life is satisfactory, we should avoid death for as long as we can. The reason why this sounds familiar—just as Aristotle's systematization of the valid forms of inference must have seemed familiar—is that all of us do it already nearly all the time. We do it when we eat, drink, drive carefully, get some sleep, visit the doctor, step out of the way of cars, refuse to take balloon rides with inexperienced pilots, try to learn more about our environment, and avoid midnight trips to inner-city parks.

The question of what pragmatists would have us do in relation to death has a simple answer: fend it off one day at a time. For pragmatists, as in real life, there is no wholesale solution to anything, so we remain in a constant struggle to prevail. Every day we stay alive is a victory over death, to be celebrated as a grand achievement. Every meal strikes a blow on behalf of life; every time we wake up in the morning, we avoid permanent sleep. Each glorious breath keeps us from suffocating and every glass of clean water forestalls infection and possible death. Schopenhauer once said that walking is but a way of avoiding falling on our face, but it was clear that he would have been just as happy to see us in the mud. Similarly, all our labors in supporting life are ways of avoiding death, but pragmatists, and the rest of us, delight in its success.

In addition to private efforts to stay alive, the strategy also includes support for social measures to extend our days. The criminal code, police and courts, public sanitation, mass immunizations, pharmacological research, and institutions devoted to treating the ill are powerful instruments of extending life. They have been strikingly successful and as a result we live healthier, longer, happier, more pain-free, and more secure lives than any previous generation. That we die in the end is less significant than when the end comes; the ideal is to put off the moment until our ebbing energy gets us ready. At that point, we may experience the satisfaction of having lived well and the prospect of permanent peace.

Rescher's Cognitive Pragmatism

Dictatorships are not the only sites of mysterious disappearances. The history of philosophy is rife with theories that drop from view, in some cases never to be heard from again. Leibniz's preformationism, Hegel's astronomical ideas, and Spengler's theory of the decline of the West disappeared from the scene without a trace and so quickly that hardly anyone noticed. This may be an appropriate fate for many views. It is just as well if they go unresuscitated, and it is indeed unlikely that someone would have the bad judgment and leisure to bring them back.

Unfortunately, from time to time even worthy and interesting views slip from sight and leave us impoverished. That is what happened to pragmatism around the middle of the twentieth century. It went in short order from one of the dominant traditions of the day to a curious view no one wanted to take seriously. The usual reason offered for this sudden shift, namely the arrival in the United States of positivist philosophers inspired by the Vienna Circle, is clearly inadequate to account for the decline. Factors internal to philosophy and sociopolitical circumstances also played a central role.

Throughout the modern era, physics envy has been a powerful motivating force in philosophy. The explanatory success of physical theory left a deep impression on thinkers from at least John Locke on; many of them attempted to replicate the sweeping nonteleological theorizing of their hard-science colleagues. Pragmatism, with its insistence on the centrality of purposes and its refusal to honor the fact/value distinction, appeared to be a relic of the past, fatally tied to Hegelian views of context and totality. The pragmatic interest in social and political matters, moreover, played itself out in wrongheaded support for Stalinist dictatorship and became dangerous in the hysterical days of McCarthy. Philosophers thought it best to retire to their ivory towers and focus their efforts on abstract, value-free inquiries.

For about forty years, pragmatism was out of step with the times. Its sudden and striking revival was due to complex and multiple causes, among them the growth of interest in applied ethics, the renewed concern of the professoriate for public policy as a result of the Vietnam War, and a growing unease among intellectuals about the value-free operations and applications of science. Not the least among the reasons for the revival was the intellectual curiosity and perceptiveness of a few thinkers, who discovered in pragmatism rich resources for dealing with both philosophical and practical problems. Nicholas Rescher was, as always, in the vanguard of those exploring new terrain. His embrace and development of pragmatism aided the renaissance and made available a new, well-worked-out, and intriguing version of the position.

Pragmatism is an anti-essentialist view, so it is unhelpful, and certainly unpragmatic, to worry about who is and who is not a pragmatist. There are no necessary and sufficient conditions that, if met, constitute credentials, and accordingly the amount of information we can derive from calling someone a pragmatist is sharply limited. There are so many sorts of pragmatism—more in fact than the thirteen Lovejoy distinguished—that the serious work of understanding thinkers begins rather than ends with classifying them as pragmatists.

One way to think about pragmatisms is to arrange them from Peirce's realistic version that takes truth seriously to Rorty's postmodern, relativistic reflections. On this continuum, Rescher falls close to Peirce. His devotion to the scientific method and his insistence that there is an independently existing world concerning which we may eventually be able learn the truth are clearly reminiscent of that first great pragmatist. Rescher sees little value in a Rortyan pragmatism queered by postmodern accretions and finds himself so far from social constructivism that Dewey's name does not even appear in *Methodological Pragmatism* and *Realism and Pragmatic Epistemology*.

I will say more about Rescher's relation to pragmatism a little later, but first I want to explore the remarkable and unsuspected similarity of his postulate of realism with George Santayana's philosophy of animal faith. I do not know if Rescher is aware of this resemblance. He makes occasional references to Santayana, though more for his pithy quips than for the major philosophical system he developed. The connection to Santayana, who was a realist and in certain respects a pragmatist, will help me elucidate Rescher's philosophical position and lead me to the fundamental objection I want to raise to it.

The realism Rescher embraces in *Realism and Pragmatic Epistemology* is the view that, in Peirce's language, there is an "external permanency" that constrains our beliefs. This "order of mind-independent reality"[33] serves as

33. Nicholas Rescher, *Realism and Pragmatic Epistemology* (Pittsburgh, Pa.: University of Pittsburgh Press, 2005), p. 21. Hereafter *Realism*.

the object our cognitive efforts explore and the standard by which the truth of our beliefs is measured. Any of our current convictions about the objective universe may prove false because its processes—ready to be explored yet unaffected by what we think or hope—comport themselves differently from what we believe. The enveloping natural world both motivates inquiry and stands as the silent judge of our methods and results. Without it, the enterprise of knowledge would be in vain and human communication impossible.

Rescher is keenly aware of the power of skepticism and the arguments of such idealists as Berkeley. He thinks it is clear that the existence of an objective order cannot be proved. Yet it is equally obvious, he believes, that without such an independent world, truth, knowledge, and even inquiry would not be possible. So the epistemic status of realism is not that of an "empirical discovery but of a presupposition."[34] The postulate is required by our cognitive practices for which it is vital that we distinguish truth from falsity and appearance from reality. Without this backdrop of real objects or facts, communication and common inquiry could not exist and the fallibilistic enterprise of science would never move ahead.

One could raise questions about the requirement of an objective world for communication and about the importance of a grand distinction between appearance and reality for conducting our ordinary cognitive affairs. Arguing about such matters is the delightful privilege of philosophers. But, though detailed criticism may be useful and appropriate here, that is not my present purpose. I want to examine the structure, appreciate some of the strengths, and criticize a major weakness of Rescher's pragmatism. I cannot accomplish that if I challenge every one of his interesting but questionable claims.

Rescher proposes two justifications of his postulate of realism, though he seems to conflate them. First, he maintains that its "ultimate justification" is a transcendental argument from "the character of our conceptual scheme to the unavoidability of accepting its inherent presuppositions."[35] He also argues, however, that it is warranted because of its utility; through the results we achieve by adopting it, the view receives "experiential retrovalidation."[36] These two attempts at justifying the assumption of realism do not strike me as identical or even very closely related. The appearance of a transcendental argument in the work of a pragmatist is, to say the least, surprising. However that may be, arguing from something actual (in this case, the conceptual scheme with which we presumably work) to the conditions of its possibility seems altogether different from justifying a belief by its salutary results.

34. Ibid., p. 22.
35. Ibid., p. 21.
36. Ibid., p. 33.

I note this issue also as worth exploring but not germane to my current interests. I want to focus on the similarity of Santayana's justification of his philosophical views, including realism, with Rescher's validation of realism. The connection is best observed by attending to *Scepticism and Animal Faith,* Santayana's detailed discussion of epistemology. That book, as the title suggests, is a work in two movements, the first destructive, the second restorative. In the first, Santayana assesses the power of skepticism; in the second, he re-establishes the beliefs of common sense on the basis of the philosophy of animal faith.

The skeptical reduction features a savage attack on every belief open to doubt. As it turns out, this includes all beliefs, from the perceptual to the historical, from the scientific to the mathematical, and from the public to the personal. The criterion by which convictions are evaluated is that of immediate and indubitable presence; on the basis of that high standard, everything we think true fails the test. Santayana concludes the first movement by what he calls "solipsism of the present moment,"[37] in which we give credence to nothing beyond the immediate content of consciousness. This content, however, is inert and unmeaning. It is what it is, but validates nothing other than its self-identity.

Although such a reduction spells cognitive disaster, it also offers a way out of the grips of skepticism. It points to the irrelevance of wholesale skeptical doubt and the artificiality of the standard on which it rests. A philosophical position cannot be right if it invalidates all of life, even while we continue in the happy pursuit of our values and purposes. Confident human action displays the fatuousness of universal doubt and unmasks it as nothing more than an intellectual exercise. One can hear overtones at this point of Peirce's distinction between genuine doubt and feigned hesitancy.

Abandoning the skeptical enterprise leaves Santayana with the need to establish a different criterion of knowledge. He proposes a new philosophy of animal faith, consisting of the adoption of all and only those beliefs implicated in our actions. The independent existence of a world, for example, is affirmed in our attempts to influence it. Our actions suggest that this universe is deployed in space and time and that, as agents in it, we are both causally efficacious and mortally vulnerable. Other beliefs to which our actions testify include the continuity of the field of agency in which we operate, the difference between animate and inanimate inhabitants of that field, and the identity through time of substantial existents.

37. George Santayana, *Scepticism and Animal Faith* (New York: Dover, 1955), p. 15. Hereafter *SAF.*

According to Santayana, a sensible and honest philosophy will focus its efforts on articulating the tenets of animal faith. These are the beliefs animals (including human animals) would adopt if they thought in propositional form and learned to generalize. To the discerning eye, actions reveal beliefs, and the most general of these beliefs constitute a philosophy we can safely adopt. Its tenets carry the highest level of assurance humans can provide, namely the confidence that comes of success in operation.

Santayana clearly agrees with Rescher that realism and other fundamental beliefs are not susceptible of proof. Initially, they are experiments animals make, and the success of the experiments establishes them as habitual modes of operation that, on their intellectual side, can take their places in the philosophy of animal faith. One might well say that the propositions expressing this "empirical confidence" are postulates justified by the felicitous results obtained through acting on them. Santayana puts it in a way that is close to what Rescher has in mind by retrovalidation when he says, "When once I have admitted the facts of nature . . . then indeed many excellent reasons for . . . belief . . . will appear."[38]

Santayana's view of what justifies the tenets of animal faith can, interestingly enough, also be put in terms similar to Rescher's transcendental argument. As for Rescher, the premise of the argument is the description of certain human practices. The search for the necessary conditions that make such practices possible should yield the same results as does starting with the examination of tacit animal beliefs. An independently existing spatiotemporal world the agents of which enjoy reciprocally effective causal powers is one of the first conditions of engaging in the practices of hunting, fleeing, hiding, and eating. Other conditions can be derived in a similar way.

At this point, however, we arrive at a crucial parting of the ways. When Santayana speaks of practices, he has in mind the rich, embodied activities of animals trying to survive in a treacherous environment. He views even the human "psyche"—his word for the agent animal in us—as primarily engaged in parrying the blows of the world. Our lives are taken up by acting on our desires and pursuing our plans, preparing for trouble and repairing the damage we suffer constantly. We use our surroundings to meet whatever need arises. The perpetual demand for nourishment reminds us, says Santayana, that "matter is essentially *food*."[39]

38. *SAF,* p. 186.
39. George Santayana, *Realms of Being* (New York: Cooper Square, 1972), p. 288.

When Rescher speaks of practices, on the other hand, he has in mind activities of inquiry and communication. He operates on the level of thought, and his transcendental argument for realism is built on "the character of our conceptual scheme."[40] The reason for postulating an independently existing world is that without it inquiry and communication would be impossible. Practices of information gathering and information sharing are, therefore, the central activities in which humans engage. They suggest that we need intellectual accommodation in the world no less than we need physical accommodation.[41]

Further, Rescher is not satisfied with the sort of inquiry in which a bird might engage in looking around for predators and the kind of communication common among monkeys when they warn each other of danger. He wants a much higher level of intellection, consisting of inquiry and communication that provide good reasons for beliefs. The reasons and the beliefs they support must, of course, take propositional form; this is what it means for humans to be "intelligent beings"[42] who search for sound information and guide themselves by it.

This model of human intelligence is well-known and enjoys a certain plausibility. The phenomenal success of social life and the ubiquity of the communication on which it rests support it. People today are in love with information. They want to learn about themselves from psychiatrists, about celebrities from gossip columnists, about the weather from meteorologists, and about the future from astrologers. The vast investments we continue to make in science provide momentous quantities of information, some of it useful for the purposes of life. So it is not implausible for Rescher to focus on the clear and perhaps even quantifiable fruits of research and to isolate our cognitive practices as our most significant and most promising activities.

The prevalence of information goes hand in hand with the dominance of language in our society. The growth of universities as institutions devoted to the cultivation of talk provides support for the impression that human beings operate in a verbal medium. Some people have actually come to believe that all differences among us can be talked out, that finding the right words resolves or eliminates conflicts of value and belief. The informational content of talk is measured in propositions, and the majority of people believe that science is the single most effective instrument for generating information-

40. *Realism*, p. 21.
41. Ibid., p. 27.
42. Ibid.

STOIC PRAGMATISM

laden sentences, for providing reasons to believe them, and for evaluating especially those among them that are suitable to guide our conduct.

In spite of the plausibility of building a philosophy—a "cognitive pragmatism," as Rescher calls it—on the centrality of intellectual practices, I believe that such a system rests on the wrong foundation. Rescher says again and again that our beliefs ground or determine our actions,[43] introducing a tacit but questionable separation between intelligence as manager of information and action as force in need of direction. This is an artificial distinction that is likely to mislead us about how we operate. Even Peirce, Rescher's mentor in pragmatism, maintained that beliefs are simply habits of action or tendencies to behave in certain ways. To say that such tendencies express values or beliefs is not to maintain that values and beliefs exist independently of the actions; on the contrary, they are thought to exist only in the activities expressing them.

Dewey makes a related point when he reminds us that intelligence is not substantival but adjectival. This is a stilted way of calling it wrongheaded to suppose that there is any intelligence apart from intelligent participation in practices. Moreover, a psychology that thinks habits of action can be changed by providing new and perhaps better information to the agent is at a distance from understanding how human beings behave. We may be able to substitute new and possibly better habits for old and undesirable ones, but only in the rarest circumstances does that occur as a result of recognizing the superior truth of novel information.

These considerations, gleaned from Rescher's fellow pragmatists, clearly cut against his view. Since Peirce failed to provide a detailed analysis of the notion of habit, it may not be surprising that Rescher pays little attention to his theory of belief. His distaste for social constructivism renders Rescher's disregard of Dewey understandable, but nevertheless unfortunate. Rescher's deep grasp of science would have made the encounter of the two instructive for the rest of us, and Dewey's subtle account of psychological and social phenomena might have succeeded in convincing Rescher not to make his pragmatism too intellectual.

Although I think Dewey is right in arguing against a sharp distinction between intelligence and action, that is not the ultimate reason for my unhappiness with the foundation of Rescher's pragmatism. A great deal of philosophy today displays the influence of the mode of life of its author. As professors, we live in universities sheltered from the external world. Economic downturns leave our salaries largely untouched, and we enjoy job security

43. Ibid., pp. 62, 105.

and protection from capricious bosses. We are expected to read books and to write them, to criticize and to think up new ideas. Much of the travail of life is alien to us. Sickness might strike, but with fine health insurance, we can afford every treatment of promise.

The major activity in which we engage is the manipulation of words. We argue with each other, give lectures, discuss policies in committee meetings, contribute to reports, write books and articles, and instruct graduate students. We live in a sea of words and get paid for talking, not unlike preachers and comedians. But talk is a thin veneer covering the surface of events, which tends to turn our attention away from the underlying physical and biological realities. In the world of words, a trip to the grocery store may seem like a pleasant journey to meet friends and chat with the butcher. We forget, if we ever knew, what goes into the presentation of steaks at the meat counter. The violence of slaughter, the labor of people who live hand-to-mouth, the pain of working in dead-end jobs, and the insensitivity to the suffering of others that seems endemic are easily submerged in what appears to be a civilized exchange of words and of money for food.

As philosophers and members of an isolated academic realm, we are understandably tempted to think that words are omnipotent and that inquiry and communication constitute the central elements of life. This conviction, however, is not borne out by the experience of the vast majority of humankind. Most of us always and all of us most of the time engage the world on a nonverbal level. We eat, drink, walk, drive, buy bananas, and pick lovers without verbalizing. The choice of what we do, the skill of doing it, and the expected consequences are rarely if ever verbal. Words cannot capture the griefs and exhilarations of living, and dying is a mode neither of communication nor of inquiry.

Of course, it is possible to see a rudimentary form of inquiry in many of our activities. We can suppose that tasting food and checking the weather before dressing are proto-scientific acts involving hypothesis formation and experiment. This idea may be useful for some purposes, but it grievously overintellectualizes the processes of ordinary life. We are not logic machines or mechanisms that attend to and obey rational rules; we just do what we do and let those who wish extract theories from acts. Least of all do we formulate propositions to ourselves or "self-communicate" as we go about the business of daily life.

We may see here a philosophical version of what William James called "the psychologist's fallacy." James noted that psychologists were apt to project the analytical products of their investigations into the minds of their subjects. In fact, of course, psychological processes do not take place in a way that matches their dismemberment and rational reconstruction at the hands of scientists. Similarly in philosophy, investigators try to understand everyday practices by analyzing them into their elements and articulating the principles on the basis of which they operate. This leads to severe error when philosophers suppose that the practices involved actually look like their reconstructed counterparts. Laying bare the logical or epistemic structure of what we do may help the cause of understanding, but it is gravely distorting to suppose that that is how events actually devolve.

Rescher takes a bold step beyond the overintellectualization of everyday practices. He asserts that "a scientifically sophisticated and technologically advanced civilization is itself largely geared not towards the conduct of everyday life but towards the enlargement of knowledge."[44] Of course, as a pragmatist, he adds that one of the purposes of this expansion of knowledge is the improvement of life. Yet this pragmatic concession appears to be of the nature of an addendum; though Rescher clearly means it, there is no denying that what draws him is cognitive improvement.

If purpose is determined by investment, our society is at best modestly committed to the development and dissemination of knowledge. But even the professional search for information is grafted onto the trunk of ordinary life with its roots in the soil of biological and social struggle. Scientific research presupposes and is more than somewhat motivated by the vicissitudes of life and by the need to overcome them. Our admiration for cognitive mastery is so great and the academic world is so distant from the hurly-burly of existence that we tend to enjoy the flower and overlook the root. Yet even scientists are people first, foremost, and throughout their investigations. Romantically, we might imagine them as unrelenting searchers after truth. In reality, however, they have ambitions and fears, needs and wants, conflicts and hesitations. Their days are structured by relations to parents, children, partners, bosses, neighbors, and rivals, and only in a relatively minor way to research paradigms and the truth. This takes nothing away from their achievements as scientists; it simply puts their cognitive activities in the broader context of their multifaceted empirical lives. To suppose that we search for truth much of our lives is to overlook the bulk of what we do and to overextend the ideology of the academic world.

My objection to taking inquiry and communication as paradigmatic practices is that doing so gives a distorted picture of human life. The overt search for knowledge does not occupy a central position in the broad range

44. Nicholas Rescher, *Methodological Pragmatism* (New York: New York University Press, 1977), p. 24.

of our activities. Our behavior is not well-understood as governed by beliefs and principles and is not readily changeable as a result of increased information. Beliefs are not separate realities that govern actions, and knowledge of a propositional sort plays a relatively minor role in the processes of life.

I am aware, of course, that pragmatists do not believe there is a single right place for philosophical reflection to start; they enjoy the privilege of setting out from whatever place they happen to occupy or judge productive. But they do acknowledge an external standard of success even if it is not the correspondence to reality Rescher extols. That standard is deployed in the future in the form of consequences. What are the salutary results of focusing on the intellectual practices of human beings as their primary activities? I can think of very few, other than glorification of the overly optimistic Enlightenment supposition that knowledge solves all problems. This is to gainsay neither the immense value of knowledge for the improvement of life nor the delight and glory of learning about the world. But even in the age of the Internet, the search for knowledge and the dissemination of information are incidental practices embedded in and built upon our wide-ranging social, practical, emotional, and personal activities.

On the other hand, the cheerleaders for reason lose a great deal as a result of their focus on explicit knowledge. First and foremost, they forfeit the opportunity to form a balanced picture of human life. Contrary to what Peirce said, man is not a sign, and only importantly but not primarily a sign-making animal. Insistence on the cognitive tacitly delegitimates other areas of life and forms of activity. It establishes a hierarchy among human beings, with workers and businesspeople near the bottom and intellectuals at the top. Judging by its historical ubiquity, such a pecking order might well be the favorite self-indulgent fiction of professional thinkers; one can see it from Plato's theory of the philosopher-king to Peirce's disdain for everyone whose primary commitment is not to the pursuit of inquiry.

This unfortunate and unfair stratification of persons and activities rests on a suspicious value judgment, whose source may explain its nature. The eloquent make a case for eloquence, the smart for intelligence. The dominance of thought and talk among the literati misleads when it is generalized to all humanity. Focus on the cognitive makes us overlook the obvious empirical fact that humans are ruled by unuttered and largely uncontemplated desires, passions, emotions, drives, longings, strivings, aspirations, fears, and avoidances. Our behavior may be intelligible on some level, but it is not controlled by intellect and for the most part is not open to the suasion of reason.

By contrast with the overintellectualized versions of pragmatism we find in Peirce and his followers, stoic pragmatism does not make the mistake of restricting itself to a theory to be debated and, if possible, proved. Battles over theories constitute nearly the entire history of philosophy; even those thinkers who boldly demand the unity of theory and practice end up trying to establish that unity only in theory. Cognitive pragmatism may be viewed as an attempt on the part of traditional philosophers to rationalize and thereby to subvert the vitally practical orientation of pragmatism. Rescher's idea is to reduce philosophy to a number of propositions and then give the best reasons he can for each of them. In this process, the human realities he sees are those that come nearest to the exercise of intellect. That is the reason he takes inquiry and communication as central to human life.

Stoic pragmatism is also a theory, but that is not all it is. It serves also as a description of sound practices, along with an account of largely unintellectualized attitudes. The theory derives from the discovery of these habits and attitudes. It is, therefore, thoroughly empirical, converting the facts it uncovers into normative recommendations for action. Stoic pragmatism takes human existence in all its nonintellectual complexity as its datum and the quality of life it can secure us as an indication of its value. Although statable in propositional form, it points away from theory toward action, from philosophy in the academic world toward work in hospitals and other places where humans struggle and suffer. Philosophy must deal with the whole human being, not only with the mind. When that happens, the unity of theory and practice will have at last been achieved in practice.

There is hardly a better demonstration of the power of arational forces than the way philosophers themselves adopt and defend their views. If we were governed by reason, our theories would tend to converge and those with the better arguments would little by little win over their colleagues. Nothing like this is actually the case. Philosophers embrace ideas that seem particularly plausible to them. They hold nearly every conceivable view and cling to their positions with unflagging devotion. The energy and inventiveness with which they attempt to justify their ideas suggest that they are less interested in pursuing the truth than in protecting their favored versions of it. The conclusion seems unavoidable that the central organ of many whose profession requires commitment to untrammeled inquiry is not reason but the will, with its infuriating obstinacy. Even those who deride the method of tenacity display great stubbornness in their judgments, remaining for the most part altogether unconscious of their motivations.

Focusing on our social predicaments and on what we share with other animals, by contrast, enables us to develop a picture of human life in all its complexity. This picture must display humans as they were thousands of years ago and as, for the most part, they still are today. The struggle with others, the struggle with nature, and the struggle for life antedate, encase, and outstrip whatever role talk and reasoning play today. Engagement with the world by means of our hands is a fundamental fact about humans; what inquiry would be possible and what would be the value of communication if, like sparrows, we could operate only with beaks? Spontaneous social cooperation, the foundation of human success, prepares the way for systematic inquiry, not the other way round. Information gathering and information sharing are belated and specialized arrivals on the scene, showing us what humans are capable of doing but telling us relatively little about the compass of their lives.

It is understandable that Rescher the philosopher's splendid dialectical mind would make him fall in love with science, books, and thought. But Rescher the grandfather knows that the function of poems is not to gather or transmit information. He also knows that embracing your grandchildren is something deeper and more meaningful than any knowledge numbers and words convey.

Primitive Naturalism

Experience, even of a primitive sort, even the experience of primitive, untutored people, reveals a world continuous with our bodies. The hunted beast is vulnerable to our weapons, but when it turns in anger, we are the ones endangered. The symmetry of causal influence, known to all as mutual endangerment, serves as the foundation and curse of animal life; we seek food and are food, in turn. This is the primitive naturalism of ordinary people who know, unreflectively, that they live in the same world as is populated by everybody and everything.

This world may have surprising regions, accessible only through special openings, such as the mouths of caves, or as a result of special events, such as death. Mysterious holes in the sides of mountains can open our eyes to a magical world of crystals and rivers, which is soon understood to be a part, a very special part, of the ordinary world. Similarly, death may reveal to us a fabled province of happy people given to singing the praises of God, or else a dark realm marked by screams of pain. These regions are also parts of the ordinary world, even though they can be reached only on condition that we die, just as Columbus could visit the West Indies only on condition that he leave Spain behind.

Primitive naturalism, which is the inarticulate conviction of all, is amply confirmed by our actions. We live in a single spatiotemporal world that is largely regular in its habits and hence somewhat predictable in its behavior. Beings that may seem supernatural—elves, spirits, guardian angels, and leprechauns—are all parts of this world. If they exist at all, they exist here and now or somewhere else at some other point in time, always ready to engage in mischief or protective action. Even if mental events are different from what takes place in the brain, they belong in this world and obey its laws. They exist at a time and for a while, they exercise influence over such portions of the world as the human body, and since Locke is right that when we travel we don't leave our minds behind, they are clearly associated with certain regions of space.

Is there anything that does not belong in the natural world? God does if he listens to prayers, rewards the righteous, and punishes the wicked. So also do ghosts, poltergeists, and the Virgin Mary, who ascended to heaven and lives there with her son. Possibilities expand this world immeasurably, though they are not existing powers. Numbers pertain to the world as applicable abstractions, as do hypotheses and relevant errors. Ordinary people have few ontological problems; they know where to turn to deal with entities of virtually any sort.

Such a naturalism is undermined by those who wish to raise one part or another of this crowded world to prominence. They may want to call special attention to God and his angels, control mystical powers, or stress the prerogatives of mind. In doing so, they think they establish grand dualisms or display the ontological priority of one world-region over all the rest. In reality, however, they overlook the fact that in making the supposedly independent regions relevant to ours, they strip them of prerogatives and render them continuous with the mundane. So long as any being has a purchase on space and time and stands with what exists in them in causal relations, it cannot escape being a part of the single world in which we all live.

Philosophers who associate naturalism with the universe as described by science tend to forget about this more primitive, pervasive, and inclusive version of the view. Naturalism is not the position that there is a single world populated by entities that are the proper objects of science, but the unuttered conviction that the world is one and all its parts have access to all the others. The job of science is to determine the constituent regions of the world and to learn the nature of their populations. The Russian cosmonaut who returned from space informing us that there is no God, for he had been "up there" and had seen only darkness, was not altogether foolish. He was right that if there is a God, we should be able to find him, or at least feel his influence. But he may well have looked in the wrong place or failed to perform the proper rituals to invoke the presence of God.

Primitive naturalism makes all issues of existence empirical questions and provides reassurance that a being whose presence and influence cannot be ascertained need not be counted among the existing. The connection of the sciences to this view is primarily through their efficacy in resolving empirical problems. They can trace the source of hidden influences and more often than not provide definitive answers to the question of what exists and what does not. If deviation from the expected path of Neptune suggests a previously unknown object, astronomers can calculate the location of that body and identify it on their telescopes. Other specialists with the relevant expertise can determine whether there are quarks and muons, reproduction across species, and gold deposits under the sea. The evidence for the existence of ghosts and telepathy and for the efficacy of faith healing and prayer must be examined by the best available methods, which typically are—but may not always be—scientific ones.

The conditions for obtaining empirical evidence may, of course, be deadly. Anthropologists have been cooked and eaten by their subjects, and the astronomer who tries to determine the temperature of the sun by carrying a thermometer to it is vaporized long before arrival. Similarly, some areas of the world may exist behind trap doors, permitting the investigator to enter but never to return. Black holes may function in this way, along with death as a condition of studying the afterlife. Once we realize this, we may be satisfied with never trying to enter, or else employ these limitations as spurs to inventiveness. The important fact is that what we want to explore lies open to our efforts even if we must be cautious and clever in how we investigate it. However difficult and dangerous it may be to get to some parts of the world, they can in principle be reached.

What we think of as mystical powers and miraculous events are no less natural than the most mundane forces and happenings. Lack of imagination and the desire for security make us believe that the sequences of the world are always regular and hold no surprises. In fact, the opposite of this is the case: even the most common of ordinary things, the weather, can be astonishing. Extraordinary forces and events surround us, due not to the intrusion of supernatural beings but to the natural operation of the restless world. If shamans know how to cure diseases by words and dance, and if the cures are not accidental, then they must have found a shortcut to the relevant mechanisms of nature. If some people know how to raise the dead by calling on them to rise, the sensible response is to learn the right words so we may be able to do it as well and to believe that some verbal rituals are more effective than resuscitation by pumping the chest or administering chemicals. And it is no miracle if only some people can do it and the rest of us can never learn: no one else can write music the way Mozart did, and only one person could paint like Mondrian.

Much has been made of the ineluctable privacy of minds and feelings. And indeed, my cousin who tends to bore me to tears has no idea of what I think of him. But the impenetrability is not intrinsic, or else I could dispense with making sure that my drooping eyelids and painful urge to yawn do not betray my secret. If the world is continuous with my body and envelops it, thoughts and feelings must find their places in the orders of space and time. Some think that naturalism is an inadequate view because feelings of anger and sensations of red cannot be discovered in specific areas of the brain. But the expectation that everything must be like mailboxes and Christmas trees, located in unique places with sharp spatial boundaries, is groundless. Radio waves spread everywhere and lack definitive borders; actions such as calling a friend in New Jersey are not located in a single place; and summer heat can suffuse an entire continent.

Philosophy suffers from an impoverished selection of examples. Sometimes it operates with a single model and is quick to create dualisms when not everything fits that mold. But there is no need to invent arcane substances and a private world. When I get excited at a football game, I know exactly where my feelings are: they were admitted to the stadium with me and on my ticket. Worries about the existence of other minds and about our ability to communicate with them appear to be the specialty of loners too much in love with themselves to notice the movements of the world. The rest of us know how to get in touch with other people to monitor their feelings, to learn their thoughts, and to annoy them. I could not drive home if I were unable to gauge the intentions of others on the road, and I would never kiss anyone if I thought they lacked feeling or experienced it as a stabbing pain. Success in our physical and social operations provides ample support for the one-world thesis of primitive naturalism.

The primitive naturalism I have described is the tacit belief and operational guide of everyone. We think and when we act we suppose that the world is a single place, all of the inhabitants of which are, potentially at least, within our causal reach. Philosophically sophisticated versions of naturalism are derivatives of this mindset and of such experiential enactments. Is there anything that could disconfirm our silent belief that the world is a continuous field? Only repeated frustration of our plans due to the failure of actions to be efficacious could convince us that reality is, in structure at least, not an even playing field, and this conviction would dawn on us slowly.

If, for example, one day we manage to cross the Potomac on Memorial Bridge but the next, inexplicably and irremediably, we cannot, our faith in the one-world hypothesis may suffer damage. Imagine that the bridge is there, we can walk, no one is holding us back, and yet, as in a dream, we make no headway in getting to the other side. A few days later, we get across without trouble, but then the nightmare scenario repeats itself. We would of course invent a hundred naturalistic explanations for our failure and propose an equal number of remedies. But what if none of the explanations accounted for the irregularity and none of the remedies accomplished what we want? We would over time come to view ourselves as caged beasts, feeling our power yet witnessing our impotence. Since we can imagine many such disconfirming instances, primitive naturalism is not a view to whose truth we are committed no matter what. It lives or dies, as we do, by the success of our actions.

A point worth stressing is that primitive naturalists believe, first and foremost, in the efficacy of action in a field of agency continuous with our bodies and only derivatively in the regularity of the world. So what would concern them about Memorial Bridge–type experiences is not that they subvert the accustomed sequences of nature and even less that what goes on is difficult or impossible to understand. The problem as they see it is that we cannot do what we intend, that even well-executed actions bear no fruit. The idea that the order of nature has changed serves only as an explanation of this failure, and the desire to grasp why and how it has done so is part of the attempt to re-establish our power. Primitive naturalists are not theoreticians. They do not believe in the primacy of action in theory but by enacting it. Their interest in understanding and in the regularity of nature is practical to the core: they want to be able to achieve concrete results.

The claim that ordinary people unreflectively embrace primitive naturalism raises the question of how it is possible for them to be unaware of their commitment. If what I have said so far is anywhere near right, even people who take religious texts literally believe that the world is a unified system of interacting forces. Why, then, do they profess to believe in supernatural agencies, thinking of heaven and hell as discontinuous with the mundane realm? Would they not be aghast if presented with the idea that the natural and the supernatural form a single universe with identifiable doors or transfer points?

In fact, unreflective people are much clearer about what they believe than philosophers make them out to be. They know perfectly well that the realms religion describes are appendages to the world of the everyday. If they were not, heaven would hold no reward and hell no threat. There is an analogy between misbehaving students being sent to the principal for punishment and nasty adults finding themselves on the way to the nether regions. Religious people believe such things unproblematically and they get the ontology right: the natural and what is claimed to be supernatural are equally real elements of the one world in which we live. God is, for such people, a force that can strike you down and a person with whom conversation is possible.

The confusion about the status of the supernatural comes not from people who believe in it but from those who do not. Nonbelievers think that since the world they know contains neither heaven nor hell, believers must have transcendent realms in mind. Yet that is not an accurate depiction of the religious perspective. God-centered people live amid signs and meanings in a world whose "supernatural" regions complement the mundane and rectify its moral failings. But though outcomes in the supernatural realm are just, and hence different from the way things work here, the causal mechanisms bringing them about are identical: companionship and love provide heavenly satisfaction and the fires of hell bring unremitting pain.

Disagreements between religiously and scientifically inclined people concern not the unity or continuity of the world but the inventory of its elements. The former assert and the latter deny the existence of beings such as God and of places such as heaven and hell. Everyone except rationalist philosophers agrees that such matters must be decided by methods that are empirical in a broad sense of the word, that is, by positioning ourselves in the way required to get or fail to obtain certain experiences. Individuals committed to Enlightenment values tend to think that forms of consciousness serving as evidence for the existence of religiously significant entities cannot be obtained. Their opponents charge them with insensitivity to divine signs and impatience in not wanting to wait for evidence that may be presented upon death. When called on to reflect, religious people have no trouble realizing that they are primitive naturalists, even though enlightened spirits want to disallow their claim to naturalism altogether.

A central job of philosophy is to uncover the basic structure of human beliefs. I do not mean, of course, that philosophers are to study the opinions of sundry individuals. They need, instead, to pay attention to the beliefs enacted again and again in daily life, such as the active convictions that food nourishes and that what is lost does not go out of existence. Primitive naturalism is one such deep-seated and frequently verified belief, as is the realism that asserts the mind-independent existence of objects surrounding us. Such an examination of the general beliefs on which people are willing to act keeps philosophy safe from frenzied speculation and the irrelevance of clever moves and hairsplitting distinctions.

I know of only one thinker who has argued that philosophy can make headway by attending to the action-oriented general beliefs of people. George Santayana proposed to establish a philosophy of "animal faith," consisting of the excavation and critical examination of the beliefs behind what people confidently do. This, he thought, would reveal to us "the shrewd orthodoxy" of the human mind and undermine the contrived problems of professional philosophy. The identification of primitive naturalism as a shared belief we continually enact is a step in the direction of developing the tenets of animal faith. Although various other beliefs implicated in action are also in need of study, this one stands out as a central view that honest philosophies must explore, acknowledge, and adopt.

To be sure, there is dishonesty in action, as when we pretend to be friends with someone we despise. In fundamental matters, however, actions reliably reveal people's beliefs. We cannot pretend for long to get by without food or to disguise our habit of situating our bodies with a careful view to other objects, such as trucks that hurtle by. We can say that the trucks are ancient chariots or comets sent by God; such descriptions—picturesque and perhaps symbolic—can usefully call attention to certain features of the objects. But considering what we do, we cannot deny that such things occupy spaces continuous with those inhabited by us and that we believe they have both helpful and harmful causal properties.

Dissembling in philosophy, by contrast, is easy and attractive. We can pretend to doubt everything, maintain that space and time are illusions, invent substances, or announce the discovery of human world-creative categories. All the while, of course, we sincerely believe that our books reach other human beings, take time to lecture in distant cities, find ourselves satisfied with the possession of ordinary objects, and accept the world pretty much as it presents itself, without our contribution. The call for honesty in philosophy is a plea to have our actions serve as the test of our convictions and to give no professional credence to what we cannot enact, that is, to bring our philosophical lives into line with our lives as agents in the world. Honoring the call does not close the chapter on philosophy in the intellectual history of our species. To the contrary, it places the field on a sound footing by giving it a new and clearly achievable task.

The idea that belief is, among other things, a tendency to act has been with us since the days of Plato. Oddly, however, the connected truth that action is or reveals a tendency to believe has escaped the notice of philosophers. Calling attention to it and laying bare the beliefs implicit in ordinary action can eliminate insincere and implausible theoretical views. It can also establish at last the primacy of action in philosophy. A great many thinkers have avowed their commitment to this primacy. Kant, for example, announced that reason cannot gain satisfaction in its theoretical employment; only in

STOIC PRAGMATISM

the sphere of action can it be fulfilled. Yet his reason takes no instruction from activity as we know it in this world. Kant develops instead his own idea of what action, properly conceived, should be. So it is not empirical acts that acquire primacy in his system but only the idea of action, or action as it is thought in philosophy. The distinguished thinkers emerging from Kant and reinterpreting his ideas have not succeeded in establishing more than the primacy of practice *in theory*, that is, of the *idea* of practice. They have not surrendered themselves to the examination of real-world action and the implications it holds for the theories we should embrace in philosophy.

Primitive naturalism is an important part of the philosophy that explores the generic beliefs suffusing action in a space-time world. In fact, it is the central tenet of the philosophical system derived from "empirical confidence." Although Santayana was the first to develop them, it is important to note that this view of the task of philosophy and this notion of naturalism are independent of the ontology he attached to them. His categories of essence, matter, truth, and spirit or mind have merits of their own, but they neither imply nor are implied by primitive naturalism. This means that the weaknesses of the ontology and the current unpopularity of such conceptual structures leave primitive naturalism untouched.

There are at least two reasons for the separation of primitive naturalism and its connected philosophy of animal faith from the ontology of different "realms of being." The first is that though Santayana attempts to make them a seamless whole, they are nevertheless quite distinct, the former gaining expression in *Scepticism and Animal Faith* and the latter appearing only in the later books, collectively titled *Realms of Being*. The second and more urgent reason for detaching primitive naturalism from ontology is that the ultimate issue worth exploring is not the truth, adequacy, or usefulness of Santayana's system of thought but his proposals for how we might understand naturalism and, more generally, how we can develop a method by which philosophical thinking might profitably be conducted.

Our age is one in which philosophy has, once again, lost its way. Some believe critical thought can sweep clean the Aegean stables of mistaken religious, popular, and scientific opinions. Others despair of the ability of philosophy to accomplish anything at all, with the possible exception of its own burial. Still others attempt to employ outlandish methods to come, not surprisingly, to outlandish conclusions. At such a time of crisis, modesty and good sense are hard to come by and desperately needed. Examining human actions for the time-tested beliefs they reveal is a promising way to conduct philosophical inquiry. Primitive naturalism as the first fruit of this method re-establishes the social usefulness of philosophy and points in the direction of sensible and lasting results.

Learning about Possibility

The physical world is a vastly complex place; human institutions, history, and traditional practices make it even more involuted. It takes the young many years to learn to operate in this environment. They get everything they know from others and from personal experience, but much more from the former because the latter is slow and limited in scope. Every human being we meet is in one way or another our teacher, conveying valuable information about the forces that surround us. But some humans educate us systematically or as a matter of their profession: their job is to teach us about how things stand in some area of life.

Such teaching can be part of an institution, though it need not be: marriage partners teach spontaneously and over many years what they will not accept from each other. The support educational institutions receive from their communities is due to the need to convey in a speedy and organized way the knowledge, values, and accepted practices of the culture. Professional teachers impart information and help their students develop useful skills for dealing with the complexities of the world. The emphasis is, understandably, on the actual; the function of education is to enable people to live longer and better lives.

In spite of the charge of irrelevance, undergraduate courses are devoted to the exploration of reality. Physics, chemistry, and biology deal with aspects or elements of the physical world; history lays bare what happened; sociology and economics uncover vast sets of interactions among human beings; even much of mathematics is focused on how it can help us understand the world. It may seem that fields of investigation specializing in the works of the imagination escape this tyranny of the actual, but students of literature are less interested in the luminous unreality depicted in stories than in how these symbols contribute to our ability to deal with the actual.

This interest in reality is natural and appropriate. "What else is there?" one could reasonably ask. Since human life is precarious and easily snuffed out, we have a more than adequate motive for learning everything we can about how the world works and for trying to tilt it to our advantage. Those who know more are typically, though not always, better at bringing about desirable outcomes. The likelihood of their controlling their environment and obtaining what they want is higher than that of people operating without special skills and information. The philosophical tradition has always maintained that the object of knowledge is the real. The veneration of knowledge, to which Nietzsche so vehemently objected, is therefore at once the veneration of reality, a quiet surrender to what unquestionably IS.

As Leibniz and others knew, however, the actual is but a tiny fragment of totality, surrounded on all sides by possibilities. Reality is embedded in an infinite field of what might, or might not ever, be. This is the world of the imagination, though among humans even the imagination is finite and can never do justice to the richness of the absurd, the baffling, the unforeseeable, the unintelligible, and the mind-numbingly large or complex. We cannot wrap our minds around the millionth prime number and cannot give content to how life might be different a hundred years from now.

The unfortunate oversight of possibility is supported by the general sense that the actual is natural—that there is something right about how things are and it would be inappropriate to try to change them. This feeling is ubiquitous, showing itself in how we relate to the house in which we grew up, the language we have been taught to speak, and even the table manners to which we have become accustomed. Alternatives to these and other habits tend not to occur to us. We simply don't see that anything we do is a selection from innumerable other things we could be doing and that even *how* we do things is optional and has only the weight of actuality to recommend it.

Educational systems are so busy teaching students about what is that they have no time and no taste for exploring alternatives. In any case, awareness of alternatives tends to make people think that everything is contingent, which might lead to questioning the status quo and thereby to destabilizing the entire system. Surely one of the reasons for discouraging speculation about how things could be different is that we might take matters in our own hands and change things to suit our desires. Even vision that differs from the conventional is considered illegitimate, as when her first grade teacher upbraided our daughter for having drawn a marvelously imaginative picture of the sun, in place of the conventional yellow orb with lines representing its rays. Hers was just an innocently different aesthetic vision; the presentation of alternative institutional arrangements, rules, and values is met with far more vigorous disapproval.

The guardians of the status quo do not welcome the consideration of possibilities because they make their living from existing arrangements. Institutions resist change even more mightily. They are conservative systems interested in safeguarding the actual, of which they are salient parts.

Everything in the world seems to want to hold on to existence, which can be accomplished only by rejecting all other possibilities. Change is death to what exists now. Since it consists of the embodiment of some other possibility, the best way to stave it off is not even to acknowledge alternatives: the actual operates as if the myriad possibilities ready to replace it were not nipping at its heel.

Schools typically reinforce the tendency to suppress the possible. Social and political changes, for example, are presented as matters of the past whose sole legitimacy lies in having conducted us to our current, excellent system. Language is taught as it is supposed to be written, scientific theories are presented as facts, and even literary criticism restricts itself to a small number of canonical interpretations. Thomas Jefferson and his friends were inventive in how they spelled words; for us, any nonstandard spelling counts as error.

To be sure, some teachers announce proudly that they reject satisfaction with the actual and think of theirs as a subversive profession. They use ridicule or critical questioning to undermine the unthinking acquiescence of their students in whatever shape the world takes. They feel emboldened in their classrooms to say nearly anything they want and delight in creating the impression that in their opinion nothing is sacred. It seems invigorating to see them challenge every orthodoxy and question the legitimacy of all authority.

Young people speak and act as if they wanted to revolt against the authorities that surround them on every side, but they learn to treat power with respect early in life. Their talk of rebellion is no more than that, and soon they make their peace with whatever institution accommodates them and however many mad rules it imposes on them. Rebellious undergraduate drugheads become lawyers in three-piece suits; anarchist artists who painted obscene frescoes on dorm walls learn to photograph cakes for magazine ads. Hardly any of them can imagine what will become of them precisely because no one taught them how to deal with possibilities and thereby fend off surrendering to what in their salad days they would have thought a nightmare.

Sadly, the bold talk of teachers has no more substance than the rebellious grumbling and foot-dragging of the young. Supreme courage in the classroom is little more than talk—in the hall and in the dean's or principal's office, teachers act as obedient officials of the institution. Principles seem to belong in the realm of discourse; reality demands compromise and adjustment. In this way, teachers learn to enact the living contradiction of mighty words and petty deeds, of never quite doing what they say one should. When students notice this, they lose all respect for their teachers. What good are words that never inspire acts?

All of this goes a long way toward explaining the tenuous life of possibilities in human society. They are difficult to envisage in detail and it is never enough to articulate them in words. The actual surrounds us on all sides. In stable societies, the weight of the status quo is such that we can hardly believe anything could be different from what it is. The possible can gain a foothold against the everlasting IS only by being embodied in at least one life. It acquires credibility only by becoming actual or at least by having someone demonstrate the steps that will take us there.

The demonstration must be concrete and visible. Teachers who speak eloquently of social or institutional changes but never act on them fail to teach about possibility; outlining a future without embarking on bringing it about makes it look distant and unattainable. Literary critics who explain how novels should be written but never write one, social critics who stand on the sidelines observing the birth struggles of the new, and psychological counselors in the business of giving advice on which they tend not to act are enemies of the possible who masquerade as friends. They cheapen it by showing how little power it has to engage the soul and how easily those who profess allegiance to it can be discouraged from its pursuit.

Not surprisingly perhaps, those devoted to possibilities of harm appear more ready to take vigorous and steadfast action in pursuit of their vision. The literatures of heaven and hell are uneven in their specificity and quality: we can describe the tortures of the damned in exquisite detail, but find ourselves oddly bereft of ideas when it comes to the rapture of the saved. Tamerlane, Hitler, and Saddam Hussein entertained clear notions of preferred futures for their victims, as do thieves, rapists, and sadistic bureaucrats all over the globe. Such people have little trouble motivating themselves to act; their deeds and their imaginations appear to be welded together into a seamless nasty whole. People of goodwill, on the other hand, tend to be faint of heart when it comes to doing what they know they should. They suffer from self-doubt, hesitate, and talk themselves out of allegiance to a shining possibility by bringing to mind innumerable other alternatives. In the end, many of them find a proxy for action in an avalanche of words.

This discrepancy is particularly puzzling because in many instances benevolent people are protected from the consequences of their actions taken on behalf of ideals. College and university teachers, for example, enjoy the benefits of tenure, meaning that they can be fired only for crushing incompetence or gross moral turpitude. Such job security is the perfect cover for speaking one's mind and acting on one's convictions. Criticism of the institution and of the society beyond is protected speech, and so long as correlated actions do not violate the laws, they can be performed with impunity. Given the threat of bad publicity and expensive lawsuits, the likelihood of institutional retaliation is slim; its consequences are negligible.

For, after all, what could the administration of a university do to punish tenured in-house critics? They may be scheduled to teach at inconvenient times, forced to move their offices to the basement, and have their salaries frozen. In the grand scheme of things, however, *when* one teaches is of little significance. If one's office is a windowless cubicle, one can simply reduce the time spent there to the mandatory hour or two a week. Moreover, tenured professors earn a substantial salary, so making do without the annual 2 or 3 percent raise should not present a problem. At most, university administrators can make the life of critical faculty members uncomfortable, which is a small price to pay for doing what a teacher should, namely explore possibilities so that a suitable ideal may be found and enacted.

Relative invulnerability does not embolden faculty to think and teach the possible. Tenure protects much more than classroom speech. Public criticism, peaceful protest, and investment of one's time and money are among activities one can support by evidence derived from one's field of specialization. Yet teachers show themselves to be a timid lot, always ready to sidestep commitment and find an excuse for not taking a stand. This lamentable lack of courage defines them as distant from the concerns of life and shining only so long as empty words suffice.

Timidity makes it impossible for teachers to fulfill their mission. Teaching the young involves activities that pull in different directions: the culture's practices and values must be handed on, but they must also be criticized and suitably revised. In doing the former, teachers act as servants of the past, giving a favorable account of the fruits of long experience. In doing the latter, they labor for the future, presenting ideas for how our practices can be improved. The first activity is centered on sketching the geography of what exists and explaining the rules governing it; the second is about the ways the possible can bring improvement to the actual. The first without the second yields stagnation; the second without the first creates chaos. When properly related, the two preserve what is of value from the past even as they encourage active dreaming about a better future.

Making established practices look attractive is a favored activity; this is what makes teachers beloved in the eyes of students who grow up to be pillars of society. Criticizing our comfortable values, on the other hand, makes instructors seem alien in their own world or troublemakers ungrateful for the good that society lavishes on them. They need courage not so much to give voice to their own beliefs, which can range from the idiosyncratic to the absurd, but to express their dreams and thereby point to possibilities that may otherwise escape us. Without daring, teachers can only repeat the well-worn wisdom of the past, much of which is, in any case, available in books.

The critical stance toward current practices is as necessary in the sciences as it is in the humanities. Established methods and theories in physics, chemistry, and biology invite periodic challenge; at least some of them may have served us well in the past but now stand in need of imaginative revision or replacement. The social sciences are in a unique position to offer ideas concerning novel economic, social, and political arrangements, and the humanities have traditionally been a hotbed of new values and thoughts about better ways of treating our neighbors. At the very least, practitioners of all fields can have something useful to say about improvement of the institution in which they serve. Sharing those ideas is a minimal obligation and involves the development of possibilities considered, as it used to be said, under the form of the good.

Tenure in universities and colleges was instituted largely to protect faculty members in their vital activity of offering unpopular possibilities to their students, to administrators, and to the public at large. Some may think that tenure confers a right to speak on faculty members and a collateral obligation on the institution not to fire them for the views they hold as professionals. This, however, is only part of the story. The right conferred carries with it a duty: faculty members are not only permitted to speak their minds without retaliation, they must do so. By extending tenure, an institution of higher education hires critics and pledges to pay them for the trouble they give. Those who do not present possibilities constituting at least tacit criticisms of the status quo fail to meet the conditions of their employment.

This failure is so widespread that at one point I suggested the possibility of requiring each tenured faculty member to advance at least two critical initiatives a year.[45] Not surprisingly, this idea captured the imagination of no one. Administrators did not want to have to deal with in-house critics, and teachers were concerned about their next raise. Artificial as the method may be, it addresses the real problem of faculties taking little interest in the governance of their institutions and timidly avoiding criticism of deans and presidents. Such behavior may make more time for advancing one's research

---

45. John Lachs, "Intellectuals and Courage," in *A Community of Individuals* (New York: Routledge, 2003), p. 9.

agenda, but it does not improve the university one serves and whose care should be in all its employees' hands.

A more natural way to enhance the role of possibilities in our lives is to make teachers fall in love with them. The changes must begin in kindergarten. Fortunately, in young children the imagination is as strong as the sense of reality; all we have to do for them is not to crush the free play of their images and thoughts. Beyond puberty, when the actual lays siege to their minds, we must aid their resistance by showing that their teachers know how to think alternatives and rewarding them when they do likewise. The undergraduate curriculum needs to be changed to teach not only how things are, but also how they might have been, and may yet become, different. Even graduate and professional training have to be imbued with a sense of what is not, in order to take a full measure of the nature and limits of the real. The education of teachers in the love of possibilities must thus stretch from the time they first enter school as young students to the time they take retirement.

Embrace of possibilities may be confused with ready adjustment to inevitable change. But adjustment is serious work that belongs to the world of the actual. It lacks the free-ranging playfulness of considering alternatives and the excitement of the what-if. Moreover, there is a great deal of irrelevance in the range of possibilities: some have little or nothing to do with the world in which we live. We can imagine beings with eighty-two heads and kidneys, large as balloons, that encase them. We can think that clouds of methane gas sing the national anthem while small molecules scratch their tiny heads. Such fancies are certainly possibilities and they may have some use in the realm of humor. But they have little relation to the task of making life better and they make no contribution to recrafting reality. The possibilities we must always keep in mind are those relevant to the real but not now actualized, alternatives that help us understand the world in which we live or offer a blueprint for desirable change.

The most intriguing possibilities, which are at once the most difficult to bring into focus, cluster around our current fashion of conceiving the world. The way things appear to us has the authority of the objective and the natural. This takes attention away from the contingency of current arrangements and the contribution our thoughts make to how things seem to be. The French and the American revolutions opened our eyes to the possibility of new social and political orders; Darwin made it possible for us to view biology, and human beings, in a novel way. American pragmatism and postmodernist challenges are bringing home to us that how we think about the world is a vital element in its constitution and that such thoughts are within our power to change or to retain.

Inevitably, each new way of thinking freezes into place and, appearing natural and right, resists challenge. To counteract this tendency, we must keep reminding ourselves that modes of thought, no matter how entrenched, are optional. We can think of sex, for example, as a duty within the context of holy matrimony or as casual recreation; of doctors as superior humans with unique access to the mysteries of the body or as useful health consultants; and of bureaucrats as powerful agents of obstruction or as servants of the public. Each mode of thought defines appropriate behavior and leads to consequences we may or may not desire. In the end, how we think should be determined by the consequences we want to achieve. This requires that we stand ready to exchange conceptual structures as if they were useful instruments. This is what the contemplation of possibilities is all about: in thinking of alternatives, we add tools to our tool chest. Nothing has a more profound effect on the world than a good idea.

CHAPTER 3

INFINITE OBLIGATIONS

Human Blindness

In writing about *a* certain blindness,[1] William James proves himself less than sharp-sighted about the variety of human intellectual-ocular impediments. He thinks he has identified a single disability when in fact he is focused on a broad range of problems. I do not want to be grudging in my praise of James; it is always cause for joy when philosophers tackle issues of moment for daily life. James is superb at this. His essays, such as "What Makes a Life Significant" and "The Moral Equivalent of War," illuminate issues of great personal and social importance. But he is notoriously reluctant to draw distinctions, even when they are vital for clear vision or for the outcome of his argument. In the case of the essay on blindness, failing to see the diversity of phenomena he addresses garbles the message he wants to convey. Human blindness is far more widespread, far more variegated, and far more insidious than James represents it, yet overcoming it, even if it were possible, would create as many problems as it would solve.

The primary form of blindness in James's line of sight is the failure to see how others view the world. This actually consists of two disabilities, the first that of not being able to see the world the way others see it, and the second that of closing our eyes to the divergent devotions of other people. James conflates the two through his example of coming across a hideous house and clearing in the woods that the mountaineer sees as his beautiful home. James finds shocking the realization that someone can value something so primitive. But he thinks the woodman's perception of his bit of reality is equally dismaying.

---

1. William James, "On a Certain Blindness in Human Beings," in *Talks to Teachers on Psychology and to Students on Some of Life's Ideals,* ed. Frederick H. Burkhardt, Fredson Bowers, and Ignas K. Skrupskelis (Cambridge, Mass.: Harvard University Press, 1983), pp. 132–49.

Our view of the world is deeply influenced by our values, but perceptions differ not only as a result of embracing different goods. Color-blind people, for example, cannot even imagine what a world of reds and greens might be like. Similarly, individuals lacking a sense modality, such as hearing, operate in an environment not easily understood or replicated by people without that deficit. And I doubt that any human being can experience in the rich olfactory fashion common to dogs. One's condition or circumstances also serve as perceptual determinants: in a child's world, even short parents appear as towering giants. Social conditioning influences the look of the world no less. South American Indian parents taught their children to see invading Spaniards as creatures, each of whom, with his horse, constituted a single animal.

The influence of values on our view of reality is profound. Love offers a striking example. It can make ugly children and toothless spouse appear as creatures of magic and light. A similar chemistry renders it difficult to see ourselves as others see us, or others as they see themselves. If we don't share the values of people, we remain strangers to their worlds. Yet embracing what others prize is a rare achievement. For the most part, even a sympathetic grasp of why they hold their values eludes us. Such incomprehension may lead to overt conflict; at the very least, it fuels a quiet antagonism to much that is not ours.

There is also a third form of blindness, that connected with the emotive tone of experience or the way life feels to other people. We encounter this, for example, in the excited activity of the lantern bearers James describes, hiding their lights under their coats. The problem is that our view of the excitements of others is always external; we see the things they do but not how it feels to be doing them. Yet, James correctly avers, much of the joy of life resides in the rich emotive feel that accompanies our activities. Without it, we are rocks in the meadow or the burnt-out hulls of meteors.

When a new dog joins the pack, it sniffs with delight and its tail wags happily. In a similar fashion, laughter and smiles spread readily from one person to another; it is difficult to escape the contagion of the group. But existentialists, though dour, are right that each person smiles alone, that the feel of the smile, the smile of the inner face, is open only to one. So it is with suffering, as well, both in the form of pain and of the anxiety that casts a shadow over life. We simply don't know what exhilaration and depression feel like in our neighbors. We view them and deal with them as though we were behaviorists, attentive to their outward movements but unmindful of their inner life. Distance from others exaggerates this blindness to their pain, yet—paradoxically perhaps—close presence does not enhance our access to their joys.

The inevitable corollary of such ignorance is a fourth sort of blindness, namely that to who others are. This does not mean that we fail to remember the names of people or don't know them by their social positions or their jobs. What we lack is a clear view of what makes them tick, that is, of what we might appropriately call the constitution of their souls. Ignorant of their motivations, surprised by their purposes, and unlettered in their principles, we live near them the way birds and squirrels share a tree as home, each in its own nest, indifferent to all the rest. Thus we see spouses of fifty years realize that they are married to a cipher. A trusted partner is not necessarily a person whose soul is known; loyalty in marriage may give the relationship stability, but the routine that reassures also induces sleep, inviting people to go through life blind in their intimacy.

Our sightlessness is by no means limited to such subjective elements of the world as persons, their views, their feelings, and their values. Sometimes we are victims of a fifth kind of blindness, that of operating in ignorance of objective parts of reality and their meanings. Such undiscerning ways differ from those we have discussed so far in a variety of ways, among them by being relatively easy to remedy. In subjective matters, there is a wall between persons that may be scaled only with much trouble; the *facts* we overlook, however, tend to stare us in the face. The attitudes of people are reflected in their eyes and in their acts; it is not difficult to discern changes in their moods. Yet many marriage partners feel crushing surprise at infidelity even though they had ample early signals. Similarly, we may not notice danger on the road, the missing coffee table, or that someone cleaned the house. Such inattention is fed by routine, falsely suggesting that our corner of the world is adequately explored and can therefore be disregarded.

This problem of what James calls "the jaded eye" naturally leads to a sixth sort of blindness, one that makes us view the world as old and boring. This is a tragic loss: it colors our days gray and fills life with ennui. We miss a great source of happiness when we no longer see the world as ever new. The joyous symmetry and asymmetry that pervade the real, the energy with which each being occupies its slot in the scheme of things, and, in the end, the delightful improbability of everything should be enough to amaze us for the few years we are here. Yet we meet people who can summon no ideas out of what I just said and see the world as if through dead men's eyes.

A Mozart can love every note and endlessly caress their sequences. A Picasso may be in love with shape and color, and a Frank Lloyd Wright with how walls articulate space. But we don't have to be artists to see the marvelous riches of the world; attention to details is enough. The swirl of lines in wood and the way water runs downstream can make children of adults. The construction of insect bodies and the grand complexities of a single molecule are simply astonishing. The explosive growth of bamboo is as fascinating as the slow deterioration of wood on the forest floor. There is hardly a thing or a relationship that fails to offer food for reflection or at least to induce amazement. All we need is eyes for it, that is, a receptive and energetic appreciation of what surrounds us. Blindness to the beauty of the world is blindness to what is best in our earthly lives.

A seventh sort of unseeing is easily confused with failure to connect with the vibrancy of the world. James refers to this blindness only briefly in his essay, though it is a recurrent theme in his other writings. We detect the beauty of the world by enhancing our sensations, by living—we might say—through the senses. But our "sensorial life" yields much more than beauty, and if we efface it, we lose more than the eye-opening newness of existence. When we downplay it, we become crippled by concepts, people who live in their thoughts or fall prey to ideologies. Like D. H. Lawrence and others, James is a champion of sensory life and an implacable critic of abstraction. This form of blindness is the failure to notice the concrete, the specific, and, on the reading of empiricists, the *real* in the world. Since concepts are so much easier to deal with than recalcitrant facts, people gladly turn away from harsh reality to thin and pliable ideas. Our sensations may be "powerful and ineffaceable," but they do not command the attention our favorite notions do. They are constantly overruled by being interpreted, so that we end up seeing what we think.

Blindness to our sensations suggests an eighth and altogether different sort of inattention. The desire to be considered a member of "the elite" turns us away from our simpler functions toward a celebration of sophisticated but derivative activities. We enjoy going to dinner parties, for example, but overlook the joys that come from chewing and swallowing. We seek to engage in conversations but forget to savor the delight of pronouncing words or of the togetherness of quiet cuddling. Children take pleasure in the simple functions when they first master them; adult attention turns that way only when we have to relearn them on account of illness or accident. Yet life would be immeasurably richer if candidates for president worried less about what they say in interminable debates and took time to show the electorate that they know the value of silently breathing.

There is a ninth, special sort of blindness that besets spectators. One might suppose that the spectatorial stance, devoted to observing everything of moment, is particularly well-suited to overcoming sightlessness. Yet its very nature sets obstacles in its way, limiting onlookers to the benefits of perception and denying them knowledge of the feel and consequences of action. Dogs in the act of love have access to experiences sadly unavailable to their packmates looking on. The same is true of soldiers, whose exploits on the battlefield remain their private possessions and cannot be captured by those who stay at home. This blindness is not a matter of choice or the habit of inattention; it is the inevitable outcome of failing to be in a certain position. Its remedy is not enhanced awareness but shouldering the burden of agency by going to war or plunging into love.

This leads me to the tenth and last blindness, which is the greatest and most lamentable. We can be so taken with the past and the future that we become unmindful of the present. The young see the failures of the past, the old its victories. In either case, what has been casts a long shadow over the only thing real, which is what exists *now*. Expectations can terrorize life or else charm it; when they do, we live for what is not yet and will perhaps never be. The present always ends up as the victim, seen only as residue or preparation, appreciated only in its passing. What we seem not to understand is that the present never passes, that its riches are inexhaustible, and that in spurning it we discard all of life.

Objects tend to be of interest to us for their instrumental value. The more we view things, people, and relationships as means to ulterior ends, the less we are concerned with their intrinsic properties. We can quickly reach the stage where we hardly notice what is immediately present, reading it only as the sign of things past or yet to come. The firstness, as Peirce would say, of whatever we deal with tends to give way to its secondness and thirdness; the immediacy before us is quickly mediated. The genius of James, Peirce, and Dewey is that they did not go down the road of Hegelian mediation, maintaining instead a keen consciousness of the importance of unmediated presence. Hegel, however, was more prescient of the common mind than were the Americans. Busy people don't linger over the appearance of things, savoring each marvelous aspect of the world. They turn a blind eye to how things look and feel and thereby lose the most direct contact we can develop with the real. This is the blindness of people who have no trouble finding their way, but haven't a clue as to where they have been.

I have distinguished ten different sorts of blindness, undifferentiated by James, all of which, however, are hinted at in his essay. Some of the blindnesses are connected with each other in a variety of ways; others remain essentially independent. They are different from each other because their objects, causes, organs, processes, or remedies differ. But they tend to travel in company so that, for instance, the person who is blind to immediacies is likely also to be nescient of how others see the world. Similarly, persons who take no delight in our simpler functions probably also fail to lead an intense sensory life.

Should we be distressed at seeing so much blindness built into the human frame? If blindnesses are deficits of a cognitive, valuational, or emotive sort, it would presumably be much better to be without them. James certainly conceives his essay as a call to action. He laments our inattentions and implies, even though he does not state, that we must work to overcome them and try to see the neglected riches of life. Surprisingly perhaps, he says nothing about blindness to ourselves in the form of self-deception and the sort of subconscious impulses Freud worked so hard to bring to the light of day, but he clearly considers unseeing a severe human failing. He may not go so far as his colleague, Royce, and say that the willful narrowing of attention is the very definition of sin, but he is convinced that we would be better off if we lived in total conscious possession of our world or at least significantly expanded the range of our sympathies.

Can we rid ourselves of what James calls the "great cloud-bank of ancestral blindness"? By the time he writes the next essay in the series of his talks to teachers, James is ready to declare that we cannot. He avers that it "is vain to hope for this state of things to alter much,"[2] for practical-minded beings such as ourselves are "necessarily short of sight." He is clearly right that considering the demands of animal and social life in a precarious environment, eliminating all our blindnesses is impossible. I don't mean of course the dry logical impossibility of contradiction, but impossibility measured by who we are and what we have to do to secure our existence. Sensitivity to different perceptions slows up response time, and constant empathetic access to the sufferings of others makes action odious. Could we kill animals if we had a vivid perception of their anxiety in the slaughterhouse? Could we compete for mate or promotion if we felt the disappointment of the loser? Could we prefer our own values if we saw justification for everybody else's?

In speaking of blindness, James does not distinguish the voluntary from the unavoidable. Unseeing is voluntary when we have the capacity to

2. William James, "What Makes a Life Significant," in *Talks to Teachers on Psychology and to Students on Some of Life's Ideals,* ed. Frederick H. Burkhardt, Fredson Bowers, and Ignas K. Skrupskelis (Cambridge, Mass.: Harvard University Press, 1983), p. 151.

behold or understand an object but we refuse to look or choose not to try. The nescience is ineluctable whenever we lack access to the objects or experiences it would be good to know. Sometimes this is momentary; the blindness that comes of the spectatorial stance can be overcome by engaging in action. At other times, however, there is not much we can do to achieve clear vision. People who hide their feelings or who are at a great physical, cultural, or temporal distance from us may simply never be known.

Such intellectual or emotional blindness is similar to the limits to sight we experience in physical operations. We cannot see what lies around the corner or on the other side of the globe. Temporal situatedness restricts vision in roughly the same way: we cannot behold the consequences of our actions two hundred years from now or enjoy a clear perception of battling Athenian triremes. Such limits to the range of emotional and intellectual responsiveness constitute another reason why eliminating all our blindnesses is impossible.

Of course, we can make a little headway and overcome inattention here and there. And, indeed, ridding ourselves of some of our blindnesses, reducing their scope or increasing our voluntary control over what to overlook, could make for a somewhat better life. If we bathed the values of others in the same warm light as we bathe our own, there would likely be less conflict in the world and more understanding. If we appreciated the immediate presence of things, our lives would be richer and significantly more carefree. And if we focused on the simpler functions of life, we would have a surer source of joy than sophistication or competition can provide. This much is clear and it seems sensible to encourage people to open their eyes a little wider so they may improve their condition.

Unfortunately, however, every benefit has a seamy underside. If we saw the world as forever new, we could not develop work-reducing and life-saving habits. If we were party to everyone's grief, we would be tortured and immobilized by the horror. If we attended to the immediacies of life without reference to instrumentalities, we would lose all practical sense and find ourselves gaping at the world. And if we gloried in our simpler functions, we would have little use for the sophisticated activities unique to humans and productive of satisfactions unavailable otherwise.

So we should take thought before we recommend the elimination of blindness or, for that matter, any other general measure as a solution to the problems humans face. Opening our eyes a little here and there, selectively resisting sightlessness in certain contexts, can help us move in the right direction, bringing us closer to loved ones or to the vivacity of the real. We should work vigorously to make ourselves more perceptive in our intellectual life and more generous in our responses. But we must not forget our finitude and we must try to remember that as much as blindness is, in the abstract, a lamentable condition, in concrete life it protects us from being overwhelmed by reality.

Moral Holidays

Let me begin with what may well be fighting words. Josiah Royce's intellect was doggedly one-directional; William James's mind, by contrast, showed signs of playful creativity. His relentless focus on evil places Royce among the most serious of philosophers; one can imagine him thinking with gritted teeth. James, on the other hand, displays moments of winking fun, such as when he invents the idea of moral holidays.

In his usual fashion, James does not spend much time explaining what moral holidays are. Aiming his comments at Royce, he assails the role of the Absolute in the moral life: if our obligations are infinite but God picks up the slack and completes what we leave undone, then we might as well break from our labors and let the Deity take over. The urgency of moral action abates the moment we feel assured that God presides over a universe in which the good inevitably prevails. In his infinity, God can do it all even if we "drop the worry of our . . . responsibility."[3] We can then take a moral holiday and "let the world wag in its own way, feeling that its issues are in better hands than ours."[4]

This leaves us with an intuitive but not very precise idea of what a moral holiday might be. A few moments of reflection reveals that there are at least four different notions of moral holiday and that James is not careful to draw distinctions between them. The first idea is the rejection of all moral rules and limits, the second the elimination of obligations, the third the disregard of what is supererogatory, and the fourth the lessening of effort usually associated with vacationing.

Only sociopaths of exceptional resolve and concentration can sidestep *all* moral constraints. Ordinary mortals find it nearly impossible to sustain immorality on a grand scale: even the cruelest and nastiest people tend to pay for their groceries and refrain much of the time, even if not always, from burning down their neighbors' houses. Suspending all moral rules is hard work and goes against the grain. Leading a thoroughly immoral life is as exhausting as

3. William James, *Pragmatism,* ed. Frederick H. Burkhardt (Cambridge, Mass.: Harvard University Press, 1975), p. 41.
4. Ibid.

being through-and-through moral: each of its constituent actions requires scrutiny, and we must make sure that the temptations of decency never prevail. This is hardly a holiday. It sounds more like the labored efforts of a conscientious person whose values became lamentably inverted.

The second notion of a moral holiday takes aim at obligations and announces that, for a while at least, they are suspended. Individual duties may be suspended for many reasons. Illness may make it impossible for us to do what we should, and greater obligations may overshadow some minor, ordinary duty. This concept of a moral holiday, however, goes far beyond lifting an obligation or two, sanctioning instead the wholesale temporary disregard of *all* obligations. So when I am on moral holiday in this sense, I can let my baby cry in the crib and the accident victim lie in a pool of blood—I am going to the beach and have, for the moment, no interest in doing what I should. Of course, not all of my actions are liberated from the rule of morality; I can still do good gratuitously, so long as it is not in response to a duty.

The third notion of a moral holiday is significantly narrower than the first two. It leaves us in the thrall of obligations but removes actions of supererogation. People on this sort of holiday remain, in a narrow sense of the phrase, moral agents, meeting their obligations and obeying obvious moral rules. They refuse, however, to go beyond the call of duty: they fill their roles adequately but are out of the office sharp at five o'clock. Perhaps more than half the world is on such a holiday pretty much all the time, following rules but never going even a small part of the extra mile.

The last notion of a moral holiday is a little more difficult to articulate. Part of what a vacation means for many people is the opportunity to take a break from doing things for others. One might be inclined to help if help is desperately needed, and one would certainly not want to slough off important obligations. But life on vacation lacks the busy urgency of the everyday. The strenuous striving of the rest of the year is laid aside for the moment and one can kick off one's shoes and head for the hammock. This is a time when one does not look for things to do and considers it acceptable to be doing little or nothing. The fact that people on such holidays resist helping others does not mean that they go out of their way to serve themselves. Even activities of self-improvement are shelved, and what is perceived as a healing and wholesome laziness overtakes the soul. This is something like what James calls "the easy-going mood" that lets the world go its way without moving a finger to intervene.

I suspect that this fourth sense of the phrase comes closest to what James has in mind when he speaks of belief in the Absolute justifying moral holidays. His point is that if evil will inevitably suffer defeat and has already done so from the standpoint of eternity, then we may well declare a moratorium on effort; we *can* head for the hammock to contemplate the victory secured by God as we slip off to sleep. The name "moral holiday" may well be a misnomer for this attitude, for though it is a holiday, it is not an obviously or pre-eminently *moral* one. The people who enjoy such breaks from exertion do not dismiss the legitimacy of moral rules and obligations, they just don't feel called upon to follow them for a stretch of time.

If we take the matter further, Royce (as the friend of the Absolute James targets) is in even deeper trouble than it at first appears. Why should moral holidays be temporary events rather than permanent dispositions? Royce maintains that God makes up the difference between our noble aims and feeble efforts; he accomplishes what we set out to do but cannot achieve on our own. Royce inherited from Fichte the fateful idea that whatever demand can be satisfied does not constitute a proper duty, that Kant's idea of "ought implying can" must be set aside for the deeper and beautifully romantic notion that we are called upon to do what we can't. Anything finite might conceivably be attained, so the only way to assure that our obligations are worthy of us is to make them infinite. Royce declares that there is no rest in Zion: our struggles never cease so long as we are mired in finitude, which means that they never cease.[5]

But what motive do we have for engaging in the struggle with vigor? The distance between the finite good we can do and the infinite demanded of us is itself infinite, one that only an infinite being can traverse. This opens a marvelous opportunity for reducing our labors: if we do twice as much as we did last year, we are still infinitely removed from the goal, and if we reduce our effort to 10 percent of that next year, we will be no further from meeting our obligations. Moreover, God must provide the same boost in both cases—he needs to close the gap between finite and infinite. Since only he can do that, why should we exert ourselves? If we do less, in one sense God does not have to do more than he would otherwise, and he will, in any case, do it all. The conclusion that we can do as little as we please and yet not imperil the perfection of the world seems inescapable. To load infinite obligations on finite beings is to let them escape with none.

5. Josiah Royce, *The World and the Individual, Second Series* (New York: Macmillan, 1908), p. 407.

James's attack has at least two prongs. Morally, it is repugnant to demand infinite achievements of the finite. Psychologically, if God supplements what we do and thereby raises it to a level adequate to meet our obligations, we have no incentive for doing much at all. Do these lines of reasoning raise fair objections to Royce? They would if he did not have a system of metaphysics and as a part of it a full account of human nature. But he clearly does, developed beautifully in *The World and the Individual,* and a central element of it consists of the claim that infinity is inscribed in our souls: the search for it is constitutive of what it means to be human.

"It is not satisfactory to be finite,"[6] Royce declares. All finite acts and facts are evil, and as such "leave us in disquietude, searching still for the Other, i.e., for true Being in its wholeness."[7] Having this drive or platonic *eros* for completion is precisely what it means to be a self, and the fact that the self's task in the finite world can never be fulfilled serves, astonishingly, as the premise that points to our immortality. In striving for union with God, we seek to be like him, broadening our attention and expanding our loyalties. Royce can thus readily respond to James that there is nothing morally objectionable in letting human nature develop and express itself, and it does so in the search for the eternal. And as to motivation, we need no additional incentive if by nature our will is focused on the infinite.

I leave to one side the strikingly romantic nature of these ideas and offer only one comment. Remarkably for someone devoted to the expansion of attention, Royce pays little heed to what Hegel called mere "empirical details." Relentless and endless striving may well characterize commercial, industrial, and knowledge-based societies in the temperate zone, but it is not a feature of human beings everywhere. Ancient Athenians were satisfied with much less than infinity, significant numbers of medieval Christians seeking union with God did not hope to find it through restless search for evils to defeat, and incessant yearning is alien to many cultures even today. The actual blinds us to distant variety and elevates the local into the universal.

One might suppose that James, respectful of human finitude and devoted to exploring the details of motivation, might be a friend of moral holidays. Even if our limits can expand, there is only so much good we can do: one person cannot stop the spread of AIDS or defeat starvation in Africa. Perhaps all of humanity acting in concert cannot either. Moreover, everyone needs some breathing room from obligations; we do better tomorrow if we spend an hour relaxing tonight. Moral holidays look, therefore, as useful and per-

6. Ibid., p. 363.
7. Ibid.

haps necessary breaks in the routine of life, enabling us to gather our forces and return stronger to the fray.[8]

This is the message James might have conveyed in his article titled "The Gospel of Relaxation." And, indeed, in that essay he bemoans the breathlessness, anxiety, and convulsive "over-tension" he detects in the American character. He calls the intensity and agony of our approach to the world "bottled lightning"[9] and deplores the "absence of repose" in our lives. This is promising because it focuses on the hyperactivity that wants to correct everything in the world and leaves no time for quiet reflection and healing. He goes so far as to recommend to the students he addresses that they "fling away" their books the day before the exam and learn not to care about how well they do.[10] This sounds like an endorsement of moral holidays not only in the fourth sense of wholesome inactivity, but also in the second sense of failure to meet one's obligations.

By the end of the essay, however, it is clear that that is not what James has in mind at all. He does not want to reduce our labors or exempt us from what Royce would be happy to call "doing the Lord's work." He objects to our "absurd feelings of hurry" because they are inefficient. "If . . . living excitedly . . . would only enable us to *do* more . . . it would be different," he says.[11] As it is, the tension and anxiety that weigh on us because there is so much to accomplish "are the surest drags upon steady progress and hindrances to our success."[12] Instead, James suggests, the better way to do everything we must is to clear our minds of worry about whether we are doing it or not. Then we will be "calmly ready for any duty that the day may bring forth."[13] If we manage

8. James flirts with the idea that moral holidays are wholesome and valuable. In "On a Certain Blindness in Human Beings," for example, he exalts the mysteries of "sensorial life" and asserts that "the holidays of life are its most vitally significant portions, because they are, or at least should be, covered with just this kind of magically irresponsible spell." William James, "On a Certain Blindness in Human Beings," in *Talks to Teachers on Psychology and to Students on Some of Life's Ideals,* ed. Frederick H. Burkhardt, Fredson Bowers, and Ignas K. Skrupskelis (Cambridge, Mass.: Harvard University Press, 1983), p. 149. But he does not say that the holidays of which he speaks are *moral* holidays, and he generally shies away from endorsing breaks in our earnest efforts to improve the world.

9. William James, "The Gospel of Relaxation," in *Talks to Teachers on Psychology and to Students on Some of Life's Ideals,* ed. Frederick H. Burkhardt, Fredson Bowers, and Ignas K. Skrupskelis (Cambridge, Mass.: Harvard University Press, 1983), p. 122.

10. Ibid., p. 128.

11. Ibid., p. 125.

12. Ibid.

13. Ibid., p. 129.

"genuinely" not to care about attaining what we should, we are more likely to succeed at our tasks than if we are dogged by perpetual concerns about our performance. What sounds like an invitation to take moral holidays quickly turns in this way into a recommendation of how to be maximally effective in the work that keeps us from going to the beach. James seems interested in improving our output rather than in limiting what we are supposed to do.

James thus appears imbued with something resembling the same moral fervor that animates Royce. In "The Moral Philosopher and the Moral Life," he makes his admiration of the strenuous mood clear. He argues that every desire is a demand for satisfaction and the essence of good is to satisfy these claims.[14] Demands are not directed at particular persons; anyone in a position to satisfy them is under obligation to do so. This throws the floodgates of generosity wide open, with each of us facing a universe that imposes an indefinitely large number of duties on us. Such profusion of responsibilities leaves no room for moral holidays. Only the strenuous mood, teaching us to disregard stress and pain, makes it possible to meet our obligations. The endless labor of the Protestant ethic seems as central to James's moral metaphysics as it is to Royce's.

The similarity does not end there. The last few pages of "The Moral Philosopher and the Moral Life" suggest that God is no less significant for James than he is for Royce. James avers that finite demands are inadequate to evoke the deepest self-sacrificial commitments; it takes an "infinite demander"[15] to engage our sympathy and mobilize all our energies. He goes so far as to suggest that if God did not exist, we would be inclined to, and indeed ought to, "postulate" his existence. The Divine Being makes for a systematic moral universe in that his way of ordering the demands of living creatures is "the finally valid casuistic scale,"[16] and sincere belief in him sets free the habits of endurance and courage necessary to do everything we must.

Yet these similarities, intriguing as they may be, do not go very deep. James is ready to wax poetic about the value of believing in God, but rarely does he give us more than a hint concerning what this Deity might be like. He is certainly not the Absolute of the idealists and, most important, he is not a being who compensates for our failures. For James, God does not play a consolatory function, assuring us that he will supplement our imperfect

14. William James, *The Will to Believe and Other Essays in Popular Philosophy,* ed. Frederick H. Burkhardt, Fredson Bowers, and Ignas K. Skrupskelis (Cambridge, Mass.: Harvard University Press, 1979), p. 153.
    15. Ibid., p. 161.
    16. Ibid.

efforts. Contrary to Royce's view, we are left alone to do what needs to be done; all the action comes from human beings trying to make the world a little better. We postulate God for inspirational reasons. He is indispensable for letting "loose in us the strenuous mood."[17] So God's function in James is motivational, while in Royce it is metaphysical.

The contrast is even sharper in relation to our moral labors. The tasks that weigh on us, according to Royce, are infinite in number. We must defeat all evil and that, in the end, means that we must overcome finitude altogether. This remains forever impossible, and as a result we cannot escape frustration at our impotence. James, by contrast, burdens us only with an indefinite, but finite, number of obligations. Ideally, we are to satisfy every desire and meet every need. But James does not let philosophical enthusiasm obscure his marvelous sense of reality. He knows that gratifying some impulses is incompatible with satisfying others. Many parts of the ideal must, therefore, be "butchered," reducing the number of desires whose fulfillment falls to us. As a consequence, we can make genuine headway. Although hungers continue to arise, we can find technologically sophisticated ways in which many of them can be satisfied quickly; human intelligence is powerful enough to reorganize the world. If we want water, James reminds us, all we need to do is turn the faucet, and similar, equally forgotten but radical breakthroughs have occurred on many levels to make life immeasurably better. Even though he would not let us, in James's world we can afford to take a moral holiday.

The sorts of things we must rectify and what rectification consists of establish the final break between Royce and James. Royce sports a keener sense of evil than many of the medieval philosophers whose names begin with "Saint." He sees evil in the world and in the human soul; in the end everything limited and partial falls under suspicion and requires to be corrected by integration into a larger whole. Royce's drive for overcoming evil, both moral and metaphysical, is so all-encompassing that it attempts to unite three elements that are difficult to reconcile. He welcomes concrete improvements in the human condition: the broadening of loyalties, the much hoped for elimination of aggressive wars, and the possibility of a great community delight him. We might call this his American temper.

His soul, however, also harbors a romantic German metaphysician. To that Royce, all finite improvements count as nothing. Finitude itself is tainted and can be redeemed only by union with the infinite and the eternal. Halfway measures are of no value; empirical advances leave our condition morally—

17. Ibid.

really metaphysically—no better. In addition, there is the third Royce, whose plight is best understood in terms of Hegel's unhappy consciousness. When evil is thought to have penetrated the soul, we become our own enemies. The discord that comes of viewing oneself as both sinner and saint, of hating one's loves and loving one's hates as Royce puts it, rends the fabric of the self and makes satisfaction impossible to attain. As a result, nothing can be done with a good conscience and, though we are made in the image of God, nothing about us is holy. Under these circumstances, we cannot even *think* of taking a moral holiday. Finitude and wickedness must be battled day and night. And yet the evil we fight cannot be overcome because the ones fighting it are evil.

James's thought, by comparison, is far simpler. He sees the concept of evil as derivative from the ideas of desire and satisfaction. If there is any room for the notion of evil in James's world, it is merely to mark that a need went unrequited or a want failed to be met. Evil is no more pervasive than the good; if anything, the opposite is true. Reasonable self-control in choosing, vigorous labor, social cooperation, and a bit of luck should enable us to satisfy many of our desires. Of course, we cannot satisfy them all: our wants notoriously conflict with one another, and when they do, some have to die shriveled on the vine. This, however, is just what comes of the innocent, natural profusion of life, and it is up to us to trim the luxuriant growths. The outcome may be tragic, and James boldly calls it that, but it is not nasty or disgusting or depraved.

James believes that each of our desires is justified from its own point of view. This contrasts nicely with Royce's idea that "an evil is, in general, a fact that sends us to some Other for its own justification."[18] The full force of this difference is best brought out by focusing on the sharply divergent reactions of the two thinkers to the defeat of evil. For Royce, this is cause for jubilation, for taking delight in crushing an enemy. Evil is a force without legitimacy and intrinsic value, a disobedient energy to be wiped out. In defeating it, we accomplish a divine mission and the heavens smile. If there is an equivalent in James to gaining victory over evil, it is the satisfaction of a desire too long denied. The proper response here is empirical enjoyment; what we had long wanted has at last come about. Royce glories in the elimination of an alien, negative reality, while James grieves the death of every impulse and being. In the end, it is not inappropriate to say that Royce believes in the fallenness of both humans and the world, while James, a child of the Enlightenment, affirms the fundamental goodness of everything that strives.

18. Josiah Royce, *The World and the Individual, Second Series* (New York: Macmillan, 1923), p. 380.

Several ideas offer themselves at this point as worthy reflections. The first concerns philosophers committed to radically different ideas living together in harmony. Despite superficial similarities of view, James and Royce are nearly as far from each other philosophically as two thinkers can be. Nevertheless, they managed to live for decades in the same department, respecting each other's talents and praising each other's achievements. Although James called Royce's *work* "a rotten tissue of reasoning,"[19] he also wrote:

> How, then, O my dear Royce, can I forget you, or be contented out of your close neighborhood? Different as our minds are, yours has nourished mine, as no other social influence ever has, and in converse with you I have always felt that my life was being lived importantly.[20]

Severe criticism of others' views is compatible with the most cordial of human relations and a hearty appreciation of their philosophical excellence in their chosen style and idiom. There is a lesson to be learned here.

A second reflection relates to the disturbing presence of the Absolute in philosophical systems. Royce's work is replete with striking ideas, interesting arguments, and illuminating analogies. Again and again, however, he is hampered in developing his insights by antecedent commitment to an Absolute that is supposed to be both person and totality. His philosophy would have been more consistent had he allowed it to develop from the vital finite realities that he, in his best moments, recognized and embraced. It would have been also more sensible had he not felt himself carried to the obvious but unfortunate conclusion that everything finite is radically evil. James, burdened with his own inconsistencies, saw clearly that the Absolute was philosophical dead weight, and he wisely dispensed with it.

Third, preoccupation with evil and with the struggle to overcome it distorts moral philosophy and stunts our generous impulses. Royce's idea that an infinite process converts rottenness into perfection is satisfying to contemplate but suffers from three ruinous flaws. It postulates a linear infinity, whose problems were thoroughly aired by Hegel and whose motivational hold on finite beings is negligible. It makes us view all things as broken and ourselves as never quite able to mend them. And it burdens us with infinite obligations that we can never hope to meet. Seeing anything as evil is one of the forms of

19. *The Correspondence of William James,* vol. 9, ed. Ignas K. Skrupskelis and Elizabeth M. Berkeley (Charlottesville and London: University of Virginia Press, 2001), pp. 120–21.
20. Ibid., pp. 320–21.

blindness James was so good at unmasking; it is the inability to see the world from the perspective of that being and to understand its self-justification. James was much better at the imaginative extension of his sympathies than was Royce.

That takes us back to moral holidays. To fight an infinite battle with not a day off to let the smoke clear and to listen to the birds is nearly the most terrible fate I can imagine. The fact that I might yell "Victory!" makes little difference; Sisyphus also thinks he is winning before the rock crushes his foot on the way back down the mountain. After a day of doing good, I want to listen to Mozart and drink a beer with unblemished conscience and in the secure knowledge that this will make me a kinder man in the morning. Royce does not allow me that, and James would like to forbid it too. For Royce, there is more evil to be vanquished in the evening; for James, unmet desires continue to cry out for satisfaction. Royce cannot accommodate my leisure; James could but feels disinclined. I can appreciate the pressing urgency of need and want, but can one live a life of ceaseless service? What would life be without the song of birds, and what is the value of a philosophy that makes me feel guilty for listening to it?

What might a theory of moral holidays look like? It must start from the recognition that we have many obligations to others, but reject three views of these duties. Contrary to what some earnest moralists believe, our obligations are not infinite in number. The idea that our duties and our ability to meet them can never reach balance is devastating for the moral life. Moral psychology cannot be built on the perpetual frustration of our efforts. The thought that no matter how much we do, it is not enough extinguishes motivation and leaves us disillusioned with trying to make the world better. A limit to the demands on us, on the other hand, holds out hope of completion and sets clear and achievable objectives.

We must also repudiate the Fichtean view that even if our obligations are limited, they include tasks we cannot ever discharge. Our inability in this case is based not on the sheer volume of the demands on us, but on their nature. Fichte supposed that we have a duty to substitute laws of freedom for the mindless laws that govern the natural world.[21] This task is pompously momentous and logically impossible: our agency flows through the body, yet the body itself must be eliminated if freedom is to replace necessity. The duty some might suppose I have to change the foreign policy of my nation involves

21. J. G. Fichte, "Second Introduction to the Science of Knowledge," in *The Science of Knowledge*, trans. P. Heath and J. Lachs (Cambridge: Cambridge University Press, 1982), p. 83.

another sort of impossibility—"political impossibility," we might call it—but it frustrates sustained effort no less.

The third view of our duties a theory of moral holidays must repudiate is based on a curious inversion of the famous "ought implies can" proviso. Kant was right to insist that duties presuppose the ability to discharge them: we are not obliged to do what we cannot. With wildly generous spirit, however, some people insist that "can implies ought," meaning that it is mandatory for us to do all the good we can. This makes every valuable service we can perform for others a moral requirement and renders us slaves to our talents and possessions. So if I can use my lunch money for hunger relief in Darfur, I must do that, and the time I have after work ought to be spent caring for homeless people. Personal cost is irrelevant on this view. All that matters is that we employ our labor and inventiveness for the benefit of others.

Could one think of a demand more destructive of inner peace and joy in life than this? It reaches into the private recesses of our being and denies us the rest, the play, and the freedom that make the grinding instrumentalities of life worth enduring. It tells us to sacrifice everything we like because others need it more than we do. It declares playtime with one's children unworthy by comparison with tutoring illiterate strangers. It denies us sleep and drives us mercilessly to emergency rooms, soup kitchens, and orphanages to help the distressed and the diseased. Everyone's needs must be addressed under this regime but one's own; the relative privilege of those who have means and time must be paid for by self-sacrifice.

The idea that can implies ought travels in the company of a universalist ethics that refuses to distinguish obligations to those near and dear from duties to unknown multitudes around the globe. If I owe everything I can provide to everyone who can use it, I must not prefer meeting my children's needs to feeding the hungry in East Timor. Health care for my family cannot take precedence over curing the sick in India, and paying taxes to a nation-state is unjustified if the money could go to Oxfam. There is no end to the mischief such views cause in the name of morality by imposing unreasonable demands on givers and creating outrageous expectations among recipients. These are the demands from which moral holidays are meant to shield us and preserve our integrity if we choose to do less than everything we could.

A friend who works three jobs to support his family once told me, "It is so important to have a little time to do nothing." What he had in mind was a moral holiday in two senses of the phrase: a temporary turning away from moral demands and an inactivity that is morally justified. He saw the point of moral holidays, intuitively grasping that taking time out from moral concerns is, under certain circumstances, morally acceptable. Downtime is necessary in the way sleep is for animals, and serves as eloquent affirmation of our finitude. We simply cannot do everything and cannot remain active without cease. The limits to our nature are neither evil nor something of which we can be proud. They are simply facts, like the rotation of nights and days, that we must learn to accept.

Under what conditions is time away from moral efforts justifiable? The easy answer is: Whenever a person needs it and circumstances permit. The need must be genuine and not contrived, occasional and not permanent. Extraordinary developments cancel moral holidays the way war terminates shore leave. But even an emergency of the magnitude of 9/11 is inadequate to command ceaseless service; the aid workers need time to eat and rest, or else they will soon join the victims. The difficult reality is, of course, that all these matters require judgment, as does everything that relates to morality. The need for respite must be assessed and measured against the need others have of help. From the standpoint of suffering people, everything looks like an emergency, yet there is no algorithm to determine when all holidays must be put on hold.

The uncertainty that surrounds such judgments is no greater than what we face in nearly every corner of life; at any rate, they are inadequate to bring the legitimacy of moral holidays into question. The case for them seems weaker, however, when clear duties are ignored to create private time. We do not think it all right to play the fiddle while one's neighbor's house goes up in flames, and there is something repulsive about overlooking massive suffering in the quest for spiritual peace. Yet even in such circumstances, the case against moral holidays is by no means compelling. One might distance oneself from the fray because of inability to do much good; we may not have access to food to combat starvation or to water to quell the fire. Physical distance and cultural difference may also stand in the way of reaching out to those in need. Individual situations vary widely and there is no general principle on the basis of which those on holiday can be condemned.

The most objectionable cases of turning away from obligations may well be those in which people have the wherewithal to help others, yet choose to spend their substance in another way. Some years ago, a member of the Detroit Ford family hosted a wedding that cost more than a million dollars. Newspapers wrote with outrage about what they saw as a gross display of selfishness. Editorial writers calculated how many people could have benefited if the money had been given to charity. Of course, no one noted that the money was *spent,* meaning that large numbers of people who provided useful services for the wedding were in fact benefited. But that consideration aside, were the parents justified in overlooking the urgent demands of the needy as they celebrated the beauty and good fortune of their child?

I find it hard to avoid the conclusion that they were. The money was, after all, theirs to use as they saw fit. There is nothing intrinsically immoral about large weddings; as over the top, they may offend our aesthetic sense, but constitute no moral violation. It may of course be true that the money could have been put to better use. That, however, is a matter of judgment, and such judgments leave room for discretion and personal taste. The most we can say about them is that they may fail to maximize the good even though, or perhaps precisely because, they permit significant freedom.

This casts a new and different light on moral holidays. They may be nothing more than temporary refusals to maximize value, that is, occasions on which we are satisfied with the good without seeking the best. Limits to our energy, time, attention, and readiness for self-sacrifice all point to a need for such events, and James at any rate should have seen this clearly. Royce probably saw it but attributed it to the imperfection of our nature, which must be combated at all costs. For him, we are not allowed to take a moral holiday from suppressing our desires for moral holidays.

Good Enough

No matter how well things go for us, we tend to dream of ways they could go better. Our love affair with the perfect may be an expression of Western restlessness or, more generally, the result of human desires in over-drive, but it unquestionably structures much of what we hope for and work to achieve. We want not only *more* of everything but also *more perfect versions* of the goods we have and the experiences we enjoy. We seem to think that the world falls short of the ideal and that therefore everything needs to be improved.

This belief has become the grotesque mantra of the manufacturers of commercial goods, who advertise their products as "new and improved." But it is also embraced in cooking where we seek surprising ways to enhance the taste of meals, in human relations where we try to find the perfect friends, and in raising children where they can never quite meet our expectations. It is not that we fail to know what is good; we just believe that nothing is good enough.

A particularly harmful version of the view that nothing is good enough hides in the claim that our duties are unending. Such diverse philosophers as Fichte, Royce, and Levinas maintain that no matter how much we do, we cannot fulfill our obligations: our efforts remain forever inadequate. The reason may be that what we are supposed to do is intrinsically impossible to achieve, that it exceeds our powers, or that we have simply too many obligations. In any case, the best we can offer in moral exertion is not good enough. This reveals perhaps more clearly than anything else what is at stake. The demands on us are infinite even though our resources are clearly finite.

The perverse desire to heap infinite obligations on finite individuals guarantees moral failure. Similarly, demanding perfection of our experiences and relationships is a certain way of making life miserable. We do much better if we heed the counsels of finitude and refuse to seek what cannot be obtained. This involves both judgment and resolve: we must be able to decide what is good enough and be willing to embrace it as sufficient for our purposes, that is, adequate to satisfy our desires. The romantic quest for the perfect destroys human relationships and converts what could be happy lives into the misery of endless seeking and striving.

The first task in exploring the geography of the good enough is to distinguish it from what merely will do. There is actually a double distinction here, encapsulated in the ideas of that which will do and that with which, in the absence of better instruments and experiences, we can make do. The latter clearly announces compromise: when we do not have what we need or want, we satisfy ourselves with something less that may serve as a substitute. As a child, my grandfather lacked Band-Aids and so had to put spider webs on cuts and bleeding bruises. Knives are plausible stand-ins for screwdrivers, and we settle for CDs when a live performance is unavailable. After a grand but failed love affair, people make do with whatever partner happens to be on hand, just as the threat of hunger inclines them to accept jobs for which they are overqualified.

To say that something will do, by contrast, is to endorse it as adequate. This judgment can express a broad range of attitudes, from finding something barely satisfactory to thinking of it as fine. The variety is reflected in the many ways in which we say, "This will do," sometimes conveying resignation, and at others delighted surprise. The adequacy asserted means that some object or experience reaches at least a minimum level of acceptability, though in some cases it may be significantly better.

At the low end, for example, looking for cherry pie in the refrigerator but finding only a cookie, we might well decide that that will do. It may not be what we wanted, but it will still the desire for something sweet. At the other end, when searching the Internet gives us five million web pages on a subject, we may well decide after the first couple of dozen that that will be enough.

The latter example makes it clear that the idea of something being adequate is not a judgment concerning a substitute; when tools or experiences are satisfactory, they are so on their own account. The way a lover kisses can be perfectly fine without the need for comparisons and without thinking that it is a replacement for someone else's style.

Considered as a continuum, the upper reaches of what will do adjoin the area of what is good enough. Things good enough are truly *good* or colloquially speaking, even *great,* in fact so good that they do not need to be better. This does not mean that they are perfect or that they could not perhaps be improved. But they are *good enough* for me or for us as finite, thoroughly limited beings operating under circumstances we may not be able to improve. It also does not mean that those satisfied by what is good enough settle for the dregs or live a compromise accepting shoddy goods. They enjoy what is fine and permit themselves to feel fulfilled, refusing to search for some elusive ideal.

Chess pie can be flawed in a variety of ways. The crust may be too soft, the taste not sweet enough, the consistency of the filling too loose. My wife and I were once given a pie that seemed to have none of these problems: it was sweet and soft and crunchy in all the right places. Conceivably, there can be better chess pies; a little extra lemon in the filling could tease the palate, or a slightly crunchier crust could give more work for molars. But these were abstract and irrelevant considerations in eating the pie. It simply did not need to be better than it was; it was plenty good and thus good enough. The same was true of a sunset I once saw on the shores of the Gulf of Mexico. The light danced on the waves, the huge orb was bathing in the water at the end of sight, the rest of the sky was white with terns and gulls. It is possible that the experience would have been better if the sun had set exactly where the water kissed the land or if the waves had been a little higher or the birds less numerous. But the moment had its integrity. The sight was magnificent and thus good enough. It did not need to be better.

The search for the perfect and the search for the permanent seem to have an oddly close connection. In seeking the flawless, we seem to want something we will be able to remember forever. Perhaps we think of this permanence of memory as a warm home in the coldly changing world, something stable that will always welcome, accept, and shield us. Touching the perfect, even if only in one of its minor manifestations, gives the sense that our lives are justified, that something we have been or seen will always endure. This is one of the primary uses of the concept of God. The deity is supposed to hold all the achievements of the world in an eternal gaze, never permitting the perfect to sink under the waves of time. The flawless thus provides permanence or at least exemption from decay.

Whether true or not, this is a reassuring view, depicting the world as a cozy realm responsive to the good. The consolation is largely annulled, however, by the companion view, popular since Plato, that in ordinary life we can attain nothing perfect. To those committed to the search for some final good, this is a devastating prospect. Plato tried to counter its demoralizing effects by glorifying *eros*, the *drive* for perfection, even though it could deliver only meager results. Hegel understood the terrible contradiction between the dream of perfection and the fact of failure, of our being made in the image of God and yet succumbing to finitude and sin, and he exposed it convincingly in the dialectical involutions of the Unhappy Consciousness.

What is there about perfection that exercises such a magical influence over the human mind? The traditional view has it that only in the infinitely perfect—that is, in God—can we find rest and satisfaction. But why should this be the case? Why should we not break off our search for the good when we find something good enough, without reference to whether it or something else could be better? Why is the good enough not good enough for us?

Some have thought that our very notion of the good is an idea of perfection, that we cannot know the value of anything without an absolute standard or exemplar. But where would we get such a standard? What we consider good is too closely tied to empirical desires to yield a notion that is pure or divine. Justice, power, mercy, and knowledge are matters of degree first; we have no idea of what a perfect version of any of these properties might be like. We can recite empty formulas, such as that omniscience is knowledge of all true propositions along with knowledge that each of an infinite number of false propositions is false. But this tells us nothing about lived omniscience—how it is, for example, for someone so well-informed to be denied the delight of surprise.

In any case, we must first determine what it means to know anything at all before we can grasp the idea of knowing everything. This suggests that omniscience and with it superlative levels of other desirable qualities are abstract extrapolations of ordinary empirical achievements. We know that in this difficult world everything is tenuous and changing. The insecurity this begets drives us to imagine unfailing wisdom and goodness. Nothing shows better that perfection is a derivative ideal than the fact that we know so little of it. We have a precise idea of what it is to know that tomorrow is Sunday or that it is raining, but only the vaguest notion of an intuitive grasp of all reality.

The pursuit of perfection, therefore, is not the search for something definite and well-known. The limits of human capacity and the vagueness of the ideal make attainment of perfection impossible, yet its lure ruins our satisfaction with what is clearly excellent and therefore good enough. Even if this is right, however, and I believe it is, one can sensibly ask for an account of the marks of the good enough. How can we know that an action, process, or experience does not need to be better? Are there generally recognizable signs that distinguish what is just good from what is so good that it is good enough in the sense of needing no improvement?

The wide compass of human natures, the differences among our likes, and the broad range of our experiences make the search for universal standards futile. A music lover may experience a performance of Schubert's Trout Quintet as divine. Superior knowledge and acquaintance with other interpretations of the score may reveal to a music critic a host of problems in the same performance. To one, the evening may have been a luminous and exhilarating experience; the music was so good that it did not need to be any better. To the other, the tempo may have been too rapid or the pianist's playing mechanical. The same is true of virtually any experience; nothing is good enough in an absolute or nonrelational way. One has to be ready for the experience, possess an adequate background of appreciation, and believe that events of the sort are attractive. So to find something good enough is a spontaneous feeling evoked or judgment made on the basis of a relationship among events, persons, and their values.

Because determining that something is good enough involves a judgment, we may suppose that it is open to correction. And indeed it is, though only in the sense that what we find good enough at one time may not qualify as such later. This is the natural development of taste as we become weary of repetition and may seek higher standards. There is, however, also an ineradicable feeling component in the experience of the good enough, and correcting that is impossible. We may never feel the same way about a similar experience, reserving enthusiasm only for what is rarified and finer, but that cannot annul the fact that at one point in our lives some process or event was thoroughly satisfying.

The spontaneity of our feelings distances the good enough from the highbrow by attaching, unpredictably, to commonplace sorts of objects and ordinary kinds of experiences. Nevertheless, we can be educated by being shown that what we thought good enough is easily outdone. A fine dish of home-cooked coq au vin can pale by comparison with what is available in good restaurants in France, and the next performance of Schubert's Trout Quintet may put to shame what we once thought divine. This does not eradicate the fact that what we now think weak was at an earlier time experienced as splendid. Although improvement of taste is in certain respects desirable, appreciation is a time-bound fact. Arguing that in light of some later judgment an earlier experience could not have been wonderful is futile, because what counts in the end is the direct enjoyment and not the then unavailable knowledge.

Can we then be wrong when we say that some experience is good enough? Only in the limited sense of thinking that we would not have found it good enough had we had a richer trove of experiences or had we known more at the time. Since there are no objective standards in such matters, however, we cannot say that we *should* have held back our appreciation. Further, we cannot assert that it was a mistake to view the experience as good enough. We cannot even say that it would have been better had we not done so, because the experience of the good enough is valuable on any level of sophistication. We have no business grieving over the past; instead we can cheer ourselves by thinking that we are getting less simple and more discerning.

Some may suppose that such a generally tolerant attitude is an invitation to settle for too little and thereby miss what is truly good enough. This objection originates in a stubborn misunderstanding of the notion of the good enough. Persons with the requisite faculty of appreciation and an appropriate set of values can experience events and objects of virtually any sort as good enough. This means neither lack of standards nor lack of judgment. Some people find thin beer and raw wine marvelous; others buy airbrush art for their homes. Although we may not agree with their choices, they are discriminating and selective, rejecting many objects as unsatisfactory. If experiences of their choice evoke in them the sense that drink and art need never be better, we can cheer them on in their enjoyment and leave the matter at that. Otherwise, we attempt to substitute our judgment for theirs by maintaining that what they think need not be better should be better, after all. The occurrence of experiences of the good enough deserves celebration independently of their content.

This, of course, does not hold for destructive processes. If some Serb commander announced that the ethnic cleansing his soldiers were conducting went so well that it needed no improvement, we would be rightly horrified. Our dismay, however, would be directed not at his experience of satisfaction but at the awful source of it, and at that only because it involved murder, rape, and kidnapping. However electrifying they may seem to some, such activities must be proscribed. But to tell people that they should take satisfaction only in sophisticated activities and performances amounts to a reaffirmation of the hierarchy of values that has perfection at its apex.

How, then, should we think of the relation of the good enough to hierarchies of value? Are some experiences that are good enough of their kind better than good enough experiences of another kind? We have no reason to believe that that is so, at least from the standpoint of the feeling of satisfaction involved. It may nevertheless be true that some sources of satisfaction are deeper or richer or more variegated than others. Music lovers may experience no more than a general sense of delight at hearing Schubert's Trout. Music critics, by contrast, can concentrate on the details and take pleasure in the flow of the melody, the interplay of the instruments, and the crystalline sound of the piano. Knowledge of relevant details enables critics to focus on more that they can find good enough—more that can satisfy—than ordinary people, and that makes their experience richer.

Yet nothing is gained from excoriating music lovers for their shallow understanding of the performance. Those with greater knowledge may present them with the possibility of a more detailed grasp of what the music offers, and they may—if they wish—gain an education in auditory pleasure. People who know human nature, however, will do little more than nudge them in a direction; embarrassing them or lecturing them is of no avail. And too much knowledge of details and alternatives has its own problems. Critics find it more difficult to surrender to the experience and may know so much that they judge something good enough only on rare occasions. It may be best, therefore, to encourage enjoyment and create opportunities, but exert no pressure, for deepening its source.

Relatively little harm is likely to come from experiencing what to others may seem an inferior performance of music as good enough. But, moralists often urge, major disasters can result if we extend the idea of the good enough into morality. We may then experience middling efforts to make the world a better place or to respond to the needs of others as sufficient and thereby perpetuate evil and injustice. Such halfhearted attempts at amelioration are, for them, never enough. Nothing short of a full-fledged war on poverty, ignorance, cruelty, discrimination, and illness can be considered a good enough response to the evils that surround us. Anything less is neglect of our obligations to ourselves, to others, or to God, an unconscionable preoccupation with our limits in the name of lessening our burdens.

I cannot think of myself as a moral monster, yet I am unable to detect any universal duties that tie me to humanity or the world. I have no problem identifying and acknowledging obligations to many people near and dear, and to animals whose care I have voluntarily assumed, but not to anyone and everyone, including individuals I have never met and those whom, for one reason or another, my agency is unable to reach. Such obligations, unlimited in scope, might be the ideological invention of persons devoted to keeping others miserable through failure or guilt-ridden for lack of trying.

Alternatively, the source of the idea of universal obligations may be a well-meaning and proper sense of horror at all the suffering in the world. The notion is supported, however, by a serious confusion. It would be better if there were no disease, poverty, and injustice; if people could live in peace with each other; and if we did not have to eat living creatures to live. But the fact that the world could be better than it is does not imply that we are obliged to make it better. Even if it would be better if we tried to make things better, we cannot conclude that it is incumbent upon us to spend our lives in service to the good. The promise of improvement is inadequate to impose a moral obligation, which requires a closer or more stringent relationship between sufferer and agent, such as we have with family members and people we have promised to help. Being human or sentient or a fellow being in the world is close enough for concern and sympathy that may lead to action but not for the demands of duty.

Up to a point, it is appropriate and good to encourage people to assume more obligations. But it is important to keep in mind that when they embrace them, they do so voluntarily and that there is a sharp limit to what they can do. Moreover, if world improvement is what we have in mind, it is worth remembering that cleaning up one's little corner of it is a mighty start. Some can do much more, but no one can accomplish everything. So what counts as a good enough effort depends on the capacity of individuals and their circumstances. Bill Gates can offer heaps of money and the Mother Teresas of the world give much of their lives, but many others do all they can, and should, by raising a family and being kind to their neighbors.

Although occasions may arise in which we surprise even ourselves, most of us are neither saints nor heroes. Yet the world gets better if we do our share, if only we make an effort that is good enough. Feeling that we must fix everything is surely due to a perverted egoism propelled by the thought that nothing short of infinity is big enough for us. In reality, much less than infinity or perfection is good enough—must be good enough—because more we cannot reach. Of course, we can always take on one more task, support one more dependent, and do one more good deed a day. The cat lady who has saved fifty-four cats may well find room for the fifty-fifth. But much as we can stretch, there is always a limit, and when we reach it, we should be able to look on what we have done and sincerely feel that it is good enough.

Here we see the advantage of the idea of the good enough. As affirmation of our finitude, it negates our Faustian tendency to want to have and do everything. It rejects the relevance of the ideal of perfection and strikes at the root of our compulsion to pursue unreachable ideals. It liberates us to the enjoyment of the possible without eliminating standards or moral effort. It enables us to still our will by achieving what we can and celebrating what we do. By no means least, it dissolves the eternal dissatisfaction that permeates Western industrial society and substitutes joy in the immediacies of life for all-encompassing guilt.

Leaving Others Alone

Imagine a world in which there is only one sort of fruit, say, apples. There are, of course, several types of apples, yellow and red delicious, Jonathan and Granny Smith; occasionally one even encounters a bad apple. The people in this world learn to appreciate apples, eating them raw and baking them, flavoring them, juicing them, turning them into sauce, and making them into filling for wonderful pies. As a result of their cultivation, apples become available in a surprising variety of flavors and as ingredients in a bewildering array of dishes.

What should we say of these people? First, that they took advantage of the possibilities of their raw material, creating something fine out of what, left to itself, would be common and boring. Should we feel sorry for them because they were impoverished, never having enjoyed the glory of a pear? Such feelings seem appropriate when we contemplate our good fortune in having a hundred different types of fruit available year-round. But if the apple people lead impoverished lives, so do we because we must get by without another hundred fruits whose names we don't know and whose flavors we cannot even imagine. Just as we can say to the apple people that they would be better off if they could get some grapes, so people from a richer planet could lecture us that our lives without their favorite fruit must be sadly hollow.

What we should tell the apple people is that we are impressed by how much they made of what they had. Their attitude is surely right. We must use what is at hand, enhancing it intelligently to make life a little better. Notice that enhancement consists of diversification; humans tend not to be like cats happy with dry food morning and night. As Leibniz knew, variety is a great good—so great in fact that without a measure of it life becomes unbearable. Sensory deprivation, solitary confinement, and isolation in the dark of polar winter can drive people berserk.

Variety in the form of diverse experiences can make existence satisfying, perhaps even exciting. People generally agree that a world in which there are many different sorts of cuisines is better than one in which we have only goulash to eat. The reason for this is twofold. Different tastes add to the modalities of our satisfaction, enabling us to experience surprising delights. Further, the spread of alternatives gives play to choice, so we can enjoy the satisfactions not only of savoring unforeseen textures and tastes, but also of freely deciding what to eat. In such a world, one can still eat goulash every day, but only if one so chooses.

Who could take offense at seeing French, Chinese, and Ethiopian restaurants opening their doors side by side? The more the better, I am inclined to say, even though I cannot imagine ever wanting to visit some of them. Normally, we are happy to let such harmless competitions play out and consider ourselves fortunate to have a choice of where to eat. Plurality does not bother us in such contexts, and we show a commendable readiness to leave others alone. We are simply indifferent in these matters, and that indifference serves as the condition of others pursuing their goals in their own ways.

Not only do I fail to be bothered by the variety of restaurants in the neighborhood, but I also have little concern about what they do in their kitchens. The secrets of kitchens are like the secrets of bedrooms; sensible people do not want to know how their strange neighbors prepare food or for love. Such wholesome distance makes for good relations, enabling us to enjoy fine meals and our neighbors' satisfied smiles. The resultant relationships permit people to flourish on the basis of their own efforts and the voluntary cooperation of others.

Distressingly, when it comes to some matters, the distance is difficult to keep. Some people cannot abide seeing young men with long hair or earrings; others call the police to stop lovers kissing in the park. Individuals dressed in a way deemed tasteless or unkempt earn social censure. Those who voice opinions out of favor or choose unconventional courses of life are viewed with suspicion. Bodies that don't meet prevailing standards are thought to be in need of correction, and people whose religious preferences differ from the norm arouse the sense that they are unreliable.

Xenophobia is a comfortable state: it is vastly comforting if everyone looks the same, feels the same, and expresses common sentiments in a shared language. This enables us to exclude the different as abhorrent or morally flawed or unnatural. If the different should find its way into our midst, we feel entitled to shun it or to stamp it out; surely it and it alone must be responsible for whatever misfortune befalls the community. Generosity soon comes to consist of saving people from their awful selves, and we spare no effort in criticizing, correcting, and converting them. But conversion may be too kind or impossible; women cannot readily be turned into men, nor blacks into whites. As a result, oppression and obliteration appear, from time to time, as justifiable ways of dealing with minorities of race, religion, and ethnicity.

We can see an important difference between the apple people and many closed communities. The former work to diversify their meager supply of fruit while the latter do everything in their power to limit diversity to a few acceptable forms of the same general type. One is hard put to think of a society that has promoted a plurality of values among its members. On the contrary, by design or unconsciously, communities shape young people and immigrants in their own image, heaping rewards on those who conform and making deviance a source of pain. Even when the United States was wide open to immigration, it thought of itself as a melting pot in which new arrivals would burn off their foreign trappings and, through education in English and in a new way of life, could soon become indistinguishable from the locals.

Why do we gladly diversify our food but avoid the different in people, values, and behavior? The reasons are many. The unfamiliar is uncomfortable and the strange makes us feel out of place. Seeing people do what for us is taboo may be threatening or, precisely because of its attraction, a source of resentment. Moreover, the different heralds a possible need for change, and even in a society such as ours, given to the veneration of the new, change is kept within narrow limits. In the case of religion, sexual practices, and family life, differences are disquieting and touch the deepest recesses of our being, evoking visceral responses and sundering the world into "them" and "us."

Historically, the most powerful factors in developing an antagonistic attitude toward the different have been a desire and a conviction. The desire is to exert power over others and thereby to put our stamp on at least a small portion of the universe. The justifying conviction consists of the claim that our values and our ways of behaving are natural and right. The desire is familiar to all of us, though rarely acknowledged. The conviction seems innocent and therefore unsuspected, yet it structures much of what we think and do.

Controlling others is actually more than a desire; it is a burning urge. Its source may be evolutionary: in this dangerous world, those who can channel the aggressions of others or can at least enlist them to their aid improve their chances of survival. But the drive is generalized and roils behavior long after ordered social life makes the struggle for physical existence unnecessary. Accordingly, parents want to make their children "behave," the police often exercise overweening power, and bureaucrats take delight in forcing everyone to obey their rules. Salespeople want us to buy their goods, solicitors maneuver donors to give more than they wish, and neighbors often seek to impose arbitrary limits on what their neighbors can do with their land.

The desire to exercise power over others is so great that children find it difficult to escape the domination of parents even after they grow up, politicians resist term limits with all their might, and individuals who built businesses want never to retire. That people seek others to tell them what to do—paying fortunes to hire interior decorators, personal trainers, and consultants of every sort—may appear to be evidence against this view. But in fact it is further confirmation. In hiring them, they do our bidding and though we listen to them, *we* determine what we want, and thus the last word is always ours. They let us wield power over them for a fee.

The conviction that seems to justify our lording it over others is that what we, and people like us, do is natural and right. The customary defines the natural; the food we ate as children has not only the warmth of familiarity, but also an astonishing appropriateness. Some think that goulash is a dish invented by God and it is only perversity that keeps people from eating it; others believe that the paradigm of food is pasta or lamb kidneys or the lungs of cows. We tend to feel the same assurance about clothing, table habits, raising children, sexuality, ambition, profit, the treatment of women, the range of acceptable life plans, and religion. We grow into thinking that our tradition articulates the requirements of nature and that we do things exactly as it has ordained. I was raised to believe that God spoke Hungarian, as did everyone else uncorrupted by the misfortune of being born and raised in foreign lands.

I cannot overemphasize the significance and power of this innocent social egocentrism. "Innocent" in this context means the unintentional or unreflective intuitive embrace of a certain way of life, which happens to be the only one offered as a model. Anointing our ways as natural, however, loses its innocence when it begins to serve as the foundation of xenophobia and illusions of grandeur, leading genders, tribes, classes, races, and nations to develop a hierarchy of worthiness, each awarding itself the top spot. That way lies the history of humankind, which has certainly not been an innocent affair, spread out over millennia of injustice and exclusion. The cruelty and the horror of it far exceed what animals do to each other in response to the call of hunger; humans crush one another not as a result of justifiable need but in the name of establishing the natural order of things.

Schopenhauer saw as clearly as anyone that will seeks to overpower will and that it takes a relatively high level of moral culture to resist getting one's satisfactions that way. His recommendation of universal sympathy as the antidote to this cruel self-seeking, however, goes too far. We have no business cheering on oppressive wills, and it is in any case too much to ask that we invest ourselves in every failing cause. Something much less strenuous and therefore much more doable is adequate to make the world a better place: we have to learn to leave people alone. Although this sounds like an endorsement of moral isolation, it is not. Leaving others be as a pervasive moral disposition is perfectly compatible with living in a community with them, caring for them, and responding to their needs. All it forbids is uninvited interference in their affairs, that is, making them do what we want, even if we think it is justified by being good for them.

Philosophers have not been excellent at acknowledging the importance of leaving others alone and reducing our obligations to a sensible level. Josiah Royce declared that there is no rest in Zion: the moral person must be engaged in doing the Lord's work without cease.[22] We must right all wrongs, meet every need, and vanquish the evil that surrounds us. We are familiar with the hyperventilation to which this gives rise; it defines the moral tone of the reformer. We would have to be gods to meet such Herculean tasks and, indeed, Royce knows that the work is infinite. That is why he avers that God completes what in our finitude we must leave undone, making the gradual perfection of the world the joint venture of the human and the divine.

The introduction of God is at once the recognition that the task is too great for us. Since the task is infinite, without God we face moral despair. But if God picks up the slack, we might as well leave him a little more to do and thereby make our lives a lot more comfortable. Caught between the demand to exhaust ourselves and the temptation to throw in the towel, we face the problem that however much we do, we know we accomplish much less than we should. The magnitude of our duties makes guilt a certainty, and such certain failure weakens moral resolve. William James, even though he believed in the importance of what he called "moral holidays," did not do much better. He thought that every conscious need imposes a demand on all the world, and in particular on anyone who can help, to meet it.[23] Here again the resultant obligations are potentially infinite, with only finite resources to discharge them.

The contemporary version of certain moral failure and unavoidable guilt is James Rachels's view that there is no relevant moral difference between failing to aid people in a distant famine and killing them on the spot.[24] If that is true, our duties never end; tithing to Oxfam still leaves us murderers. All

22. Josiah Royce, *The World and the Individual, Second Series* (New York: Macmillan, 1908), p. 407.
23. William James, "The Moral Philosopher and the Moral Life," in *The Will to Believe and Other Essays in Moral Philosophy*, ed. Frederick H. Burkhardt, Fredson Bowers, and Ignas K. Skrupskelis (Cambridge, Mass.: Harvard University Press, 1979), p. 145ff.
24. James Rachels, "Killing and Starving to Death," *Philosophy* 54, no. 208 (1979): pp. 159–72.

the moral marvels for which we are responsible must, of course, be done in accordance with our own ideas of what is in the interest of distant and deeply different others. Our aid to them is wrapped in our values; in availing themselves of it, they see their desires, habits, and traditions beginning to change. Worse, we find ourselves rushing around in the futile attempt to intervene everywhere, attempting to fix what cannot be corrected, or what cannot be corrected by us, or what we have no business trying to correct. The frustration and mischief that arise can be eliminated only if we embrace our finitude, respect the integrity of others, and allow people to conduct their lives as they see fit.

Letting others pursue their goods according to their own lights is a vital condition of autonomy. But even those who value self-determination or liberty tend to think of leaving others be as a special duty imposed in certain circumstances rather than as a pervasive moral disposition. The better view is to conceive neutrality with regard to others as the foundational moral attitude of which obligations constitute a temporary suspension. The justification of this attitude and the grounding assumption of freedom is that human beings are self-moving agents capable of recognizing, seeking, and attaining their own good. If we deny human intelligence, drive, and competence, we will naturally wish to take over the lives of others to help them along. But this assessment of human ability is scurrilous and flies in the face of facts. If even dogs in heat know what is good for them and often attain it, there is little reason to suppose that humans don't and can't.

Of course, those who speak of the good tend to have high standards in mind, explaining to all why they should seek what, left alone, it would never occur to them to desire. This however is but another case of imposing values on people who may well want to have no part of them. I do not wish to deny that under special circumstances others may know more about one's good than one knows oneself. But this is exceptional and rare. For the most part, being oneself day and night gives one a privileged view of what satisfies; there is little basis for substituting the judgments of others for our long experience and considered opinions. What appear to some as errors in valuation may in fact express the deep, authentic, and internally justified commitments of different others.

Establishing the disposition to let others be as a fundamental moral attitude is not capitulating to selfishness. Egoists typically maintain the dominance or the sole legitimacy of a single good. People who gladly leave others alone tend to do so, admittedly, to pursue their own projects. Their focus on their plans does not imply, however, that only their own projects are worth pursuing. On the contrary, the attitude makes sense solely on the assumption of the legitimacy of a plurality of goods. This multiplicity of values, each centered in a feeling agent, is what makes the need not to interfere in the lives of others compelling. For each life has a native judge and advocate; each person is in the best position to determine his or her interests and to devote energy to their pursuit. People who let others work for their own good unimpeded simply act out their respect for the self-defining agency of which personhood consists. Claiming to know what is good for others and attempting to make them live up to it look much more like the work of selfishness than does keeping ourselves benignly removed.

Distance from people may be motivated by indifference to them. I am perfectly happy to leave the lake alone, because it simply does not matter to me. I don't rush over to tend it when a speedboat slashes its face and I don't grieve when it freezes in the cold. An attitude of this sort toward human beings, however, strikes me as horrendous; connected to one another from cradle to grave, we cannot be indifferent to each others' fates. The distance I advocate has its source not in cold unconcern, but in caring. Humans tend to do particularly well when they can make their own decisions and enjoy enough operational space to carry them out. If we wish others well, we let them flourish as they will, cheering them on from a distance. Good wrestlers and runners need no help from us. All we need to do is stay out of their way.

Leaving others alone because we want them to do well has as its flip side helping them when the need arises. If we wish everyone well, we must be ready to aid them in emergencies or when obstacles are overwhelming. The wise wait until the desire for help is obvious, if not through overt request then through crushing circumstance or pleading eyes. To give true help is to become an instrument of the other's will, honoring the integrity of what the needy want instead of telling them what they ought to have. Moral wisdom consists largely of knowing when to leave people alone and when to help them and, when helping them, how not to subvert their aims.

In addition to being morally suspect, taking over other people's lives is also strategically unwise. The bears of Yellowstone National Park got used to tourists bringing them food. As any intelligent creature would, they quickly abandoned foraging and took up favored spots near the highway, rendering themselves dependent on the kindness of people. We can find a trace of this tendency in human beings, some of whom raise no objections to being provided with what they need. Those wishing to interfere in the lives of others must therefore be ready to acquire permanent dependents who require continuing attention. The social welfare system operates in disregard of this fact of human nature. Instead of helping people over the hump, it offers ongoing support, tempting individuals to surrender responsibility for their own fates.

Helping others, therefore, is a far more complicated affair than it may at first appear. It must not be done in a way that impedes acknowledgment that people are intelligent choosers and independent agents. Paradoxically perhaps, providing for others may be of no help to them; it may invite them to surrender their independence and throw themselves on the mercy of strangers. The consequent inactivity, vulnerability, and collapse of self-respect interfere with even minimal satisfactions and make for a disconsolate life. The art of helping others begins with the recognition that giving does not always help. Just as courage does not mean tackling every danger, so caring does not demand that we answer every call.

But, it can be objected, is this not substituting our judgment for that of needy people, and if so, do we not wrongly interfere in their lives? The answer is no to both questions. Although refusing aid has important consequences for the people seeking it, it is primarily a decision about the activities of the donor. Such decisions are exercises in self-determination. In making them, we form an opinion only about how we ought to act, and say nothing about what anybody else should do or aim to be. One's actions determine, first and foremost, one's own life. To leave others alone is simply to keep one's distance, and not a subtle way of exercising power over them.

Permitting others to seek their goods in their own ways tacitly acknowledges the existence of multiple perfections, that is, of many ways in which good lives may be led. Since all these lives seem natural and appropriate to the people attracted to them, it becomes easy to recognize any claim of exclusive naturalness as a local illusion. Like each language, every life is natural when viewed from the inside but alien to the unfriendly observer. The ubiquity of the natural destroys extravagant assertions of universal normativity. If natures differ, so must the values they seek and the experiences that satisfy them. We can match aims, values, and fulfillments to natures, but there is no independent standard in terms of which natures can be ranked.

Curbing our desire to rule over people and abandoning the error of supposing that ours is the only natural or worthy way to live would go a long distance toward making this a more decent world. There is an attitude to life that makes attainment of these difficult goals a little more likely, though it is itself not easy to sustain. The attitude I have in mind expresses the conviction that though some things matter intensely, most things don't much matter at all. In its current state of development, the human psyche is easily riled. Powerful emotions are released by relatively trivial events and observations:

good looks engage our sexual machinery and earrings worn by a male child can subvert peace within the family. Deviations from the customary evoke disproportionately violent responses, as when gay-appearing gestures lead to physical assault and casual criticism plunges sensitive people into deep despair.

We live as universal sensoria tuned to react to everything untoward in the world. We seem to have preferences about all things and get "bent out of shape" whenever things don't go our way. We seem never to ask the question, "What is that to me?" and in good conscience remind ourselves that a host of things are simply not our business. We like it better if we can feel outrage or at least anger, and minimally worry and concern, about the ways of the world. We don't like to admit that there is much we cannot change, and even if we could, it would make little difference to us except to please our prissy sense of order. Why should we want the world to line up the way we imagine it right? The conceit that we know how people should behave, events work out, and the stars align themselves is laughable, yet we never seem to find it hilarious.

I want to be sure I am not misunderstood. There are plenty of things that should concern us in the most profound way. Suffering and joy matter, as does the humaneness of human relations. Undeserved ill, cruelty, injustice, and early death should engage our efforts. We must be ready to take a stand against activities that threaten to harm humans and other living creatures. But many of the things that most exercise our minds are as nothing compared with such serious business. What religion others choose to practice, their private sex lives, their eating habits, their manner of speech, the way they click their tongues and roll their eyes, the veritable cornucopia of their peculiarities amount to less than is worthy of mention, never mind of outrage and retaliation. If someone chooses not to bathe, we have the option of distance; if people want group sex, we can decline to join the crowd. The joy of choice is that we can look the other way. Instead of trying to crush those of a different persuasion, we can affirm our own values by clinging to them tenaciously as the right ones for us.

We cannot calculate the harm that has come from the conviction that everything, or a large number of things, matter for our welfare and that therefore the world should operate just so. Yet how can it affect my good if others worship the wrong god or the right god in the wrong way? Is it really a disaster if my neighbors enjoy open marriages and members of some political parties closed minds? Does it make sense to fight over what to eat for dinner, where to put the couch, and whom never to invite again? These and many other issues have no significance and, in any case, whatever arrangement prevails soon passes away. But even nonexistence fails as a haven: some couples can't leave their history alone, rehearsing old hurts in the quest to wound again.

If anything doesn't matter, it is the past. A modest amount of reflection is adequate to learn what one can from old mistakes; for the rest, we need to liberate ourselves from concern over the unchangeable. Yet we find it difficult to forgive even those we love; new wars are started to settle old scores and people who were never masters are invited to pay those who were never slaves huge sums in reparation for what happened to individuals long dead. The impulse to view everything as significant and hence demanding rectification will not let go of our minds, converting us into restless souls grotesquely busy with the attempt to reform, adjust, and regulate the world. The result is frustration and pain, without much headway in making anything better.

The commitment to leave others alone and the conviction that many things in life do not matter are connected, but they are not the same. We may decide to get out of the way of other people even though we think that what they do is both significant and annoying. Conversely, we may believe that many things don't matter, yet invade the autonomy of others out of wickedness or as nihilistic entertainment. Nevertheless, the commitment and the conviction go naturally together, each reinforcing the other in the quest for a sensible life. Thinking that only a relatively few things should be allowed to disturb our equilibrium invites us to let others explore their own concerns. In turn, the more we see others busying themselves with their own lives, the less we are tempted to believe that what they do is of significance to us. The result is improvement in the moral tone of society and a corresponding increase in human happiness.

My discussion of what cuts against appreciation of the different can serve as an outline of the obstacles in the way of a generous pluralism. Is fostering a variety of values, styles of life, and types of person worth the price? I have already indicated that leaving others alone and believing that lots of things that happen hold little significance for us would yield important benefits. But many people love the comfort of belonging and the exhilaration of persecuting the different much more than they delight in sympathy for the alien or a just distribution of happiness. Therefore, it may well be that individuals in tightly knit, intolerant communities live more satisfying lives than those who have to deal with the disquieting challenges and demanding sensitivities of strangely different people in their midst.

That this is not a far-fetched conjecture is amply displayed by the internal concord of Spartan society and by the unproblematic calm of religious communities and of medieval Japan. Such little worlds can have their own problems and crises, but they are not typically due to the disintegration of their value consensus. What attracts people to them is that the rightness of their customs receives reinforcement from all sides; no one defies the prevailing powers or denies the truth of shared ideas. Revealingly, we think of such agreement as a hallmark of heaven, where we enjoy praising the Lord in unison. Isolated fishing villages share this unanimity with the afterlife; in spite of their poverty, they provide a satisfactory social life due to concord about everything that matters.

Such uniformity of opinion and action is not a matter of choice for us, and it is quickly becoming unavailable for other communities as well. The mobility of people, the easy accessibility of vast stores of information, and the secularization of the world make it impossible for any nation to be a closed religious community or a modern Sparta. In some places, dissent and deviance are crushed and a coerced conformity appears to prevail for a while. But before long, imposed customs begin to crack and individual choice re-establishes alternative values and discordant modes of life. Despite efforts to control immigration, much of the world is now America, mixing races, religions, and ethnicities in ways that both break down and enrich original cultures. In the United States, the pluralism of values, religions, lifestyles, characters, customs, and preferences is a fact to be dealt with, not a choice to be made. It makes no sense to ask if we should opt for a homogeneous or a widely diversified society; pluralism is simply unavoidable.

This suggests that wisdom lies in tolerating the pluralism we find, permitting African Americans, Hispanics, gays, people of underappreciated ethnicity, transsexuals, and pacifists to carve out what existence they can in a society no longer overtly antagonistic toward them. The principle of leaving others alone recommends this passive attitude to what others do; accepting them and letting them do what they wish is tantamount to welcoming them into the community. Anyone who knows the history of exclusion will think this not a small matter. Historically, minorities by choice or nature have faced insuperable obstacles to full participation in the benefits of social life. They have been denied schooling, the vote, the right to hold property, the choice of occupation and of marriage partners, free movement, medical care, and sometimes even existence itself. The moral improvement of the human race has rendered these cruelties exceptional and unacceptable events. They still occur here and there, but the weight of public opinion and the might of civilized nations militate against them. A passive pluralism, tolerating a wide variety of values and allowing people of all sorts full social participation, should be enough to fulfill the requirements of moral decency.

What duty demands, however, is inadequate for flourishing. Even the apple people sought to diversify the one fruit that fell to their lot, and they did so with good reason. Comforting as uniformity may be, in the end it does not satisfy. Boredom with the same is an attractive alternative to insecurity in times of stress, but when things settle down, we start searching for the excitement only the different can provide. This desire for variety may be inscribed in the curious, that is exploratory, nature of humans and animals. But even if it is not, we find it everywhere, suggesting that its satisfaction is a vital element of the fulfillment we seek. And, indeed, there is ample evidence that people who enjoy a combination of stability and change are more satisfied than those who enjoy either one without the other.

For this reason and for others, therefore, pluralistic society is, on the whole and within limits, more conducive to human flourishing than one that is uniform and inbred. I say "on the whole" because living in the midst of competing values is not an unmixed blessing. For people of rigid habits and firm convictions, putting up with what they may well think is wrong can entail distress. Only on balance, after factoring in the pain, is it appropriate to judge pluralistic societies to be better. And I say "within limits" because diversity can be so great, though that is certainly not a problem in our country today, that it destroys the shared values on which a society is based.

The positive pluralism to which this points requires not just the toleration of diversity, but also its encouragement. Different cuisines, divergent ways of relating to family, a variety of religious practices, and multiple conceptions of self and occupation serve as Mill's "experiments in living" without which many of the best approaches to dealing with our problems may well go unexplored. There is much to learn from the accumulated experience of other cultures and divergent traditions, and there is a special lesson in seeing that ethnic groups that were mortal enemies in their original homes can peacefully coexist in a country that values them all. Variety provides us with choice, and choice with the opportunity to develop ourselves in directions we could not have imagined on our own.

The pains attendant on positive pluralism are easier to bear if we keep in mind the principle that many things in life don't matter much. Gay marriage, for example, evokes visceral responses from many people. This may be a battle over words, in which case it could perhaps be resolved by calling legally sanctioned gay lifetime commitments "unions" instead of "marriages." But to the extent it is not, we could sensibly ask ourselves what it is about single-sex relationships that matters so much that we are prepared to throw generosity to the wind and deny them the protections of the laws. How does it affect me if two men in Seattle or two women on a Florida beach pledge to each other their eternal love? I realize that deeply felt religious beliefs play an important role in the refusal to permit such things. But does it weaken one's religious resolve if others don't agree with it and if worldly authorities don't enforce its edicts? Conversion is of value only if voluntary; conformity achieved by force cannot please a decent deity.

The same holds for many of the other fierce battles in the so-called "culture wars." The bitterness and intensity of the conflicts reveal that they are struggles for power, that is, attempts to make others do what we want. Very little in the way of substantive human welfare lies at the bottom of these controversies: no one's life or happiness hangs on whether we may display the Ten Commandments in a courthouse or outrageous paintings in a museum. For the most part, the source of the trouble is bruised sensitivities. People take offense at seeing what they don't like in public spaces and launch campaigns to stifle harmless expressions of opinion. One of the heartening moral developments of the past fifty years is growing sensitivity to the sensitivities of others. Unfortunately, however, sensitivities seem to expand in direct proportion to the willingness of people to respect them. If we recognized the readiness to act hurt as an instrument of controlling others, a calmer moral tone might begin to suffuse our public conversations.

Positive pluralism opens us to the joy of diversity. Once we overcome our dread of the different, the richness of the world engulfs us as a wave and leaves our cleansed souls with gratitude and amazement. We become like the apple people when they stumble upon a garden of bananas, strawberries, and grapes and realize for the first time all that they have missed. With them as with us, variety gives life; the multiplicity of values serves as food to build strong selves. We could never be the people we are if other people were not delightfully, resolutely, and in some cases radically different.

Operational Independence

Human life used to be cheap. In many parts of the world it still is. People were, and in some places still are, slaughtered without a second thought. They were expected to fight to the death in wars, die without complaint in famines, and perish for lack of medical attention. Women were raped and killed, prisoners were tortured, and children were enslaved. Tamerlane built pyramids out of human skulls; other conquerors competed for the honor of having butchered the largest number of people. Death could come swiftly and for trivial reasons to anyone weak or not born into the nobility.

By contrast with this, people in civilized countries have reached an advanced stage in the development of sensitivity. They sympathize with the plight of others and believe that human life represents a pre-eminent value. They have established institutions to protect the right of each person to exist and want to honor the claim of people to whatever resources a decent life requires. They punish murder and mayhem under a criminal code they try to apply impartially, and they refuse to countenance arbitrary persecutions and executions. For these people, life is longer and immeasurably better, because they care for others and live in friendly cooperation with them.

Caring for others, however, can go too far. It can lead to taking over the lives of people by making choices that are theirs to make and to relieving them of responsibility for what they do. In the name of kindness, it can also render people inactive by making it unnecessary for them to engage the world in pursuit of the things we need to live. Our protective love of children carries us in this direction. Government programs to take care of the disadvantaged and the unemployed can also turn into invitations to surrender a life of agency and become satisfied with what others do for one.

This raises the question of what we owe others. The Bible admonishes us never to harden our hearts, but it doesn't say enough about how far we have to go in softening them. In many circumstances, only a morally insensitive or blatantly wicked person would turn away from helping those in need. But in many others, help may not be necessary or may even lead to long-term harm. The cruel past of humankind and our sympathy with all who suffer incline us to want to help everywhere. We think it a moral outrage for some to flourish while others have to make do with little, so we set out to even the scales and correct nature. Doing so, however, is a dangerous enterprise: our intentions tend to be good, but the consequences of our interventions are difficult to foresee.

Focusing on what we must do for our fellows, moreover, presents only a partial and therefore misleading picture of our moral relations to them. We must also ask when it is all right to invade the lives of other people or when we are justified in not leaving them alone. One may think it absurd, of course, to consider it an invasion of people's independence if we save them from dying of hunger. But even there, conditions may obtain that make such an act morally suspect, as when the person we want to save chooses to be on a hunger strike. Further, the bulk of our interactions involve nothing as dramatic as this. Everyday incursions take the form of telling people what they should eat, instructing them on how to raise their children, and demanding justifications for their actions. This sort of meddling is a favorite and deeply satisfying activity of many people, some of whom cannot understand why others, strangers no less than friends, fail to avail themselves of their wisdom.

Decent people concern themselves with human flourishing; helping others is a fundamental moral task. But the world would be a horrible place if people spent their time telling each other what to do and helping or making them do it. For such activities take away from others what is properly theirs: decisions about how to run their lives.

Collaboration leads to the ever-growing dependence of humans on one another. Much of what we accomplish presupposes the skills and achievements of prior generations and the work of innumerable contemporaries. Medical knowledge, for example, builds up over the centuries; adding to it requires tens of thousands of researchers and treatment professionals. Improvements in transportation and communication require institutions that organize the activities of many individuals and whose existence spans generations.

This makes it look as if all skills and activities were, in the end, social possessions. The impression is supported by the centrality of education in human life. Our meager physical endowment—we come into the world without even fur or scales—is matched by how little we can do at birth. Parents know that it takes a long time to arm children with the most rudimentary skills; two decades of the efforts of teachers are barely enough to acquaint the young with a portion of the accumulated wisdom of the human race. This vast store of knowledge, built up over thousands of years of experience, is the property of no single mind. It exists in books, in communally conceived and executed products such as bridges, and in the intelligent practices of cooperating human beings. From this perspective, individuals appear to be created by social processes to which they add little and which they cannot control.

Much as we find this picture beguiling, it presents only the obvious half of the truth. In our busy communal lives, we tend to overlook the deeper reality that all activity is the work of individuals. Society is not an agent in the physical world; flesh and blood persons are. Institutions cannot continue to exist without the compliant labor of the people who constitute them, and every act necessary to summon airplanes and dams into existence is performed by some single person voluntarily. Everything hangs on what people do: a corporation would disintegrate if its employees decided not to defend its interests. The entire social world is pieced together out of the contributions of individuals and unravels when they decide to stop.

That everything depends on the actions of living persons is amply demonstrated by general strikes, which can paralyze society. Work slowdowns and employees calling in sick remind us of the same point: human practices continue only because people fall in line and show themselves willing to continue them. We express this truth about the locus of agency when we say that one can lead a horse to water but cannot make it drink, and experience it when we try, unsuccessfully, to make teenagers do what we think they should. A bank whose tellers paid scant attention to their cash, whose managers did not care about who failed to come to work, whose auditors shrugged their shoulders at signs of embezzlement, and whose board of directors met only to party would soon go out of business. It would cease to be a functioning organization because the organisms that made it work lost interest in promoting its interests. Agency resides in organisms, not in organizations.

People living in a world of large institutions, however, find it advantageous to deny that they have the power to destroy apparently omnipotent organizations. The ability to stop it all imposes great responsibilities: when institutions operate in a way that is inhumane or morally corrupt, individuals must refuse to cooperate. Since this demands great courage and can lead to grievous consequences, people decide to go along with whatever is demanded of them, hiding behind the excuse that one person cannot accomplish much by resisting.

In reality, however, the action of the organization is but the sum of the actions of its members, and there are times when the bold moral challenge issued by a single individual is enough to bring an entire house of cards to the ground. This phenomenon is what Vaclav Havel referred to as "the power of the powerless," employing that paradoxical phrase to call attention to the might of the "little" person. There is nothing paradoxical about this power, however, unless we begin with the false assumption that anything other than individuals can act. The power, exercised in the name of decency, can of course cause the individual to be swept away, but that is the inherent danger of moral action and the mark of an uncivilized society.

If Gandhi had resisted the Nazis, he would have been shot immediately, but the relatively civilized British could not find an adequate reason to remove him. The crude display of military might at Tiananmen Square was possible only because soldiers acted like machines and did not refuse to massacre their fellow citizens. This is in sharp contrast to the peaceful transformation of the Ukraine in 2005 and other silent revolutions in which no one dared give the order to fire or, when they did, no one followed it. So the greatest danger to the moral agent is a morally insensitive society. Individuals always have the power to cry halt, but their best chance of success is when their fellows realize that they, too, can resist.

Some thinkers suppose that institutions and states are purposive beings that formulate plans and take steps to enact them. People in decision-making positions can, of course, identify ends for the organization or collection of people they lead, but these are plans *for* the group rather than *of* it as a unified agency. Single-purpose institutions such as restaurants come closest to the concentrated action typical of individuals, but even their focused exertions fall far short of the effortless integration of personal acts. Larger collections of people such as cities and states display contrary currents of opinion and action; if individuals showed the aimlessness and indecision of communities, we would have to give them the protection due children and the mentally disabled.

Some visionaries fancy that the relation of individuals to their communities or nations is precisely analogous to the relation of cells to the organisms of which they are parts. They reason that both cells and persons serve a larger whole and find life and significance only in that service. The integration of the body is matched, in their view, by the order of the state, and in both cases this reveals a hierarchy of importance: cells and individuals are equally dispensable, but while they live they must serve their lord and master.

We know organisms that, observed from a distance, seem to relate to their social context in this way. Ants appear to enact a narrative of individual insignificance and bees show no reluctance to die for their hive. Possibly some future humanoids also will live in thrall of their community, surrendering themselves to the service of the larger whole. But that is clearly not how things stand now. Admittedly, people are capable of stunning acts of self-sacrifice in protecting others. But sacrifice is not surrender: it flows from private decision and is the act of a self-possessed, independent agent.

This is not to deny the influence of the social milieu on the individual. What others do is noted by children and often adopted as their mode of operation. The values of the crowd are contagious, and many people find it nearly impossible to live according to private principles or enact unconventional patterns of life. The culture in which we live stamps us with its marks to such an extent that we become easily identifiable as, say, twenty-first-century Americans or Egyptians from the age of Cleopatra. But social influence flows from person to person and the actions it incites are performed by individual agents. There are no magical social causes other than what individuals singly or conjointly do.

The ultimate reason for the primacy of personal action is biological; its fruit is moral. The human race is fragmented into individuals. Each is an agent entrusted with taking care of itself and endowed by nature with the tools to do so. Normally we can find food, defend ourselves, chart a course of life, and find mates to reproduce the species. Although there is much we cannot do without the cooperation of our fellows, the cooperation itself presupposes that we are self-moving organisms capable of contributing to what others do. We must be able to work our parts, frame purposes, and respond to circumstance, or else we are no better than logs on the forest floor. Humans, like cats, are ornery: only they can operate their bodies and they do only what they want.

Autonomous agency, then, is founded on the biological reality that organisms are self-governing centers of energy. They are not boulders in a meadow, inert and without transformative insides, but dynamic and often unpredictable wellsprings of activity. The outside world can affect them, but it gets back something different from what it offered. Just as the bee turns pollen into honey and our bodies convert fried chicken into blood and cells, so living souls build external influences into their substance. Though not detached from the world in origin and sustenance, they nevertheless operate as independent agents.

One can imagine circumstances, though not particularly interesting ones, in which agency is not nodular. In such a world energy flows as in a field from one relatively undifferentiated portion of space to another. Individuation is incomplete, with fluid and permeable boundaries between beings. Peirce conceives the relation of minds on this model, with the ideas of which they consist spreading in all directions, mixing and interpenetrating in the process. This may be a good description of how ideas behave in the public domain, where they are shared through books, newspapers, and conversations. But that is not how fully individuated biological organisms operate. They are self-directing bundles of energy, actively engaged in maintaining their integrity and developing themselves according to plan or native pattern.

Both self-preservation and self-development point to a purposiveness in the service of which the energies of the organism are deployed. The teleology is present in plants but becomes particularly notable in animals, whose exertions are directed largely at accomplishing what they want. The level of self-possession or self-control this requires marks the organism as a self-contained agent capable of operating without external help: it plans, executes, and assesses its own activities. Its independence is central for understanding its nature; it moves of its own accord and even if—or perhaps especially when—it is left to its own devices. Under normal circumstances, it needs little help to do what it wants, and it insists, as children do, on being left alone to pursue its purposes.

Reliance on the external environment for food and air in the case of the organism and for language and the skills of culture in the case of socialized humans takes nothing away from this independence. The things we need to operate amount to background conditions of life that neither act through us nor determine what we do. The enabling conditions of action do not themselves act; only organisms do. And when they do, the immediate source of their operation and its ultimate controlling force are they themselves.

This independence is on display in much of what human beings do. What we call "pigheadedness" in pursuit of a goal, dogged rejection of external interference, and the well-known but maddening insistence of people on deciding how to do things and when are manifestations of the desire to be in charge of one's life. We see the demand for self-governance even in children as they try, early in life, to wrest decision-making power from their parents. Adults retain the tendency to display it in their resentful resistance to orders from above. Even sick and old people are devoted to self-determination, attempting to control the time and manner of their demise.

Individuals, like spinning tops, live their lives with a momentum all their own. As existentialists insist, they make their decisions and bear the consequences alone. No matter how much social support they receive, in the end they enjoy their pleasures, suffer as a result of their shortcomings, and face their deaths in ultimate isolation. This does not mean that their minds are impenetrable to others or that the community abandons them in their hours of need. But no one is able to lift the burden of failure from another and none can share even a trusted partner's infinite grief at having to leave the world. There is a vast difference between knowing what others suffer and suffering those things oneself; the issue is not the knowability of other minds but the utter existential insularity of each.

All this points to an important but often overlooked distinction. *Ontologically,* that is, from the perspective of their existence, people are clearly dependent. They rely on air, food, and water, they would never have come into being without parents, and they would be worse off than wild animals if others had not cared for them, taught them, and continued to provide them with many of the necessities of life. *Operationally,* on the other hand, individuals are mostly independent. They are able to move and control their parts and to coordinate them in order to engage in the activities with which they busy themselves day and night. They frame purposes and execute them, focusing their efforts on attaining what they want. They do this without help from others and reach a level of satisfaction they deem adequate, if only for the moment.

Ontological or ultimate dependence takes nothing away from the operational independence of organisms. Automobiles cannot function without gasoline and engine, yet the necessary conditions of such operation determine neither what they do nor where they go. So it is with organisms, except that humans and other animals do not wait to have their tanks filled and their engines fixed; they take action to feed themselves and to repair the damage to their bodies. Under normal circumstances, they are in need of little or nothing beyond their own power in order to operate: they are planning, self-structuring, self-motivating, self-moving, and self-satisfying beings. Even quadriplegics enjoy a residue of this complex and marvelous ability in speaking, eating, and regulating the parts of their bodies whose moving is not denied them.

People who insist on the communal nature of all activity announce it on their own, without aid. Thinkers who maintain that since language is a social product, their ideas are not really their own, think this alone, in the quiet of their studies. Others, who are able to see only social action and no individual initiative, write their own books and get paid for lecturing about them. The operational independence of humans and animals surrounds us on all sides: the fragmentation of the life force into individuals renders it an unavoidable reality. The refusal to see it must be due to an overwrought sense of solidarity with others or to an unrealistically low opinion of one's own agency.

Every denial of individual agency or operational independence is its affirmation: the action might serve some imagined social good, but it is executed by an individual person. Why anyone would be tempted to suppose otherwise sheds light on the radical changes human life has undergone in the past few thousand years. Primitive hunters pursuing their prey, mothers in a cave giving birth, and solitary warriors struggling to survive would never have supposed that their actions were anything but their own. They could rely only on themselves. At any rate, no one could or would help them much, and instinct or experience enabled them to make it through another day. Some measure of cooperation was, of course, present even then: it took two to beget children and someone had to cook the beast the hunter killed. But the coordination of activities was minimal, rarely going beyond volunteering or acquiescing in some act in return for another.

Increase in the population, the division of labor, and the consequent growth of the scope and complexity of action have made humans vastly more interdependent. Our actions have become cooperative on a scale unimaginable to primitive peoples, and by means of them we have acquired significant control over some aspects of nature. The construction of airplanes and the operation of airlines, for example, require the precisely correlated labor of tens of thousands of people. Such activities confer immense power on us, though the power does not belong to any single person. The acts are not any one person's either: they are too large to be appropriated by individuals, each of whom makes but a minuscule contribution to them.

The natural supposition is that acts of this sort are intrinsically social, and some may even be tempted to think that they are performed by some superorganism, such as American Airlines or the state of France. In fact, however, no such superorganisms exist: institutions and nations are but interacting human beings coordinated in their voluntarily assumed tasks. The moment significant numbers of people refuse to do their jobs, the institution disintegrates like a soap bubble. Something like this happened in the Soviet Union prior to its disappearance. The acts themselves are social only in the sense that it takes many people to perform them and that some persons plan and control the activities of others. Control, however, must be understood in a soft sense, for planners cannot *make* their colleagues do what they want. They can only make it worth their while to manifest the desired behavior. This means that the causation involved runs through the choice mechanisms of workers, making them the ultimate agents performing the necessary acts.

The mistake of thinking that large-scale acts are social originates in amazement at the scope and power of the "actions" of institutions and failure to analyze them into their constituents, which are act-fragments performed by individuals. This disguises the fact that speaking of institutional actions is but a shorthand way of referring to masses of individual actions, a manner of simplifying speech that obscures important moral realities. For the belief that questionable actions are performed by faceless institutions and not ordinary persons appears to relieve people of their responsibility. The sense of personal powerlessness is at once a defense against the charge of irresponsibility. If I did not cause or cannot change the status quo, I cannot be charged with having done less than decency demands.

American English is more guilty of this problematic simplification than is the English spoken in Britain. There, words such as Microsoft, although they appear to be the names of single entities, nevertheless typically function as collective nouns, referring to the multiplicity of the people constituting the company. Accordingly, in tacit acknowledgment of the ontology of action, they tend to take plural verbs, suggesting that institutions masquerading as unified agents are in fact associated collections of activities. So, for example, "The Senate is debating" is an incorrect and misleading way of speaking. In Britain, the equivalent expression is "Parliament are debating legislation."

Debating is a complex set of activities by a large number of people instead of a single act by an institution.

Highly coordinated acts of momentous complexity and scope are commonplace in the commercial world in this age of large institutions and populous nation-states. Connecting hundreds of cities by means of air service appears to be the effortless achievement of huge corporations. In reality, however, the act is neither single nor effortless, consisting of innumerable act-fragments contributed by tens of thousands of people. Some decide which cities to serve and at what hours of the day, others fuel the planes and load the baggage, the pilots take responsibility for flying passengers safely from one place to another, ticket vendors sell seats, gate agents make sure that only ticketed passengers can board, mechanics service the planes, accountants keep the books of the company and pay its employees, and thousands of other people in hundreds of other specialist assignments take pains that everything runs smoothly.

Institutions consist of such chains of mediation, in which each participant acts on behalf of others or in concert with them. The impression of the rational agency of corporations is greatly bolstered by the experience of people working for them: the acts to which the employees contribute are so vast that they literally do not know them. Situated in the bowels of an institution, they have little understanding of the total act to which they contribute and no sense of control over it. Although they are busy doing a hundred things, they feel passive and powerless to change their routines. They suspect that the acts in which they participate may have harmful consequences, but they deflect responsibility for them by reference to the impotence they feel. They know that their fellow workers are in a position no different from theirs, so they cannot be blamed either. It must, therefore, be the institution, "the system," that is at fault.[25]

This sort of reasoning tends to create the impression that institutions are agents. But the impression is mistaken. Living human beings make the plans of institutions, and other individuals execute the plans, even if each participant contributes but a little. There is no need to postulate any agency beyond what all these individuals do. The act of the institution is fully analyzable into the constituent actions of human beings. Therefore, if there is credit or blame, it rests squarely on the shoulders of people, not on some superentity whose actions are undetectable. Although it is understandable that people in

25. I deal with this issue at greater length in *Intermediate Man* (Indianapolis, Ind.: Hackett, 1981).

mediated chains should see themselves as passive and the system in which they operate as active, this inverted perspective has the undesirable effect of allowing them to think they have no moral responsibility for the actions they perform on behalf of their nations or their employers. The past century saw this denial of responsibility in Nazi and Soviet concentration camp guards and in the silent complicity of employees in the white-collar business crimes of their bosses.

It may be objected, however, that the analysis of institutional acts into the actions of individuals doesn't go far enough. Just as social acts are made up of what people do, so the actions of individuals may be reduced to the movements of the cells of their bodies. In fact, as we saw earlier, some people think they can establish the insignificance of individuals by means of the analogy between the relation of cells to bodies and the relation of individuals to their communities, states, or nations. Cells are created to serve the larger whole, and any one or set of them is dispensable and easily replaced. Similarly, individuals are supposed to be products of the social whole, and hence their fulfillment is inseparable from the self-sacrificing service they provide. Why should we stop the analysis at individual action and not proceed to the work of cells or organs?

The question of why we should stop at the operational independence of persons is posed in a revealing way. How far we analyze and what categories we use are matters of decision, and such decisions are made for reasons. The reasons all relate to human flourishing. Humans can do a world of harm to each other, to other living creatures, and to the planet on which they live. Without a system of holding people accountable for what they do, the harm would be potentially limitless.

The practice of imputing responsibility for actions is possible only if we take the agents to be individual persons. Looking to larger centers of power does not work: how could we punish corporations for misdeeds? We may try by means of jail terms, fines, and extermination. But the company cannot be put in prison, so we incarcerate its executives. Fining it causes misery only to its employees and shareholders. Its board of directors (consisting of individual agents) may learn a lesson, but the firm itself cannot be embarrassed or suffer pain. We can try to put the corporation out of business, as the U.S. government did Arthur Andersen, but since companies are indifferent to life and death, this does not have the deterrent effect of an execution; the only ones who suffer and who could be expected to modify their behavior are the people who work there. If we want to retain a system of moral responsibility, we must reject the thought that organizations or states or races are the ultimate agents in the world.

Similarly, we must not look below the level of individuals if the practice of holding agents accountable is to remain viable. If we did, the experienced operational independence of persons would disappear in their total reliance on the movements of parts of their bodies. With operational independence would go moral responsibility for one's acts: cells cannot be jailed, it makes no sense to cut off the arm that stabbed the victim in punishment for its misbehavior, and it would be absurd to blame one's ductless glands for battery or fraud. Even without going so far as to analyze the action of cells into the movements of molecules and those into the swirl of subatomic particles, we lose the human world we know if we take our eyes off the agency of people.

This is a perfectly good pragmatic argument for focusing on the actions of individuals and declaring persons to be the authors of whatever is done. Those not satisfied with pragmatic arguments might come to the same conclusion by reflecting on what an action is. Events and happenings clearly do not qualify: actions require reference to what the agent means to do. Intentions or purposes are, therefore, essential elements of actions, as are consequences, proposed and actual. An action thus is a complex and temporally extended unity of intention, execution, and result. We cannot know what an act is by looking at the plan or at the isolated doing. We learn what we have done only by seeing how the intention, as put into effect, plays in the real world.

Freedom involves the relation between intention and performance; it consists of the ability to frame purposes and to execute them. To enjoy liberty, J. S. Mill pointed out, is to be able to do what we want, that is, to be unimpeded in planning for ourselves and to have the power to convert these plans into reality. The relation of what we do to its consequences, on the other hand, defines responsibility. So both freedom and responsibility are tied to the notion of action. The idea is that as free, we do as we want, and as responsible, we must bear the consequences. Properly understood, freedom and responsibility are two sides of the same coin and constitute indispensable conditions of education: we learn to adjust and limit our freedom on the basis of the outcomes of previous acts.

This notion of action finds no application to organs, cells, proteins, and subatomic particles. None of these is in a position to frame purposes and to consider, let alone learn much from, consequences. Things happen that involve them, but they are not self-moving organisms that plan, execute their intentions, and enjoy or suffer the results. The same is true of institutions, organizations, states, and nations: they have no minds independent of the intelligence of their leaders, no muscles apart from the people who act under their aegis, and no feeling to enjoy or suffer what they have created. Some higher animals may be able to undertake actions of the sort here described, but beyond them and angels—if it turns out that any such exist—only living human beings can act, and they always do so in their individual capacity.

A Reflection on Courage

Aristotle said that the good life requires good fortune. And, indeed, we are lucky to live in the richest and most humane country in the world, at a time when we can enjoy long and healthy lives and convert our natural talents into satisfying activities. We did not die in the World Trade Center on 9/11, have not lost the ability to move our bodies and to remember things, and will likely continue to embrace the joys of life for years to come.

I don't mean to deny any of us credit for hard work. I admire those not satisfied with good fortune who have steadfastly fostered their talents. But such efforts must be placed in the broader context of our luck, or else we lose the true measure of our contingency and necessary gratitude.

We know what it takes to rise in a profession and in the admiration of one's fellows: intelligence, hard work, and luck. But we want more than triumph in our jobs. We also desire to achieve standing as human beings. For that, we have to excel at taking care of family, not breaking faith with friends, and treating everyone with the basic decency persons deserve. We want to be responsible members of society and yet take time to enjoy those moments of eternity that open in quiet contemplation. Will this be enough for a life that, upon reflection near the end of it, we can declare satisfying or worthy?

In seeking a well-adjusted life, we must resist two great and greatly dangerous temptations. The first is to agree with the crowd, the second to elect safety as the highest value. The opinions of our society, any society, are contagious. To see others believing what we believe is a powerful confirmation, to embrace what others prize creates comfort and self-assurance. As a result, cultural values tend to go unchallenged. Shared beliefs seem, like gravity, inevitable parts of the world; they are so obvious that they hardly draw notice, let alone critique. The wisest of human beings can in this way be blinded to the blind spots of their culture or misled into thinking that the practices of their society are uniquely adequate expressions of human nature.

Aristotle saw nothing wrong with slavery and Kant did not raise his voice against keeping women in subjection. Living in a warlike nation, Hegel glorified war; in the Soviet Union, people praised the abominations of socialist realism; and—having grown up in Hungary—I was taught that the recipe for goulash was handed to Hungarians directly by God. We can easily convince ourselves that what we do and how we do it are just and right, that strangers given to other customs are mistaken or evil, and that changing anything may well subvert the natural order of things. The contagion of belief and the resistance to change beset much of our lives. I remember the bitter controversy about introducing the three-point shot in basketball. Earnest people maintained that basketball proper had no three-point shot and if one were introduced, the game would no longer count as basketball. The same argument was launched when Vanderbilt first considered adding students to faculty committees. Opponents announced that this was an unnatural and impossible feat, since student membership would strip away their nature as *faculty* committees.

One can love one's country, its language, and its customs even in full knowledge that things are different elsewhere, that as time goes on they will also be different here, and that there are ways in which what we do could be improved. We must live with open eyes, conscious of what we do well but always noting where and how we can do better. As in the university, in a dynamic society critique is a compliment and the greatest engine of progress. To criticize people is to take them seriously, that is, to respect them as intelligent friends traveling with us on the road to a less error-prone and more humane universe.

The problem is, of course, what it has always been: criticizing the status quo is costly. This is the greatest challenge. From time to time, we see that there is something wrong, perhaps even awful, about our practices. If we make a careful assessment, we realize that exposing the injustice or the violation is likely to make others view us as troublemakers and render us outcasts. Speaking up might cost us a promotion, even the job. Under extreme conditions, it may lead to the loss of our lives. Considering the price, it is understandable that people find reasons to stay silent. Perhaps things are not so bad after all; we have obligations to our families; in any case, a single person cannot do much. We hear these excuses and we sympathize. Why can't we live in peace and not be called on to take action against the wrong?

Fear is a powerful force even when there is no basis for it. After seven years of service, faculty members achieve tenure, which provides protection against arbitrary dismissal. They can be removed only for incompetence and moral depravity, the latter of which is not a major temptation for academics. At a research university some years ago, the faculty came to see the president as an obstacle to the improvement of education. Tenure, that is, the assurance of lifelong employment, imposes responsibilities on the faculty: the right to speak out without fear of losing their jobs carries with it the obligation to take a critical stance in order to improve their community. In accordance with this idea, a few faculty members formulated a petition calling on the president to resign. To forestall the possibility of retaliation against those looking for eventual promotion, they asked only full professors to sign. To avoid compromising their positions, professors with administrative assignments were excluded.

In all, sixty-three people who had voiced criticism of the president were approached. Astonishingly, only twenty-five signed. Even among the signers, some wondered aloud: "What could they do to me?" In a country that protects freedom of speech, in an institution that proudly holds to the principle of the open forum, the central issue for job-secure faculty members became fear of the consequences of speaking up. All those asked agreed that the administration was doing a poor job. Yet some used the likely ineffectiveness of the petition as an excuse for not signing, openly wondering what might happen to them if the president would not resign. Others offered to sign only on the absurd condition that the petition not be made public.

If people who have nothing to fear can nevertheless feel so intimidated, the magnitude of the task we face is obvious. A visit to neighbors to discuss their battered children or their starving dogs is difficult enough. To say no to what our employers demand or what flies in the face of the standard of practice requires far greater courage. We live in the bowels of huge institutions whose rules and habits appear as unchangeable as natural law. In the name of fairness and efficiency, organizations develop uniform procedures that justify rejecting exceptions by the devastating sentence, "But if we did this for you, we would have to do it for everyone." This mighty justification of rigor mortis forgets only one thing: that every living person is an exception. That splendid notion is the message of our great religions, which maintain that we enjoy individual standing in the eyes of God. What God readily grants us, institutions don't, resulting in a metamorphosis of human souls into crumpled numbers, treated according to general guidelines or rules appropriate to their roles.

At some point, we will no doubt feel that our institutions simply ask too much, that we just cannot, and must not, go along with what they do. Will we then have the daring to speak up, to cry halt, to say no? Will the pragmatist demand for improving the world breathe courage into us? Will stoic indifference to pain enable us to act with fortitude?

The ultimate measure of human beings is the humaneness of their souls, their readiness to aid others in their struggle for the special treatment they deserve. I put myself in the shoes of the guards of the concentration camps of Nazi Germany, the railroad workers of Soviet Russia carrying trainloads of people to Siberia, Serb soldiers commanded to slaughter Kosovars, and bureaucrats processing people, unconcerned about their private griefs. Would I, would we, be able to rise to the occasion, on every occasion of possible help, and even at great personal cost treat human beings humanely?

CHAPTER 4

AN ONTOLOGY
FOR STOIC PRAGMATISM

About Santayana

George Santayana is a major American philosopher who has been sadly neglected. In his *The Life of Reason* (five volumes), he undertook to describe the phases of human progress and, though resisting the label, he showed himself in clear sympathy with pragmatism. His later works celebrate a spirituality that consists of absorption in the present moment. Throughout his life, he was able to observe the movement of the world at a great remove, as if through the wrong end of binoculars. This stoic calm in the face of the spectacle of life and death, along with his interest in a harmonious and self-improving life of reason, brings him close to stoic pragmatism. He never quite articulated the view, but it captures his attitudes, practices, and portions of his theoretical positions.

Santayana's thought is particularly interesting to examine because his naturalism may be made to serve as the philosophical underpinning of stoic pragmatism. I took the first steps of this exploration under the headings "Primitive Naturalism" and "Rescher's Cognitive Pragmatism" earlier in this book. I continue the exploration here. Santayana's ontology provides a particularly clear and helpful way of thinking about our condition. Starting, as he does, with human animals struggling for life in a vast and indifferent world, he can view our achievements in a sobering cosmic context. He can relegate knowledge and language to their subsidiary positions in the economy of life and ground a stoic pragmatism in human desire, need, and mortality, along with the contingency of all things.

The details of a fully developed philosophy of stoic pragmatism have yet to be worked out. My sense is that its final shape will resemble Santayana's ideas in a surprising number of particulars.

The Difference God Makes

George Santayana wrote a dissertation under the direction of Josiah Royce and subsequently served as Royce's colleague in the Harvard philosophy department for more than twenty years. Both Royce and William James were kind to Santayana: as chair of the department, Royce worked hard to secure him a permanent position and a promotion. Despite tensions in the department, relations between Royce and Santayana were, on the surface, cordial. They sent each other their newly published books and exchanged friendly correspondence.

On a deeper level, Santayana's relation to Royce was anything but close. He wrote to his friend Henry Ward Abbot that "one couldn't expect anything delicate and fine from Royce"[1] and confessed that "Royce's theories of love and marriage disgust me."[2] He referred repeatedly to "poor Royce's lordly sophistry"[3] and wrote that in listening to him "you felt the overworked, standardized, academic engine, creaking and thumping on at the call of duty or of habit, with no thought of sparing itself or any one else."[4]

Deep philosophical differences lie beneath this ambiguous relationship. Santayana views himself as a materialist, "apparently the only one living";[5] Royce is proud of being an idealist. Santayana believes objects exist independently of the knowledge of them; Royce rejects this realism. Santayana maintains that the good is relative to the constitution and circumstances of animals; Royce speaks of good and evil as cosmic realities. Santayana thinks individuals are finite beings that emerge and perish; Royce embraces them as primary realities whose lifespan and obligations are infinite. Santayana attacks speaking of God as "dreaming in words";[6] Royce feels assured that God is our living partner in all the good we do. It would be difficult to find two philosophers who are further from each other in their convictions.

1. George Santayana, *The Letters of George Santayana*, book 1, [1868]–1909, ed. William G. Holzberger and Herman J. Saatkamp (Cambridge, Mass., and London: MIT Press, 2001), p. 65.

2. Ibid., p. 68.

3. George Santayana, *The Letters of George Santayana*, book 2, 1910–1920, ed. William G. Holzberger and Herman J. Saatkamp (Cambridge, Mass., and London: MIT Press, 2002), p. 105.

4. George Santayana, *Character and Opinion in the United States* (Garden City, N.Y.: Doubleday, 1954), p. 61. Hereafter *Character*.

5. George Santayana, *Scepticism and Animal Faith* (New York: Dover, 1955), p. vii. Hereafter *SAF*.

6. Ibid., p. 7.

That certainly is the usual view of Santayana and Royce, which may go a long way toward explaining why so far no one has bothered to examine their relationship in print. The general attitude of scholars is that merely noting the sharp differences between the two should fill the bill. The general conviction of philosophers is that we can book little profit for the current quarter from examining old ledgers, especially the accounts of rival companies. There is something to be said for these dispositions, but not enough to justify adopting them. The differences between Santayana and Royce are not nearly as final as they seem. And examining their arguments, their divergences, and their similarities yields lessons for us today.

Someone viewing these thinkers from a great distance may see only differences. But the closer we get to them, the more similarities emerge. Before long, the question to answer is not how, given their lives together in the same department, they could share so little philosophically. Instead, it becomes how, given the close similarity of many of the ideas out of which their systems are built, their philosophies could end up so distant from each other. Answering the latter question is the task I set myself in this chapter. In doing so, I will focus on three ideas centrally important to both: those of the specious present, truth, and individuality.

A good way to begin to see striking similarities between Santayana and Royce is by focusing on the use they make of the idea of the specious present. Both of them are indebted to William James for having developed the concept of the experienced present, which is not a point instant separating the future from the past. The specious present is, in some sense, extended in such a way as to incorporate the immediate past and the immediate future. Without the union in a single experienced event of past, present, and future, there would be no continuity in one's conscious life. We could not apprehend melodies without the coexistence in awareness of the last few notes, the current note, and a few of the notes to come. We could not understand speech if the earlier part of a sentence did not still reverberate in the mind as the current sound converts itself into future words. Philosophers have long known that the idea of succession is not a succession of ideas but a single bit of synthetic consciousness in which succession is a relation between present elements.

The phenomenology of the specious present, with heavy stress on *specious,* plays a central role in Santayana's examination of skepticism. In the first part of *Scepticism and Animal Faith,* Santayana undertakes to assess the skeptical challenge to claims of knowledge. His strategy is to doubt everything he can, to see if in the end anything remains standing. The technique is to distinguish the given—whatever cannot be denied—from what is only believed. That there is an apple-like something in the foreground is a datum;

that this is an *apple* in front of *me* is a dispensable opinion. Both apples and selves are existents with histories, and it is by no means obvious that the present datum is an element of such an apple and that there is an I to which this datum appears.

Similarly, fullness in the stomach is directly felt, but that it is due to the bacon and eggs I ate for breakfast is at best a conjecture. Is the fullness in the *stomach?* The stomach is not directly in the field of perception, so anything I think about it is a belief open to doubt. Is the feeling one of *fullness?* Possibly so, but it could also be some other feeling, misrecognized. Before long, this skeptical reduction leaves us with nothing but unutterable immediacies concerning which we cannot be wrong, but which nevertheless yield no knowledge. The linchpin of Santayana's argument is the attempt to show that if knowledge is immediate certainty, nothing changing can be known. Because the distant past is only remembered and the distant future only anticipated, they are objects of potentially wrong belief. Although the specious present promises direct access to the immediate past and immediate future, all its elements coexist, and hence it can tell us only about the present. Its vistas may be painted: it is a matter of risky belief to suppose that what is experienced now really happened or really will take place.

The specious present is thus revealed as a moment that arrests time: the present, the past, and the future exist within it as elements of a single whole. It yields a picture of succession no part of which succeeds any other or, in slightly different language, an unchanging depiction of change. The Western tradition of philosophy and theology maintains that these unmoving vistas of the life of time are eternal. Santayana acknowledges the point later in *Scepticism and Animal Faith* when he says that eternity is "a synthetic image of time."[7] He does not think that everything eternal takes the form of detemporalized succession, for numbers—to choose but one example—are timeless in the sense of showing no sequence, actual or specious. Inasmuch as we wish to understand the difference between the temporal and the eternal, however, nothing serves as a more poignant illustration of it than the form of temporal process and its actual enactment. This contrast captures the relationship between Santayana's realms of essence and matter.

Royce introduces the idea of the specious present specifically to elucidate the relation of the temporal to the eternal. He lingers lovingly on the phenomenology of poetry and music, maintaining that they show the presence of elements of the past, present, and future in a single moment of consciousness. We cannot understand a sentence or hear a melody, Royce avers,

7. *SAF,* p. 271.

without the last few words or notes reverberating in the mind even while the next several exist in anticipation.[8] This way of experiencing time strips it of succession and counteracts the loss we normally associate with it. In the specious present, the future is already here and the past is not yet gone, so we can see at least a small portion of the history of the world as simultaneous and yet as involving consciousness of movement.

Taking the passage out of time yields a view of the eternal. Royce wants to show that there are two different approaches to the travail of the struggling world: one can see it in part or whole. Viewed from the standpoint of its fragmented moments, humans find themselves in the midst of temporal passage and striving. From the perspective of the whole, however, the desperate incompleteness that characterizes the struggles of finitude is suspended and the entire history of the world grows visible under the form of eternity. All of us are capable of detemporalizing some small portion of the world-process; our specious presents enable us to glimpse moments of eternity. The magnitude of the process we can see as eternal is a function of the strength of our minds, in such a way that the more mighty the intellect, the larger the portion of the world-process it can grasp in a single act.

All minds, therefore, are continuous in nature, differing from each other largely in their power. The human mind can experience only small elements of eternity, but God's infinite intellect is able to take in the entire history of the universe at a single glance. The unchanging intuition of the changing world renders everything changeless: since this momentous consciousness encompasses all of history, there is no room for anything to happen any more. Past, present, and future coexist in God's mind in such a fashion that the story of finite striving can be seen as complete. Will finds its satisfaction and the search for meaning is brought to a successful conclusion. Our halting efforts to do what is right are supplemented and evil suffers final defeat.

Both Santayana and Royce use the notion of the specious present to develop the idea of eternity. Their conceptions of the eternal are strikingly similar, involving detemporalized succession or the conversion of passage into the appearance of change. Moreover, the eternal plays a central role in their systems: in Santayana's as defining the realm of essences that lend articulation to all existence and all thought, and in Royce's as the crucial feature of God who offers the promise that our struggles are not in vain. But a careful look at these similarities reveals profound differences as well. For Santayana, eternity is a property of depersonalized essences or forms; for

8. Josiah Royce, *The World and the Individual, Second Series* (New York: Macmillan, 1923), p. 115ff.

Royce, it characterizes a living God. Essences are without value and connection to moral concerns; Royce's God serves as the guarantor that good prevails. Santayana's forms are infinite in number but lack consciousness; Royce's divinity displays the infinity of the moral commitment and the power of intellect of a unified mind.

The idea of eternity plays a central role in Santayana's and Royce's conceptions of truth. At a time when the very notion of supertemporal truth makes eyebrows (and tempers) rise, it is particularly poignant to examine two philosophers who, as materialist and idealist respectively, occupy opposite ends of the spectrum and yet share the same vision of truth. The structuring notion behind this vision is that truth has an objective and eternal reality, one that we discover and cannot create. The objectivity of truth means that the world is just so and not otherwise, that there is, in other words, a fact of the matter in the alignment of each reality. To take an example, there is only one right answer to the question of whether termites have eaten away the foundation of my house, and that answer can be determined by resolute investigation. Since our knowledge is finite, we may know nothing about termites, and if we are ornery, we can argue about whether the cause of collapse might not have been an undetected earthquake. But none of this changes the fact or the truth that the wood of the floor is hollowed out and the supporting beams are broken.

Cleverly, Royce pivots his discussion of truth on the possibility of error.[9] "That there is error is indubitable,"[10] he says, yet it is by no means easy to explain how it is possible. Each judgment or thought must be focused on an object, and only when it fails to agree with that object can we call it false. The failure of agreement between thought and its object, however, requires that the object be correctly picked out by the thought. "Hegel died in 1900" would not be false if we thought that Hegel was Nietzsche. What makes the error possible is that we are not in error about the subject of the judgment. But if thought correctly identifies its object, in what sense can we say that the two do not agree?

The situation is even worse if we try to understand how John can err in what he says about Thomas.[11] The real Thomas makes no contact with John's mind, and for this reason, John's judgments involving Thomas are only about *his idea* of his neighbor, not the person who actually lives next door. How,

9. Josiah Royce, *The Religious Aspect of Philosophy* (Boston and New York: Houghton Mifflin, 1885), chapter XI.

10. Ibid., p. 431.

11. Ibid., p. 406ff.

then, can one be wrong without successfully identifying the subject matter concerning which one wishes to make assertions? Royce's proposed solution to the problem of accounting for error vaults him directly into the arms of the Absolute. The only way a finite thought can identify its object and yet err in its assessment of it is if a larger, encompassing thought provides that object and underwrites the comparison.[12] "Absolute," "all-inclusive," or "infinite" thought contains the truth opposed to finite error, and that truth serves as the standard by which erroneous thoughts are judged and of which they fall short.

This establishes truth as the possession of the Absolute or of God, which makes it the eternal standard of all cognitive activity. Royce's conclusion is that "[y]ou cannot in fact *make* a truth or a falsehood by your thought. You only *find* one. From all eternity that truth was true, that falsehood false."[13] The truth is independent of our efforts to change or to ascertain it. The Absolute knows the hard truth, that is, the way the world is if viewed from the standpoint of eternity: "You and I and all of us . . . all things actual and possible, exist as they exist, and are known for what they are."[14] Since truth is eternal, error is timeless, as well. So if my judgment about some future event will turn out to be false, it is false now and always has been.[15] Truth is the silent sum of everything concerning reality enshrined in the mind of God. It is the infinite, exhaustive object of exquisitely detailed yet systematic knowledge.

The similarity of this notion of truth to Santayana's is simply astonishing. The environing ontologies are, of course, divergent, but interestingly enough, they result in accounts of truth that are virtually identical. For Santayana, essences function as the forms or specificities that constitute the features of objects and the themes of thought. Things and events result from the embodiment of essences; thoughts require their presence to intuition or consciousness. Embodiment is due to matter, which is a blind force or "insane emphasis" that wrenches forms out of their native eternal realm and exemplifies them for a time in the turning world. Truth results from this interplay of essences and matter. It is, as Santayana puts it in his picturesque manner, "the wake of the ship of time, a furrow that matter must plow upon the face of essence."[16]

Santayana's idea is that every essence is either embodied/envisaged at some point in the world's history or it is not. If the former, it belongs to the realm of truth, for it is eternally the case that it was embodied or envisaged

12. Ibid., p. 431.
13. Ibid., pp. 431–32.
14. Ibid., p. 433.
15. Ibid., p. 418.
16. *SAF*, p. 227.

just then and there. Unembodied essences, by contrast, do not pertain to the world and are not parts of the realm of truth. Forms illustrated in existence may be difficult to identify, but it remains a hard and unalterable fact that they took a step or two in the dance of existence. Truth comes to serve, in this way, as the standard that measures our cognitive efforts: what we believe is supposed to capture or replicate what actually happened. To the extent that it does, our belief is true; if it does not, it falls into error. Truth or the realm of facts is the unchanging and objective backdrop of history, constituting a vast storehouse of realities. Viewed in its entirety, it is the enormously complex essence embodied by the world-process, what Leibniz thought was the form of the one possible world that reaches actuality.

Santayana agrees with Leibniz that there are innumerable other possible worlds, such as the one that shares every element with the actual one, except that in it my last strand of hair falls out a second later than it actually did. These possible worlds, however, never become actual. Of course, Santayana and Leibniz differ in their assessments of how and why the form of the actual world is selected for actualization from among an infinity of alternatives. For Leibniz, the choice is God's and the reason governing it is the search for the good. Santayana, by contrast, maintains that the selection is not the work of mind and hence no purpose defines it; the operation of matter is unimpeded by the restrictive force of principle. Royce is clearly on Leibniz's side, providing a theodicy that justifies God's choice of this evil-infested world in terms of the necessary presence of evil in the best of all possible cosmic arrangements.[17]

Royce approaches truth through the ubiquity of error, Santayana through the experience of people lying. The fact that Royce's point aims to be logical and Santayana's psychological reflects their divergent approaches to doing philosophy without undercutting the similarity of their substantive views. The truth about any fact is the standard comprehensive description of it, Santayana maintains.[18] It is a *standard* in that it establishes the goal of inquiry, a *description* on account of being articulated in essences and *comprehensive* because it includes every essence relevant to the fact. Santayana's statement that the realm of truth is "what omniscience would assert"[19] reveals the likeness of this idea to what Royce has in mind. The truth is one of the

17. Josiah Royce, "The Problem of Job," in *Studies of Good and Evil* (New York: D. Appleton and Company, 1898), pp. 1–28.

18. *SAF,* p. 266.

19. *Character,* p. 95.

names for God in "the eclectic religion of our fathers," Santayana says, and omniscience is one of God's traditional prerogatives. So the realm of truth is the cognitive totality or content of the mind of God, the residue of his omniscience after his consciousness and his personality are removed. Both Royce and Santayana want to establish an objective standard for the truth of our beliefs. As an idealist, the former lodges it in an infinite mind; rejecting the primacy of consciousness, the latter installs it as a self-standing, impersonal, eternal ontological region.

American philosophers since Emerson, or before, have taken the individual seriously. Pragmatists, however, have always thought that there is a continuity between individuals and the social settings in which they live. Peirce maintains that this continuity is best conceived in metaphysical terms: persons are concretions in the flow of experience, with porous boundaries and interpenetrating cores. He thinks of these concretions as sets of interconnected ideas and as single general ideas, and the law of mind is that ideas spread.[20] This summons a picture analogous to that of gravity: individuals are forces spread throughout regions, each strongest at a center but rippling out from it with diminishing power. The ideas or persons interpenetrate, constituting a continuous world in which each is present not only to, but also in, the others.

Although Dewey eschews such metaphysical pictures, he embraces the idea that persons are continuous with others. The continuity is established by education through which people come to share a common culture or objective mind. Moreover, experiences themselves can be shared; there is nothing intrinsically private about anything we perceive, think, or feel.[21] That one happens to be mine, Dewey argues, does not exclude its being yours as well. They are like houses in that their belonging to someone is incidental to them, or like letters in a crossword puzzle that can be elements of more than one word. Individuals are, therefore, not isolated from one another. Many of their elements overlap and they are interconnected in intricate ways, constituting collections of distinguishable but not separate units.

20. Charles Sanders Peirce, "The Law of Mind," in *Charles Sanders Peirce: Collected Papers*, vol. 6, ed. Charles Hartshorne and Paul Weiss (Cambridge, Mass.: Harvard University Press, 1978–80), pp. 86–113.

21. John Dewey, *Experience and Nature, The Later Works, 1925–1953*, vol. 1, ed. Jo Ann Boydston (Carbondale and Edwardsville: Southern Illinois University Press, 1988), pp. 178–79.

We must keep Peirce and Dewey in mind when we consider Santayana's and Royce's conceptions of individuality. The contrast between the former two, representing the mainline of American philosophy, and the latter pair could not be sharper. Both Santayana and Royce operate with the idea that, ultimately, individuals are neither continuous with one another nor overlapping in their constituents. They do not wish to deny the obvious facts of social life and influence, yet they maintain that by their nature, persons are private and insular. The experiences individuals enjoy are unique to them; in a literal sense they can share nothing with each other. In a fashion reminiscent of existentialists, Royce and Santayana believe that we form our purposes, live our lives, and face our deaths without help from others.

The basis on which Santayana embraces a view that comes near to existentialism is, oddly perhaps, biological. He thinks that each person is a psyche, and psyches are material organisms that have to find their way in a treacherous environment. Heredity and upbringing play crucial roles in making any psyche into what it is, but when the task of forming a new person is relatively complete—or, as watching the activities of children might suggest, even before—the individual becomes a unified and independent agent. Biology fragments the human race into globules of life that can operate alone and sustain themselves; we are not like the faceless wind that neither renews itself nor knows a center. In us, life adds life to life and does so in such a way that all action arises from the center and often manages to enhance it.

Psyches are organisms in the sense of self-moving and self-controlling physical agencies. Santayana insists that organizations or institutions, by contrast, have no energy independent of the energies of the organisms that constitute them; they are simply mechanisms for evoking and directing the activities of psyches.[22] This contrast between organisms and organizations is crucial for Santayana; it is the foundation of his individualism. By itself, however, it is not enough to establish that persons are insular. For that, he needs the fundamental principle of his philosophy of mind, namely that the psyche is the source and sustainer of all mental activity.[23] Spirit or awareness, he maintains, is a product of the psyche and lacks the power to accomplish anything. This epiphenomenal mind consists of a stream of "intuitions," immediacies or spectatings that constitute the conscious aspect of persons.

22. George Santayana, "The Unit in Ethics Is the Person," in *Physical Order and Moral Liberty*, ed. John and Shirley Lachs (Nashville, Tenn.: Vanderbilt University Press, 1969), p. 196.
23. George Santayana, *Realms of Being* (New York: Cooper Square Publishers, 1972), p. 562. Hereafter *RB*.

The psyche harbors the values, habits, and tendencies of the organism; spirit adds only the sense or feel of what goes on in the body.

The isolation of the psyche is physical: it is an intact animal separate in its organs and actions from everything else. Spirit is, if anything, even more insular. Since it has only a constantly renewed and not a continuous existence, nothing can pierce its privacy. Spirit cannot be affected by anything, only recreated by the psyche with varying contents or perspectives reflecting the exigencies of its existence. Conscious moments are undetectable by physical means, Santayana believes, so our feelings and thoughts are inaccessible from the outside. More, the very events, mental and physical, of which persons consist are unique to them: no event can be an element of organisms separated by space or of minds generated by different organs. Individuals are, therefore, worlds unto themselves, clearly capable of communicating with others but unable to share even a single element of their being.

Divergent as their views of the nature and fate of individuals may be, Santayana and Royce are in remarkable agreement about the way persons stand apart from others. "An individual is unique,"[24] Royce announces; there is nothing else like it in the world. Its internal meaning, that is, its will, drive, and dim vision, identifies it as an intended whole that finds its place in a fully articulated universe. From the standpoint of finite life, internal meaning and external meaning—intention and fulfillment—are forever sundered. But all of that life is a striving for the wholeness and the infinity that would complete it. Viewed from the perspective of eternity, the struggle for unity and meaning is brought to a successful end and individuals emerge as structured infinities unique in their life plans and trajectories.

The double-perspective view—seeing all things in their finite temporal context and in their changeless eternity—is a hallmark of Royce's philosophy. It recurs in striking detail in Santayana's distinction between substance and essence, the former constituted by things and events existing in the natural world and the latter by the forms of those things (along with an infinity of other essences) changelessly available in eternity. Of course, there are differences, the most significant of which is the absence in Santayana of Royce's romantic yearning for completion and moral victory. This universal teleology is the moralistic heart of Royce's vision; by contrast, the very thought of it sticks in Santayana's craw.[25] Both Royce and Santayana are indebted to

24. Josiah Royce, *The World and the Individual, First Series* (New York: Macmillan, 1923), p. 292.
25. See *Character*, p. 65ff.

Schopenhauer for the double-perspective view, but Santayana embraces what Royce rejects in the great pessimist, namely the dark vision of unredeemed suffering.

Royce's view of the uniqueness and insularity of individuals does not imply social isolation. To the contrary, he insists that the self can emerge only as a result of commitment to a cause, where that cause inevitably involves other persons. But "the willing and practical and thoroughgoing devotion"[26] of which loyalty consists is adopted in the privacy of one's soul with total autonomy.[27] To do the Lord's work is a decision by his servants. For loyalty to be authentic, the cause we serve must be embraced freely, that is, with a motive force that resides wholly in the individual. Privacy of commitment is, in this way, perfectly compatible with social orientation and public utility: the work loyalty demands is performed by self-determining, self-motivated, and self-enclosed persons.

Nowhere is Royce's view of the insularity of persons clearer than in his attempt to provide a mathematical model for individuality. Royce takes mathematical ideas and analogies with the utmost seriousness, and he obviously thinks that the model he proposes captures a deep truth about individuals. He suggests that individuals be conceived on the analogy of series of whole numbers each of which begins with a prime number and consists of successive powers of that prime. One individual might be thought of as analogous to the series 2, 4, 8, 16 . . . , another to the series 3, 9, 27, 81 . . . , and a third to the series 5, 25, 125, 625. . . . Each of these series has an infinite number of members, and because the number of prime numbers is infinite, there is an infinity of such series. The point Royce wants to stress is that these series, and the individuals they represent, are just as complex and just as inexhaustible as the series of whole numbers of which they are parts. If we think of the encompassing series as God, therefore, we have a neat model of how an infinite number of persons, each enjoying infinite life, can find a place and not lose identity in what Royce calls "the Absolute Individual."

The analogy provides a striking insight into Royce's thinking about individuals. If we take each number to stand for an element or experience of a person, no two people share any of their constituents. This is because each whole number is either a prime or a power of a prime, and no number is the power of more than one prime. Consequently, every whole number belongs in one and only one series, implying that every experience or person-element

26. Josiah Royce, *The Philosophy of Loyalty* (Nashville, Tenn., and London: Vanderbilt University Press, 1995), p. 9.
27. Ibid., p. 31.

is the possession of one and only one person. Thus not only individuals but even the elements of individuals are unique. Individuals stand altogether outside one another: each is an integral entity lacking essential connection to the others. The series never touch. Reminiscent of Leibniz, they are united only in and through God, represented by the encompassing series of all whole numbers, of which they are finite/infinite fragments.

There are obvious differences between Santayana and Royce in their conceptions of individuals. Royce thinks persons are immortal (and series are unending); Santayana believes no one escapes extinction. Royce maintains that all finite beings seek the completion that can be found only in God; Santayana, taking the empirical evidence at face value, finds no such universal striving. Royce judges individuals from the perspective of cosmically established standards of good and evil; Santayana assesses the good and bad from the standpoint of individuals whose lives and living interests generate them. These are deep and important differences. They take nothing away, however, from the profound similarities between Royce's and Santayana's understandings of the ontological isolation of individuals in a large and largely alien world. In fact, it is only in the light of this fundamental kinship that the differences acquire poignancy and require explanation.

The similarities between these two widely divergent conceptual structures point to an interesting feature of some philosophical systems. There are philosophies that consist of an agglomeration of (mainly) consistent but miscellaneous elements, such as Hume's empiricism. Others, such as Spinoza's system, pride themselves on the logical rigor of being derived in their entirety from a small number of central premises. Yet others, such as the reflections of Lucretius and Nietzsche, display the unifying influence of a single insight or vision without being logical consequences of it. The systems of Royce and Santayana represent a fourth type of philosophical structure, one fashioned out of elements in such a way that the presence or absence of a single supposition changes the entire complexion of the edifice. The impression they create is that a small difference can make all the difference, as for example the introduction of sharps or flats does in the case of a song or of a profusion of windows in a building.

The three central areas of kinship between Royce's philosophy and Santayana's thought I have explored are by no means the only ones worthy of attention. Without minimizing the differences, one could justifiably affirm that many of the building blocks of the two systems are closely similar. How, then, did the two edifices come to look so different in their completed forms? Royce's philosophy has a moral heart that consists of the uncompromising struggle with evil. Santayana's ideal, by contrast, is spectatorial; like the sages of antiquity, he wants to develop a just understanding of life. Royce is all ambition and striving; Santayana seeks to calm the human soul. Royce has bold hopes for humankind; the ground of Santayana's ideas is profound disillusionment. Given the similarity of the constituent elements, what makes for the radical difference in outcomes?

The difference, in a word, is God. Royce is predisposed to believe that there is a divine partner in our quest to overcome evil, and he makes mighty exertions to prove his existence. Although he is deeply indebted to Hegel for many of his ideas, his notion of God resembles the traditional Judeo-Christian conception far more closely than it resembles Hegel's Spirit or Absolute. Not without creating difficulties for his system, Royce thinks of God as a person with purposes, a caring comrade in battle. We can rely on him to accomplish, or to have accomplished, what still remains after we have done our best. This assures that the victory over evil is complete, even if only from the perspective of eternity. Our finite lives always remain fragmented, but a proper understanding of reality demonstrates our unity with God and identifies our resting place in the bosom of the divine.

From the time of his earliest philosophical reflections, by contrast, Santayana views religious ideas as poetic symbols for the human condition and the concept of God as a confused idea hatched in the hothouse of our hopes. The confusion is not primarily the result of the human tendency to anthropomorphize by personifying impersonal traits, but of a deeper ontological muddle. We tend to conflate first and last things by supposing that consciousness, the ultimate emergent, is identical with the primordial power of matter. This spiritual creative force is then endowed with a mind that envisages possible worlds and knows all truth about the actual one, resulting in a single being that combines in itself the divergent ontological categories of matter, spirit, essence, and truth.[28] These diverse and incompatible elements add up to an incoherent whole whose implausibility is enhanced by the invitation to attribute action to the eternal and personhood to infinity. Santayana avers that it is easy to see the origin of this jumbled idea in the vulnerable finitude of animals; God is invented to serve not spiritual but material purposes.

The difference between Royce and Santayana concerning God is of such central importance that it colors the entirety of their philosophical systems. Making room for God enables Royce to view eternity as the cognitive per-

28. See *RB,* last chapter.

spective of an infinite mind, all truth as the possession of a living intellect, and ourselves as elements of the Godhead. As a result, boundless optimism pervades Royce's work: he thinks we live in an ordered universe governed by purposes and energized by the search for the good. The drama of the struggle against evil is certain to reach a happy end and we can confidently expect both everlasting existence and eternal life.

Without God, Santayana sees only vast impersonal regions of being: unmoving forms, the boiling creativity of matter, and cool, momentary glimpses of eternity through the skylight of consciousness. His is a purposeless world whose order is always in danger of passing and in which what we call evil often prevails. The Godlike uniqueness and impenetrable privacy of individuals provide no cause for celebration; on the contrary, they constitute the source of our isolation from each other and of the sadness of having to live and die alone. Santayana is no optimist about human prospects. The foundation of a good life is partly art and partly luck, but however good it may be for the moment, ultimate extinction is inevitable.

The dividing line between Royce and Santayana runs through the land of God. The situation is no different for us today. Those who seek comfort and reassurance, a world governed by a power we can trust, turn naturally to God. Although we hear much about the decline of religion, the promise of safe haven provided by caring omnipotence continues to attract masses of people. Rejecting the hypothesis that God governs all, on the other hand, leaves us with a bleak universe of temporary joy and ultimate demise. It may be easy to adopt this attitude in the strutting fullness of life, but age and debility tend to turn the mind to searching for aid from a higher power. Remarkably, Santayana remained consistent in his naturalism to the end. Neither the closing windows of age nor the efforts of nuns and priests made him waver in his conviction that life is a temporary accident soon buried in the torrent of events.

Upon reading Santayana's early work, Royce once remarked that its distinguishing characteristic is the view that essence precedes existence. If placed in the context of their disagreement about God, this assessment proved astonishingly prescient. Royce's hallmark belief is that an existing God holds logical primacy over all things actual and possible. This means that even possibilities are but thoughts in the mind of the Deity, and therefore existence (at least God's) precedes essence. In sharp contrast, by denying the existence of God, Santayana affirms that an infinite field of possibilities, the realm of essence, is logically prior to any actual existent. This leaves us with the question Royce asked again and again: Can we conceive of the possible and the actual apart from a living consciousness that thinks them? This is the question that underlies idealism, a question that, in spite of the predominance of naturalism today, has so far received no answer.

Understanding America

There is a striking difference between how members of certain nationalities and religions behave in the Old World and how they relate to each other in the New. The changes may be situational or due to some deeper valuational transformation that accompanies immigration. In either case, it sheds light on the nature and practices of American society. It also illuminates the extent to which Santayana understood the soul of America.

Members of some nations, ethnic groups, and religions are mortal enemies in the parts of the world that are their native homes. There are historical reasons for the enmity between Pakistanis and Indians, Hutus and Tutsis, and Serbs and Bosnians. The reasons, typically taking the form of memories of ancient oppression, persecution, and murder, exercise a momentous hold on interactions among these people. The embers of enduring hatred create conflagrations of violence again and again, and each side to the conflict takes delight in waging war or at least inflicting retaliatory cruelties on people who belong to the other.

Rival groups experience much more than distaste for each other: they seek the destruction of their opponents. The struggles between Muslims and Christians, the Germans and the French, and the Greeks and the Turks display a vicious stridency that is difficult to lay to rest. From time to time, people show themselves prepared to undergo all manners of hardship to be able to cause permanent grief to their enemies. The idea of leaving others be seems not to occur to these people; on the contrary, periodically they perceive a duty to exterminate those who belong to the wrong side. Hegel's depiction of the encounter of the bondsman and the lord is a good example of this conceptual frame: seeing each other is enough for them to prepare for a struggle to the death.

By comparison with this fury, the relationships in America between Old World antagonists are surprisingly tame. Traditional enemies live at peace with each other, in many cases on the same street or in the same apartment building. Genocidal tendencies remain in check, and instead of laboring to make others miserable, people endeavor to make themselves happy. Acts of violence directed at people on account of their nationality, ethnic origin, or religion are rare. Aggression is controlled to such an extent that there is hardly an attempt to deface the buildings and stores of antagonists.

I do not mean to suggest that America is free of prejudice and of racial, religious, and ethnic tensions. People in the United States, as everywhere, have preferences, some of which, though perhaps ill-considered, show themselves, sadly, in how they treat others. Moreover, members of some groups view individuals who belong to other groups with suspicion and quiet hostility. But it is worth remarking that much of the nastiness tends to remain attitudinal, with minimal behavioral outcomes. And the bulk of the ill feeling flows from long-standing residents of the country toward newcomers, whatever their religion or ethnic background, who do not understand the local language and customs. Traditional Old World enemies live in relative peace with each other.

What accounts for this striking change of attitude and action attendant on moving from Asia and Europe to North America? A number of explanations may be proposed. Probably there are multiple causal factors at work, at least some of which are obvious and relatively easy to identify. But I suspect that there are also some more interesting and perhaps even surprising influences to uncover.

Much of the violence and destruction of organized hatred occurs through mob action. Crowds are easily mobilized in countries where there are large numbers of people with similar beliefs and emotional triggers. Demagogues can manipulate such masses, although fancied slights and ancient grievances are enough by themselves to precipitate disastrous consequences. Might the reason for peace in America be that members of ethnic groups and aggressive religions lack the critical mass necessary for violence?

This explanation is likely to be attractive to anyone who knows how anger feeds on itself in crowds and how the mood of the mob can make even sensible people act without concern for decency. In fact, however, it does not stand scrutiny. As to religions, there are, for example, enough Muslims and Hindus in the United States to create deadly clashes over their differences. Members of ethnic groups tend to live concentrated in areas where they vastly outnumber their antagonists. Since their traditional enemies usually live only a block or two away, it would be easy for them to start fights or at least to create a significant nuisance. In any case, even one or a small number of people is enough to stir up a great deal of trouble. The striking fact is that in the United States, at least on the whole and in a systematic way, no such trouble is created.

Is it possible, then, that peace is due to effective peacekeeping efforts? There is no denying that police in the Old World sometimes look the other way when ethnic or religious violence breaks out. Although America has experienced severe racial inequities in law enforcement, violence against ethnic and religious minorities is, on the whole, approached with a strong and even hand. The police in major American cities would certainly not sit back while bands fired by anger roughed up people and bombed churches, mosques, or synagogues. And timely, severe measures would undoubtedly nip disturbances in the bud.

The interesting fact, however, is that large-scale police action just does not seem to be needed. Apart from the hapless tough full of threats and boasts or the occasional thug who tries to set fire to a Catholic church or a synagogue, one sees no attempt to incite ethnic or religious violence. And, interestingly, the young or deranged perpetrators of such isolated attacks tend to be native-born Americans rather than members of some immigrant minority. The police do not have much in the way of ethnic or religious mob action to control.

Large-scale violence in the Old World tends to be evoked or supported by politicians and the press. Can the absence of these catalysts of conflict account for relative ethnic and religious peace in America? This is a plausible line of thought because politicians in the United States rarely get elected on a platform of narrow ethnic or religious concerns. From time to time, legislators are put in office at least in part because they are members of a race, a gender, an ethnic group, or a religion, but the scope of their interests tends to transcend such narrowing influences. And, indeed, there is no concentration of media in the United States that is a match for the nationalist publications bombarding the citizens of Old World countries. Without continuing agitation and demagoguery, people tend to turn their attention to pursuits other than harming their neighbors.

The last point rings true and surely constitutes one of the reasons for peace among previously feuding people after they have moved to America. But we live in a world of instant communication. Telephones and the Internet provide access for immigrants to their native lands, and in fact many of them are in close contact with sentiments "at home." Some immigrant communities print their own newspapers, and many of the religious leaders and senior opinion makers who set the tone of these enclaves are exclusivists or nationalists. So there is certainly enough leadership and communication to whip immigrants into a fury. The remarkable fact is that what would have been incendiary in the Old World falls on deaf ears in the New;

that Palestinians and Israelis kill each other in the Middle East seems not to be a good enough reason for murderous clashes between them in the United States.

This suggests another possible line of explanation. In some human affairs, context is all. We know that turning out the lights is conducive to sleep and thrusting a young man into a fraternity makes it probable that he will drink. Living in a new country may well exercise the same sort of influence on immigrants. It takes a while for them to learn the language and the customs of their new society, but they quickly catch on to what is clearly unacceptable. Systematic hate-mongering is just not a part of the culture of America as it exists today; both the legal system and the ordinary consciousness of people reject it as offensive. Newcomers might therefore shelve their ethnic or religious aggressions to fall in line with what their new home expects of them.

That some such process contributes to peace in America is difficult to deny. The adoption of local customs occurs as a natural consequence of immigration. But it does not happen everywhere. Pakistanis in Britain and Algerians in France have failed to adopt some vital customs of the larger culture. That raises the question of what there is about American society that renders compliance with local values attractive and likely. And that, in turn, points to the need for a more substantive look at what America teaches its immigrants and makes available to them. The current explanation accounts, therefore, for very little if viewed in isolation from broader issues.

What about the possibility that immigrants to the United States are selected, or self-selected, for their nonviolent tendencies? The Immigration and Naturalization Service certainly does all it can to deny entry to people who engage in ideologically motivated mayhem. Legal immigrants tend to be professionals or at least somewhat educated people who can be expected to know better than to create trouble. The political refugees among them have experienced persecution, so they are at least unlikely to want to visit it on others. The rest of them, entrepreneurs and merchants, normally focus on making money, not on achieving national or racial purity.

The events of 9/11 showed, however, that government screening is not very successful. It cannot readily measure nationalist or religious fervor, and it is ill-equipped to unmask well-constructed lies. Professionals are by no means free of ideological commitments, and many a person persecuted for political beliefs can hardly wait to return the favor. There is ample evidence that even businesspeople, if brought up to hate a group of others, can be whipped into violent action. Selectivity in immigration may account for a little of the differential in tension between the New and the Old Worlds, but not for very much.

This is a good place to turn to Santayana to see if his vision of the United States might provide the explanation we seek. And, indeed, his account of English liberty goes a long way toward helping us understand the change immigrants undergo when they arrive in the New World. Many of them come from nations devoted to what he calls "absolute liberty," which is the single-minded effort to follow one's will, however arbitrary. This absolute liberty is the freedom for persons and nations "to be just so,"[29] to follow a master passion even in the teeth of nature and resistance. Many of the cultures from which immigrants hail display an unconditional commitment to the values and practices that have structured their past; they are convinced that there is only one right way to live and it is theirs. Santayana characterizes such convictions as natural to animals[30] that are unbending in what they want and unyielding in their pursuit of it.

Absolute liberty allows no compromise. The distinction it sees between right and wrong is infinite, and it is ready to bring the house down on all the traitors and infidels that surround it. It tends to use force to overwhelm its enemies, which are many, and it is ever ready to take on all comers in its uncompromising quest to be itself. It is a newborn insect prepared to fight the world to maintain its nature and attain its purposes. Such liberty may be heroic and beautiful, but it is neither wise nor reflective, and it will certainly fail because it misreads reality. It does not understand that its energy and its values are contingent, passing phases in the life of nature, and that all its victories are temporary.

This description of absolute liberty is a splendid frame in which to situate all the despotisms that have made life awful throughout history and all the empires founded on religion and ideology. Nationalist fervor, racial exclusiveness, and ethnic strife are varied expressions of absolute liberty, which is the unyielding, egotistical drive to remake the world according to one's own ideas. The philosophical observer in Santayana sees the drive as natural though tragic, but he finds it difficult to sympathize with the inflated, absurd goals of little people and little nations. There is much about animal life that is understandable and natural, yet malodorous.

English liberty, by contrast, thrives on the spirit of compromise. It presupposes broad agreement about the goals and methods of life along with

29. *Santayana on America,* ed. Richard C. Lyon (New York: Harcourt Brace, 1968), p. 173.
30. Ibid., p. 180.

a readiness to adjust one's nature sufficiently to get along with others.[31] It is the freedom that comes of cooperative endeavors, of trusting each other and entrusting to others what one cannot do alone. Faith in the decency of people and the conviction that in the end everyone will be accommodated ground majority rule as the proper way to make social decisions. But such choices never touch fundamental issues: the values on the basis of which society operates command the unspoken consent of all.

The underlying tone of English liberty is tolerant and optimistic. Ready collaboration promises a future that is "happy and triumphant."[32] The triumph is not meant to be military; conquest that requires the application of physical force is incidental and serves mainly to protect commercial life. Contrary to countries that seek absolute liberty, the motivating force of American society is not the desire to rule over others, but "the gospel of work and the belief in progress,"[33] ideas that evoke sustained and occasionally stunning exertions. Zealous idealism permeates all facets of American life. One cannot claim to be an American so long as one lacks the spirit of cooperation and a hearty appreciation of one's friends and neighbors.

Caring for each other and uniting in pursuit of a common end come into view most clearly on the occasion of great national emergencies, such as the tragedy of 9/11. At such times, strangers from far away become friends in need of help and service. The consequent outpouring of supportive sentiment and material aid can make one believe that human nature has been transformed to answer the demands of its harshest critics. But even under ordinary circumstances, Americans tend to be wide-ranging in their sympathies and generous with their substance. They feel fortunate in their possessions and think it appropriate to share them with whoever happens to be in need. The munificence is spontaneous and personal. They are not satisfied to shift the task of aid to government, but go to the scene of disaster themselves to lend a helping hand.

Admittedly, English liberty is of a very odd sort, for Santayana claims that generous social-mindedness is compulsory in America.[34] I suspect he thinks it is a form of liberty because people embrace its elements voluntarily. "Compulsory" does not mean forced; good humor and trust are contagious attitudes supported by expectation and temperament. No one could evoke it in people with rifle butts or by threatening their loved ones. They

31. Ibid., p. 167.
32. Ibid., p. 171.
33. Ibid., p. 170.
34. Ibid.

grow naturally among individuals who are confident and successful, and they acquire hallowed standing as the right alignment to life and to each other because everyone seems to approve them. English liberty is the ethos of American society; it is difficult to escape even though no laws mandate it and the violation of its spirit does not land one in jail.

Immigrants to America enter this energetic benign world seeking the benefits it can provide. The English liberty that structures and permeates American society goes a long distance toward explaining the changes in their attitudes and values. They see the helpfulness and accommodating spirit of people around them and do what they can to enter the life of the community. To speed their assimilation, they begin to act like their new neighbors and to entertain, perhaps for the first time in their lives, the possibility that the habits and commitments with which they grew up are not uniquely and exclusively right. They move, in Santayana's language, from the absolute liberty of insisting on the rightness of their ways to the open and tolerant practices of the American landscape.

Promising as this explanation appears, it cannot constitute the whole story. Why would immigrants find embracing the ethos of English liberty attractive? When they first arrive in America, they settle in enclaves inhabited primarily by people from their Old World homes. They continue to speak the language of their childhood, eat the food their mothers used to cook, and cling to the comfortable traditions of their native culture. Change comes slowly and not without pain. Giving up the conviction that one's habits and values are absolutely right is to endanger one's identity, something no one does lightly and voluntarily. By itself, the spirit of English liberty is not powerful enough to reach into the Iraqi, Korean, and Pakistani ghettos in the hearts of many larger American cities. What moves the inhabitants of these subcultures into the mainstream of American life?

To answer this question, we must look more closely at what immigration to America involves. To those who come to settle here, the change is momentous and in some ways excruciating. The involutions of the English language, strange customs, and the need to communicate with people who, though superficially friendly, seem deeply alien make the first few months, even years, of life in the new land painful and baffling. English liberty does not seem liberating to recent immigrants; toleration appears to them as lack of principle, and in cooperating with others they worry that their partners are taking advantage of them. Suspicion and fear die slowly and would never be swept away were it not necessary for new immigrants to move into mainstream American culture.

The necessity derives not from government edict but from natural need. Immigrants, along with nearly everybody else, have to work in order to eat. The language of work is English and its habits are dictated by a tolerant but hard-driving postindustrial society. The pressure to hold down jobs and earn advancement exercises a profound influence on the human soul. One cannot spend the bulk of one's waking hours at work and shake off its lessons and demands the moment one gets home. Work teaches docility and cooperation, introducing newcomers to practices needed for success and acquainting them with the living values of the culture. Observation and informal talk at work reveal to immigrants how Americans relate to their spouses, their children, and their futures. The ever-present formal requirements of continued employment keep before their minds the opportunities and the vast costs of establishing their place in a commercial culture.

The economic system of the United States is a mighty engine of persuasion. It attracts and engulfs people, making them do what they would otherwise never imagine, in return for fulfilling their dreams. It promises rich returns on labor and champions the ideal of a carefree life. The rewards it heaps on intelligence and hard work make successful businesspeople the envy of all; even if one cannot do as well, there is reason to wait for the next raise or bonus or promotion. People assent to the old adage that money isn't all, but they believe even more deeply that there isn't much it will not buy and that lacking it makes even an idealist's life miserable. Admittedly, the economic system focuses on material values, but these are the rewards that motivate people to give up the best hours of their days and that ground their hopes for a better future.

Material values receive poor press from the guardians of high culture. They are said to be inferior and unworthy by comparison with moral, aesthetic, and intellectual pursuits. Their depiction as good only instrumentally, as merely means to our higher calling, demeans them; it shows them as results of dirty, narrowly selfish activities. To his credit, Santayana does not go out of his way to smear commercial life, but even he fails to show adequate appreciation of the central and vital roles played by material plenty in human life. Consequently, though an immigrant himself, he does not see that work and its reward constitute the hook that brings new arrivals from overseas into the culture of English liberty. The desire for wealth reaches into the tenements that house immigrants and delivers them to be shaped into compliant members of a tolerant society.

Those critics of American culture who draw a sharp line between physical well-being and the higher purposes of life seem not to understand the intimate connection between them. The comfort of owning a house is at once fulfillment of the obligation to take care of one's family. Saving money may seem miserly, but it translates into the ability to educate one's children. Grand financial success serves as the foundation and, astonishingly, also as the motivation for promoting good causes and helping those in need. Material means may make miserable ends, but properly used they are not only indispensable for accomplishing the good but actually inseparable from it.

The English liberty that suffuses America is an adequate antidote to the violent conflicts ravaging much of the rest of the world. But its spirit is not contagious. Immigrants to many countries live as strangers, never becoming parts of the surrounding culture. Why does something similar not happen in America? The New World may not be a melting pot, but it is remarkably efficient at assimilating individuals who hail from different traditions and are initially devoted to widely divergent values. Life in a new community visits frustrations on people and demands painful adjustments. Like the last snow of winter, however, the misery hides new growth: the habits and values of the Old World get slowly replaced with the attitudes considered proper in the New. Over a period of difficult years, the immigrants become Americans—sometimes even without wanting or fully knowing it.

The new values arise not through force or indoctrination but by doing what others do and especially by wanting the same things others have. Most immigrants find America a land of hard work and intense desire. Hungarians who arrived in New Jersey after the 1956 revolution were dismayed at the pace of life in their new homeland and outraged at what was expected of them in their jobs. Some of them grumbled that Soviet repression may have been preferable to having to expend so much energy every day. Yet within a few years they were taking trips to Bermuda, saving money for houses, and working their hearts out to get promoted. They realized that devoted labor brings results and that desires they would not have dared to frame in their old homes could be readily satisfied with enough of their new country's money.

The ultimate motivation of the vast majority of immigrants for becoming Americans is the promise of a materially rich existence. They want money and all that it will buy: fine food, large houses, new automobiles, designer clothing, and travel. Such desires may seem superficial, but they serve as the wellspring of the perpetual striving of animals in this cruel and deadly world. Material comfort is what we lost as a result of the misstep of Adam and Eve in the Garden. America restores the Garden by providing the antidote: through labor, it offers the possibility of a fulfilled and carefree life. The significance of this can be understood only by those who have known need and hunger.

They find it unnecessary to present excuses for wanting the good things in life and wanting more and more of them. Highbrow intellectuals, in particular, encounter difficulty in grasping the legitimacy and value of seeking the good in the quest for goods. They seem to believe that there is something wholesome about poverty, that misery builds character, and that turning away from the material world supplies people with spiritual substance.

In reality, however, there is not a shred of truth in these convictions. Need fills the mind with anxiety and resentment, and except in unusual circumstances, wretched lives make people selfish and narrow. Hunger and sorrow are not sources of great ideas, and self-abnegation shrivels the soul. Worse, destitute individuals are easily captured by vicious ideologies. They look for an easy explanation of their desperate condition and find it in some twisted set of concepts focused on available scapegoats. The result is what we have seen in Europe in the twentieth century and in the Middle East in the twenty-first: grotesquely primitive ideas propelling mass movements of violence in the name of purity, utopia, or salvation.

The values underlying the pursuit of economic well-being are, at least, this-worldly and nonideological. They turn the mind away from unproductive mischief and mayhem toward what others find constructive enough to support with their money. People who are well off tend not to fall victim to ideologies. They prefer to avoid wars and internal turmoil because they have something to lose. They like prosperity and the stability that underlies it, and reject the cheap satisfaction of making themselves better off by expropriating the resources of others. The high priests of morality ought to embrace affluence because it reduces human suffering and eliminates one of the great causes of war. Instead, they heap scorn on trade and consumption, overlooking the fact that the affirmation of human dignity through freedom of contract is the ground of commercial life and the reduction of suffering through plenty is its product. They think it lamentable that people embrace the values of physical satisfaction, forgetting that the choice is free and that possession of the goods of the world is both essential and serves as an incentive to do good in the world.

Immigrants to America appropriate local ideas of success with astonishing fervor. They work hard, seek advancement, buy cars and houses, save money for their children, and commit themselves to useful civic labors. The premise behind such actions and values is social stability, the expectation that possessions are secure and long-term plans can be effective. This means that one can reasonably hope that next year will be better than the last has been. Such hopes pervade American life and add structure, meaning, and justification to what people do. The future thus becomes an ever-present reality that offers rewards to the industrious. The conviction that tensions can be defused, problems solved, and every product and human situation improved turns the mind away from grief over the past and toward concrete steps of amelioration.

Recognition that human relations do not have to constitute a zero-sum game is near the heart of American beliefs. Warfare, violence, and persecution are zero-sum activities in which some win and others lose, perhaps everything. Commerce, cooperation, and even friendly competition are, by contrast, modes of action from which all participants can profit. Tacitly or implicitly, immigrants adopt this stance or at least come to believe that they can flourish. The consequent redirection of effort and exhaustion of energy in productive labors is the best explanation why in America immigrants lose interest in persecuting their neighbors.

The difference between past-directed retaliatory and future-directed ameliorative activities plays a central role in American philosophy. Pragmatists such as John Dewey and William James extol the value of human actions focused on influencing the future, which alone is open to improvement by our efforts. Even Royce, who recognizes the importance of communities of memory, places them in the broader context of communities of hope, suggesting that the negativities of the past must be submerged in the cleansing improvements we can make from here on. Such philosophical advice is a reflection of the broader culture, but it has the advantage of capturing in precise conceptual terms what is otherwise a prevalent though unarticulated attitude.

Is this attitude unique to the United States? It neither is nor has to be. It pervades any nation that gives up its absolute liberty and focuses on providing sociopolitical stability and the hope of material improvement to its citizens. Prosperity undercuts the complex causes of religious intolerance and nationalist fervor. Envy and destructive anger are less likely to gain a foothold among people who enjoy the present and see a happy future than among those who are hungry and destitute of hope. Even plausible ideologies find it difficult to sprout roots among individuals who have enough; such people display an interest in politics mainly to protect their happy lives rather than to impose their will on others. The Old Testament speaks of a promised land, which, if already occupied by others, can become the source of endless conflict. What people need instead is a land of promise, of actualizable hope for peace and the enjoyment of material goods, which America has been for a long time, and other nations are now becoming.

A united Europe in which cooperation and growing prosperity eliminate borders, and with them ethnic hatred, offers the possibility of another America. Some Asian nations are also working hard to provide opportunities for their citizens. Although affluence in a commercial world brings with it all the problems of overconsumption, there is in the end no alternative way to eradicate nationalist, ethnic, and religious violence. If this analysis of what makes immigrants to the New World overcome their Old World hatreds is anywhere near right, it uncovers the secret of what will make it unnecessary for people to immigrate at all. They need hope in their own lands for a better life for themselves, but especially for their children.

Not many philosophers have come out in defense of an existence of comfort and prosperity. Superbly cognizant of divergent perspectives and alternative values, Santayana comes close to appreciating the virtues of business, but in the end he veers off to praise ideal objectives and the activity of production rather than the joys of consumption. In America, "the ruling passion is the love of *business*,"[35] and not the love of money, he says. He reminds us that "business . . . will, as things now stand, look chiefly to material results"[36] and readily admits that material well-being is a necessary condition of the higher functions of human life. But he continues with the admonition that "the material basis is a basis only"[37] and requires completion in the form of "moral and intellectual functions." In the end, only speculation, the abstraction possible in solitude, and thoughts "deeper and higher" than ordinary ones justify material comfort and consumption.

That such "deeper and higher" thoughts come naturally to some people is an obvious fact. It may even be true that in certain respects the world would be a better place if more people entertained such ideas. But I cannot imagine what would justify the conclusion that a materially satisfying existence *requires* completion in the form of deep thoughts. Life is short and after it is over nothing remains of it, so it cannot be the enduring value of mentation that justifies our passing pleasures. If it were, given how few individuals choose to think deep thoughts, the lives of the vast majority of people would be pointless and vain. But this is elitist foolishness. If there is anything self-justifying, it is a good and satisfying life, even if it consists of little beyond consumption and work. Philosophers, devoted to thinking, charge shoppers

35. George Santayana, "Tradition and Practice," in *Animal Faith and Spiritual Life*, ed. John Lachs (New York: Appleton-Century-Crofts, 1967), p. 457.
36. Ibid., p. 458.
37. Ibid.

with superficiality. Rightly, the shoppers and drinkers have been too busy to reply.

Materialist and Idealist Countercharges

In the heat of controversy, fighting words tend to lose their meaning. "Christian" and "Muslim," for example, have come to signify a wide variety of beliefs and activities, as have such words as "communist" and "capitalist." In philosophy, "idealist" and "materialist," words with distinguished histories, have similarly lost their ability to designate precisely. Idealists may be of the stripe of Berkeley, maintaining that only perceptions and perceivers are real, or of the persuasion of Leibniz, arguing that the ultimate ingredients of all things are mind-substances or monads. Kantian "critical" idealists, however, assert that all but the sensuous manifold derives from human cognitive faculties, and Hegelian "absolute" idealists think they can show that the history of the world is simply the development of consciousness. There are even those, such as Fichte, who declare that idealism is the affirmation of human freedom and that those who reject it lack a self.

Similar, though perhaps less extensive, vagueness and ambiguity beset the word "materialism." The vast distance between Lucretius' conviction that atoms and the void exhaust the ingredients of reality and Marx's notion that ideas are but human reactions to prevailing economic—that is, "material"—conditions is neither suggested nor adequately traversed by using a single word. "Australian" materialism focusing on mind-brain identity and Santayana's materialism that takes an epiphenomenalist view of consciousness are incompatible, yet they are called by the same name. To say that Feuerbach, Haeckel, and Hobbes are all materialists gives no precise information about their positions.

In light of this terminological Tower of Babel, it is not surprising to find the claim that all materialists are really idealists and the counterclaim that idealists are latent materialists. One may be tempted to disregard such dialectical contortions, but to do so would be an error. A closer examination of the basis for asserting that everybody is a materialist or an idealist may actually help us get straight about what is at stake in making such wide generalizations.

In the last chapter of *Realm of Matter,* Santayana undertakes to show that although in official philosophy idealists differ sharply from materialists, they nevertheless tacitly subscribe to the fundamental tenets of their opponents. What are these tenets? Santayana identifies two: belief in the existence of a world independent of us and acknowledgment of the contingency of all things. Concerning the first of these, he says that if the idealist were to describe existence as it actually is, "this existence would still, for that very reason, remain outside of his mind and of his description."[38] Intelligent spirit, he asserts, "must assume the presence of an alien universe and must humbly explore its ways."[39] Concerning the second belief, he returns again and again to the "blind fertility"[40] of the world and asks, "Why, then, is any Idea manifested here and not there, perfectly or imperfectly, once, often, or not at all?"[41] The answer, he says, must be sought in the "pregnant and unfathomable"[42] propensities of material substance. But of course there is no ultimate answer to be found: whatever exists does so without reference to reason or the good.

These considerations on behalf of obliterating the distinction between idealism and materialism bring into focus Santayana's rather special conception of matter. His insistence on the centrality of materialism is Lucretian, though without the awkward atomism of that fine poet, in the sense that it is meant to purge the inventory of beings of all supernatural agents. The argument is simple: the material world, Santayana argues, is a spatiotemporal matrix continuous with our bodies. Every agent belongs in this world. If God and the Devil occupy positions of power in the field, they are material agencies who can affect us and who, in turn, are open to our influence. And indeed, God is presented as just such a being in the Old Testament. He tells the Israelites how to make the walls of Jericho come tumbling down and becomes angry and hurt when his orders are disobeyed.

Santayana can rightly say that his notion of matter is not any of the usual ones emphasizing atoms or other ultimate spatiotemporal realities. The reason is that matter, for him, is not a kind of being but a process permeating the farthest reaches of time and space that unites our animal bodies with the surrounding field of flux and power. Everyone is a materialist who acknowledges the everyday experience of the power of external events and the flowering of contingencies. The hungry idealist believes, with everyone else, that the food we eat does not cease to exist when it is no longer felt in the mouth, that the tragedies of life cannot be thought away, and that there are no magical agencies to change the propensities of the workaday world.

38. *RB*, p. 392.
39. Ibid., p. 398.
40. Ibid., p. 390.
41. Ibid., p. 387.
42. Ibid., p. 392.

Santayana's argument to show that even idealists are materialists is counterbalanced by Hegel's claim that materialists cannot avoid being idealists.[43] He says, "Every philosophy is essentially an idealism or at least has idealism for its principle."[44] Idealism, he declares, consists "in nothing else than in recognizing that the finite has no veritable being."[45] Hegel also presents two considerations to support his view. The first is the well-known argument that if we think that atoms or some other ultimate particles constitute the material world, we still only *think* this: the thought of matter is not matter but a thought.[46] This means that, try as we may, we can never escape the magic circle of consciousness.

Hegel's second argument is more complicated and more clearly Hegelian. The finite is the sensuous particular, he maintains, and materialists think they refer to these when they speak about atoms and matter. In reality, however, atoms, matter, and the water of Thales are not particulars but universals, because as general concepts referring to a potentially infinite collection of items they are infinite themselves. The hallmark of idealism is exalting the universal over the particular, and, unbeknownst to materialists, their theory, simply on account of being a theory stated in universal terms, is therefore a form of idealism. The only way to avoid this conclusion, Hegel avers, is to abjure the use of universals, which renders philosophers unintelligible and their "philosophies" unworthy of the name.[47]

What can we make of this remarkable controversy? The most obvious point is that Santayana's first commitment, to an independently existing world, is not enough to turn idealists into materialists. Just such steadfast realism characterized Peirce's system without his ever thinking that he had to give up his idealism. One can hold, quite consistently, that there is a world independent of all knowledge of it and that that world is nevertheless constituted by consciousness or sentience or monads. One can deny that to be is to be known and yet maintain, as Peirce did, that on the last analysis everything that exists is mind. Realism frequently accompanies materialism but does not imply it.

Hegel's first argument also fails to convince. There is no doubt that when we entertain the idea of matter we *think*, but that does not mean that we can

43. I am grateful to Michael Brodrick for calling my attention to this passage and how it relates to Santayana.

44. G. W. F. Hegel, *Science of Logic,* trans. A. V. Miller (Amherst, N.Y.: Humanity Books, 1969), pp. 154–55.

45. Ibid., p. 154.

46. Ibid., p. 155.

47. Ibid.

never get near something nonmental in our reflections. The magic of this argument of idealists was broken by G. E. Moore in his famous "Refutation of Idealism," in which he showed that the object of consciousness does not have to be, and in fact is not, something mental. Santayana rightly adopts this view and makes it a centerpiece of his account of essences, arguing that though they serve as the objects of consciousness, nothing about them suggests that they are mental in origin or nature.

One may suppose that Santayana's insistence on the contingency of the world and Hegel's glorification of the universal address altogether different issues. But, surprisingly perhaps, the two views converge on roughly the same problem and make the choice between idealism and materialism clearer and easier. Hegel maintains that thought and language operate exclusively with universals. The sensuous particular is the first thing sublated in *The Phenomenology of Spirit* where, in the section on sense certainty, Hegel asserts that no matter how much we want to get to the particular, we can never go beyond the universal. If he is right, the particular in its particularity is of no significance, and it takes only a moment of self-recognition for philosophers to realize that they are, and must be, idealists.

To say that only universals are intelligible and real means that in eating I consume food, or more specifically, steak. In the grander scheme of things, I belong to a state that, through its laws, gives structure and meaning to my life. My private dreams are matters of irrelevant contingency; what counts is the development of the human spirit, in the course of which I am likely to perish. But the death of the individual is of little moment so long as the universal aims of reason prevail. The ordinary and the everyday are below the regard of philosophers, who must keep their eyes on the grand patterns of history, from the perspective of which most everything seems necessary and the rest is dross.

What does such an idealism leave out? First, that the steak I eat was not long ago the living flesh of a particular animal; that the state gives no meaning to anyone's life; that my private dreams, though contingent, constitute my very being; that the death of the individual is no small matter to that individual who, in life and in death, has little use for the growth of spirit; that everything can seem necessary if we look at it from the standpoint of some chosen outcome; and that philosophers had better keep their eyes on the ground if they don't want to share the fate of Thales and fall into a pit.

One might object, however, that this does not address the fundamental claim that, in philosophy at least, the universal cannot be escaped. Perhaps so, but it points the way to a fuller answer. In fact, nothing is easier than to side-step the universal; we have only to quit talking. In action, *this* body crashes into *that;* in love, *this* person cares for *that;* in suffering, *these* foreign forces threaten *me.* Even if we think in terms of universals, we live as particulars in a world of particulars, staggering from crisis to crisis. We need no language to communicate our distress: feeling it ourselves and showing our predicament to others is enough for understanding and sympathy. Hegel is so taken with grand schemes and totalities that he forgets who we are.

Of course, Hegel did not forget who *he* was. He, like the rest of us, dealt with the details of daily life and weathered personal crises. These do not show up in his philosophy, for he is simply not interested in what we call "the human condition." Santayana's call, by contrast, is to attend to precisely this welter of facts. Of course, whether we attend to it or not, we are embroiled in fending off the contingencies of fortune. Santayana's philosophy of animal faith consists of identifying what we believe on the basis of what we do; that is the only way, he maintains, to stay close to the common sense or the "shrewd orthodoxy" of the human race. This is the foundation of Santayana's claim of the latent materialism of idealists. Since they act, as we do, taking into account the power of an external world in which everything is contingent, they must also believe that the world is just that way.

Does this make idealists materialists? Only in the limited sense of thinking of the world as a continuous field of action full of surprising, delightful, and dismaying events. The baffling question is why this obvious fact is devalued or denied by so many philosophers. In his daily life, Hegel did not think that sensuous particulars are unreal—he spent his days seeking and dodging them. Why, then, does his official philosophy disdain the world he in fact inhabits?

In the end, the question boils down to where philosophers are to cast their glance. Should they attend to the world as it exists in their neighborhood, displaying treacherous forces with which they must negotiate their survival, or should they look for the patterns of another world, barely adumbrated in the gritty details of individual life? This is the question of honesty in philosophy, a question no one has raised more vividly, more urgently, and more eloquently than George Santayana.

Animal Faith and Ontology

The rhetorical brilliance and philosophical energy of George Santayana's *Scepticism and Animal Faith* tends to blind readers to its profound complexity. The book presents itself as a single line of argument, collapsing all claims to knowledge through a skeptical reduction and then building them up again by means of an orderly deployment of the tenets of animal faith. Santayana is clear that the standard by which claims to knowledge are initially criticized and the standard by which they are reinstated differ from one another significantly. The skeptical reduction relies on the requirement that knowledge be indubitable presence. The symbolic beliefs substituted for the failed tenets of immediacy receive their sanction by contrast from "animal faith," that is, the confidence displayed by animals in their operations in the world. The first part of the book demonstrates the failure of the search for certainty, the second constructs an edifice of fallible beliefs.

Santayana's resolute skepticism yields a negative and two positive results. On the side of disappointment it demonstrates, better than such halfhearted skeptics as Descartes, that certain knowledge is beyond the capacity of human beings. Though negative, this conclusion is liberating: potentially at least, it terminates several thousand years of fruitless rationalist debate. On the side of promise, reduction to solipsism of the present moment leads Santayana to the discovery of essences and the invention of a new philosophical method. Essences are the immediate objects of consciousness, the *what* that appears after all beliefs are removed. Santayana characterizes them as eternally self-identical forms of definiteness. The new method of doing philosophy is that of animal faith, consisting of the identification of beliefs to which we tacitly consent through our actions.

One can embrace these two positive results without immediate contradiction, but they lead in different directions. Santayana does not examine their relationship and proceeds to use them as vital and mutually supporting elements of his system. Essences become the bedrock of which we can be certain, even though they convey no significant knowledge. Study of animal faith becomes the method by means of which the beliefs constituting the system are uncovered and justified. Santayana announces that he intends to build up his philosophy on the basis of the order of evidence, starting with minimal beliefs and proceeding from there to more complex and possibly more questionable propositions. Accordingly, he moves from the momentary appearance of essences to belief in their identity through time, in experience, in memory, in substance, in nature, and in truth. All these beliefs and more are supposed to be tacitly affirmed in action and justified by that fact.

This is a neat way of proceeding and is certain to satisfy orderly minds. Unfortunately, however, it is not the procedure proper to the philosophy of animal faith; strictly speaking, it is not even a marshalling of ideas in the order of evidence. The most compelling article of animal faith is that there are independently existing objects in space and time that we can affect, and not the attenuated thought that essences can achieve transtemporal identity. Moreover, arranging beliefs from the simple to the complex or from the less questionable to the more dubious is not lining them up in the order of evidence. Santayana himself admits that in the system of animal faith no prior proposition provides adequate evidence for embracing any subsequent one; belief in the transtemporal identity of essences is an element in our belief in experience, but not a reason for it. Ultimately, the only basis for believing any philosophical idea is that it is implicated in our actions.

When Santayana says that he will "consider what objects animal faith requires me to posit, and in what order,"[48] he does not seem to realize that although his justification of the beliefs he develops derives from animal faith, their order and reach are determined on the basis of starting with essences. A philosophy of animal faith, one honest in the sense that its tenets do not belie our actions, does not begin with essences; its point of departure is human agency situated in a space-time world. A philosophy that has its foundation in essences, on the other hand, is not a system of animal faith because eternal forms are at most distant and derivative objects in the causal continuum. That Santayana does not recognize this suggests failure to see the two distinct strains in his thought and the way they undermine his efforts to present a consistent and unified philosophical system.

For ease of reference, we might refer to the two strains as Santayana's philosophy of animal faith and his ontology. They are not immediately contradictory. Nothing in the ontology nullifies the claim that warrant for philosophical ideas must derive from action, and nothing in the philosophy of animal faith negates that essences are eternal or that matter is the source of all change. When these two sets of ideas are developed into philosophical systems, however, some of their consequences may prove incompatible. The philosophies of Berkeley and Leibniz, as an illustration, are not contradictory in their premises, yet when fully worked out they include some clashing sets of propositions. And even if, as is unlikely, incompatibilities can be avoided, the two conceptual frameworks pull the system that tries to accommodate them in opposite directions, introducing indecisions and ambiguities along the way.

We must credit Santayana's brilliant mind with inventing not one but two novel philosophies. He is due less admiration for failing to distinguish them and trying to combine the two into a single system. Had he kept them separate, he would have had a powerful naturalism built on the method of

48. *SAF,* p. 106.

animal faith and an interesting and in some respects very helpful ontology consisting, as he says, of categories "conspicuously different and worth distinguishing."[49] The naturalism would be vastly popular today because it can be worked up into an alternative to pragmatism and is in line with the temper of the times, and the ontology could be construed as a more playful, speculative enterprise the technical problems of which must not be allowed to interfere with its usefulness. As it is, unfortunately, mixing the philosophy of animal faith with the ontology has contributed to sinking both. Although there are traces of the idea of animal faith in all four volumes of *Realms of Being,* the emphasis on the ontology greatly outweighs the attention to it. The full development of the philosophy of animal faith remains a task for some enterprising young philosopher.

The confusions and ambiguities that beset the failure to distinguish the project of animal faith from that of ontology is nowhere clearer than in Santayana's treatment of matter. In his four-realm ontology, essences constitute an infinite plenum. They are the forms that serve as the properties of physical objects and the immediate objects of nonphysical thought. However, only a small subset of essences is embodied or envisaged in the world, and selectivity is the work of matter. Truth resides at the intersection of essence and matter, consisting of all the forms that receive actualization in the history of the world. "Spirit" is Santayana's word for consciousness, the light that makes for the possibility of knowledge, suffering, and joy. We encounter these four types of being everywhere; they constitute irreducibly different aspects of the world.

Viewed from the perspective of ontology, matter provides what essence cannot, namely the external relations of which existence consists. This function renders matter the other of essence, a force that, unaccountably, plunges eternal qualities and relations into the flow of time. Matter does for Santayana roughly what God does for Leibniz in creation: it selects for instantiation one from an infinite number of possible worlds. There is, however, a crucial difference. God chooses the *best* of all possible worlds whereas matter, being unconscious and hence unhampered by any consideration of value, acknowledges no principle and selects randomly.

What is the nature of matter? It has and can have no qualities or structure, for these are essences and thus cannot serve as that which wrenches essences out of their eternal slumber. The distance between essence and existence is infinite, which means that it takes God to span it. This has been the

49. Ibid., p. vi.

traditional point of the ontological proof of God's existence: in God's unique case, essence was supposed to include or imply existence. But Santayana does not accede to the hypothesis of an infinite being and thus he thinks the gap between essence and existence remains unbridged. No essence can give us a clue to what matter is or how it does its work; any nature we think we detect in its labors is but an impotent essence that cannot account for the instantiation of other essences.

The symbolic nature of cognition cannot help us here. Santayana does indeed hold that all knowledge is symbolic, but that just means that instead of being in direct contact with the essences envisaged or embodied in the world, we use other, relevant essences to reveal them. In such intellectual acts, there must be two sets of essences: those we use as symbols and those we wish to explore. The latter are missing in the case of wishing to learn about matter. Since matter has no essence, it offers nothing to cognize, no forms an apt symbol could articulate. Though we call it a force and speak of its selectivity, neither one of these essences properly belongs to it. Santayana's view comes close to Aristotle's idea of prime matter as the natureless source or ingredient of everything natural. There is not much one can do to comprehend this dark power. Santayana offers only a few metaphors as help, such as that of "the invisible wind which, sweeping for no reason over the field of essences, raises some of them into a cloud of dust: and that whirlwind we call existence,"[50] but these gestures promote little understanding.

The unavoidable ignorance should not surprise us because it is impossible to say much about the mystery of existence. Even calling it a mystery is summoning an essence to capture or symbolize not what is merely different but what is utterly other. The breakdown of intellect is a useful reminder of the arational contingency of the world, but it is of no help when one wants to write a book about the realm of matter. Accordingly, almost everything in *The Realm of Matter* concerns matter conceived as the natural world. This is a significantly different notion than the thin ontological idea we have discussed so far, and it is roughly equivalent to what Santayana normally calls "substance" or the combination of essence and matter in the ontological sense.

A close reading of *The Realm of Matter* makes it clear that the bulk of what Santayana says about the material world is appropriate only for matter as this is postulated by animal faith. As a faceless force, matter has neither indispensable nor presumable properties, and Santayana's attempt to describe the inner mechanism of the world in terms of forward and lateral tensions

50. George Santayana, *The Realm of Matter* (New York: Scribner's, 1930), p. 94. Hereafter *RM*.

cannot be read as an account of the selectivity of the principle of existence. Of all Santayana's works, this one comes closest to an account of the philosophy of animal faith. But, of course, it does not present a systematic development of this philosophy and leaves out a great deal of what it would likely say about human nature and our relation to the universe.

The eminent Santayana scholar Angus Kerr-Lawson and I have long disagreed concerning Santayana's idea of matter.[51] He champions the view that matter is identical with the natural world and is thus fully structured or formed. He rejects the ontological notion that matter is a featureless force responsible for existence. By contrast, I maintain that if matter is to count as one of Santayana's four realms of being, which is certainly his intention, it cannot *presuppose* any forms as conditions of its reality. As an ontological category, matter must serve as the condition of the actualization of essences and cannot therefore display actualized essences as the source of its agency.

There is of course an obvious counter to my claim of ontological purity. Truth is an admixture of matter and essence, the sum total of forms embodied in the history of the world, and for this reason it can be considered a derivative realm. Why should we not view matter as a mixed category also and read it as displaying all the essences embodied in the natural world? This would make matter, as Kerr-Lawson desires, essentially identical with substance or the natural world. There is a twofold answer to this, but it has unfortunately not been enough to convince Kerr-Lawson. The first part of the answer is that significant portions of the text simply do not support a mixed-category reading of matter. Santayana speaks of matter again and again as the formless other of essence. Further, if matter were reliant on essence, forms would gain absolute pre-eminence, which would lead, contrary to Santayana's deepest tendencies, to the revival of rationalism. It is precisely the irrationality of matter that safeguards his materialism and constitutes the hallmark of his thought.

On this much Kerr-Lawson and I must agree: a close study of his texts demonstrates that Santayana uses the word "matter" to indicate both the formless source of existence and "substance" or the material world.[52] But until now, neither one of us has been able to place this ambiguity in broader context and thereby render it intelligible. Focus on the two strains in Santayana's thought offers a possible explanation and thereby a resolution of our controversy. I advance it as an interesting and plausible hypothesis, directed not at

51. See Angus Kerr-Lawson, "Santayana on the Matter of Aristotle," *Transactions of the Charles Sanders Peirce Society* XXXIX, no. 3: pp. 349–71.
52. John Lachs, "Matter and Substance in the Philosophy of Santayana," *The Modern Schoolman* XLIV (November 1966): pp. 1–12.

taking anything away from the achievement of this great and greatly under-rated philosopher, but as a set of ideas that may make sense of some of those parts of his thought that are otherwise difficult to reconcile with the rest.

The hypothesis is that there are two tendencies in Santayana's philoso-phy: he wants to develop both a system of animal faith and a complete ontol-ogy. The two philosophical drives present the same objects in significantly different light. To animal faith, matter is simply the physical world that sur-rounds us and with which we interact. From the perspective of ontology, however, matter is a formless source of change and external relations. Neither idea has primacy over the other. Each fits in with a philosophical method and both express some of the same general philosophical inclinations. Because Santayana was not aware that he had two projects under way and because such words as "matter" are used in both, it was easy for him to overlook the ambiguity. He meant both what Kerr-Lawson and what I claimed that he did by "matter," and he failed to see the difference.

What can be said in favor of this hypothesis? Santayana's use of the word "matter" is unquestionably ambiguous. There are many places where he iden-tifies matter with "substance" or the physical world and provides a detailed account of its properties. In other places, however, he calls it an "unintelli-gible alloy"[53] "antithetical to essence altogether, and irrational."[54] This force of selective instantiation is "a surd, external to the essence which it may illustrate and irrelevant to it."[55] It raises some essences to an "insane emphasis," only to abandon them for no assignable reason. On this view, matter is such that "we cannot conceive it; not because our intellect by accident is inadequate, but because existence is intrinsically a surd."[56]

There is also ample evidence, adduced earlier in this chapter, that *Scepticism and Animal Faith* reveals two projects instead of one. Adopting only those beliefs we tacitly affirm in action is a wonderful antidote to the search for certainty and a hugely promising substitute for the profusion of unproductive philosophical methods that have been proposed. Although some of the propositions adopted on its basis have been criticized, ani-mal faith as a procedure of philosophical justification has never received the appraisal, and acclaim, it deserves. Part of the reason for this is that

53. *RM*, p. 82.
54. Ibid., p. 26.
55. George Santayana, *The Realm of Essence* (New York: Scribner's, 1927), pp. 109–10.
56. *RM*, p. 27.

Santayana submerges it in a sea of ontology and makes it appear to sanction such implausible views as the impotence of consciousness.

The ontology also has its deeply satisfying points, not least among them the exhilarating influence of recognizing the infinity of forms. This plenitude sets the mind free to think as it desires, without the noxious supposition that there is one and only one objective nature and order of things. One of the delicious ironies of Santayana's thought is that the infinity of his essences defeats the possibility of essentialism. Generic forms have no prerogatives over specific ones, implying that there are as many human natures as there are human beings or even life slices of which human histories consist. Nevertheless, this liberation is reined in by the unchangeable objectivity of truth also affirmed in the ontology, and it is framed by the ultimate indifference of matter to human values.

Clearly, both of Santayana's projects have a lot to be said for them. The problem is that he left the difference between them unrecognized and unreconciled. One of the virtues of my hypothesis is that it explains a variety of otherwise baffling facts, from the oddly unsatisfying structure of *Scepticism and Animal Faith* through why such implausible views as epiphenomenalism are attributed to the philosophy of animal faith and to why Santayana's use of such words as "matter" are ambiguous. It displays Santayana's philosophy not from the standpoint of its look as a completed edifice, but in order to identify its blueprint and materials. Conceptual architecture, the creation of elaborate systems of thought, is much more difficult and risky than raising tall buildings because its materials, ideas, are more volatile and richer in implication than steel and glass. That Santayana's skyscraper shows improvisation in its construction takes nothing away from its value as home address for the human mind.

What counts against my hypothesis? I will let my friends and trusted critics figure that out.

THE PERSONAL VALUE
AND SOCIAL USEFULNESS
OF PHILOSOPHY

I was born on July 17, 1934, in Budapest, Hungary. There was little in my family background to suggest a future in philosophy. My father was a lumberman and my mother, though a cultured woman, occupied herself primarily with taking care of our home. No one on either side of my family had gone to college.

Enduring daily bombings in the Second World War, the long Soviet siege of Budapest, and the subsequent Russian occupation provided ample opportunities for the development of latent reflective tendencies; nothing jolts one into thinking about life as effectively as the sight of gratuitous violence and sudden death. I started thinking about the evanescence of life and the uncontrollability of fortune even though I was only ten, and tried my hand at rendering my ideas, and my distress, in poetic form.

The "nationalization" of my father's small business by the communist government and my family's consequent passing without passports through two patrolled borders to flee Hungary created additional invitations to reflect. Immigration to Canada, and later to the United States, gave me a great deal of material for thought about language, differences among cultures, and the relations of individuals to their communities. I spent a year in a Canadian high school and then entered McGill University.

It was easy for philosophy to find me. My experiences predisposed me to be interested in momentous issues: I wanted to know about God, the meaning of life, and the right comportment toward death. I found working with ideas irresistibly attractive and wished to develop resources for effective reflection on human nature. At McGill, the only question I needed to ask was which of the many departments that vied for the attention of students dealt with the topics I wanted to investigate. Upon being told that it was philosophy, I signed up as a major.

McGill University offered me a thorough, historical introduction to philosophy. Although the faculty lacked high-profile publishers, it included a wealth of good scholars. Cecil Currie taught me Kant and exquisite attention to texts. Alastair McKinnon, whose love of Kierkegaard was contagious, engaged in a losing struggle to meet the department's absurd requirement that he teach logic. Raymond Klibansky, the scope of whose knowledge was legendary but whose thought was severely handicapped by excessive learning, set the highest standards for dealing with works in foreign languages and for mastery of the history of thought.

For a while at McGill, I thought I was called to the ministry. Reading Hume's *Dialogues* had a devastating effect on this career option; I could not imagine serving a God whose existence I was unable to demonstrate. It took me many years to realize that rational proofs don't need to play a significant role in one's religious life. I came to this conclusion partly as a result of listening to Paul Tillich in New Haven and discussing religion with John Burbidge, a fellow student, who later distinguished himself as a commentator on Hegel.

As philosophers must, I now reserve the right to interpret and to embrace the mysteries of Christianity in my own way. My recent writings attempt to articulate ways in which a commitment to transcendence can be combined with cold-eyed naturalism. My interest is in seeing religion as a celebration of life rather than as a consolation for its losses and our finitude.

The thought of George Santayana found me through the agency of T. G. Henderson, chair of the McGill department, who had written on Santayana with Whitehead and decided to teach *Scepticism and Animal Faith* in a senior seminar. I struggled for months to find the decisive weakness of the book, believing that in some fashion that kept eluding me, Santayana was clearly cheating.

I fought the book so hard that it became a part of my life. Both my master's thesis and my doctoral dissertation were focused on Santayana's philosophy of mind, and for perhaps ten years I may have been the only living epiphenomenalist in the world. The articles I published in the 1960s on this odd but permanently tempting theory did not attract much attention. When philosophers feel compelled to adopt the view, they seem to want to think through its ramifications each time anew, all on their own.

By tradition, McGill sent its philosophy graduates to Oxford; Charles Taylor, Storrs McCall, and Andre Gombay, among other good philosophers, followed this path. For me, going to Yale seemed more natural. In those years, Yale stood out as the one program that took metaphysics, the philosophy of religion, and the history of philosophy seriously. Paul Weiss boasted that Cornell's Max Black was sending his students to New Haven to point their fingers at him in amazement as he spoke of potentiality and God. Brand Blanshard was an unabashed rationalist, John Smith discussed Royce and the infinite, and both Northrop and Margenau championed international, humane, and generous philosophical ideas.

The department had been built by Charles Hendel, who was by the time I got there in rapid decline, and it impressed me and many others as exactly the kind of diversified community that could nurture many different kinds of souls. Yale students organized the University of Texas department on the pluralistic model in the early 1960s; Vanderbilt began to flourish as a Yale outpost, upholding the legitimacy of multiple philosophical methods, a little later.

Although John E. Smith was a shining presence at Yale, I took no courses with him, opting instead to learn analytic philosophy from Arthur Pap and Wilfrid Sellars, metaphysics from Paul Weiss, and judiciousness from Brand Blanshard. This work reinforced my native tendency to pluralism: the wide variety of philosophical styles and projects that flourished in the Yale department of the late 1950s convinced me that there is no royal road to philosophical insight. As if to demonstrate this belief, I chose Brand Blanshard and Wilfrid Sellars as codirectors of my dissertation.

The two of them could not have been further from each other in style and substance. They divided between them the conflicting features of a good thesis advisor: Blanshard was all encouragement and appreciation, Sellars all critical bite. I learned more from Sellars about technical philosophy, but much more from Blanshard about the virtues of loving kindness. I discovered in graduate school that I was not easily led. I listened eagerly to whatever opinions were offered, but retained the right to separate them into the potentially sound and the worthless or implausible.

I read Dewey in those years and found him terminally boring. I was expecting philosophy to reveal the hidden structure of reality, but all I found in Dewey was a description of our well-known everyday situation. It took me twenty years to realize that probably there are no arcane facts, and even if there were, philosophy would be ill-equipped to unearth them. Reading Dewey again helped me understand this.

A pounding sense of reality convinced me that language and conceptual discourse constitute a relatively superficial play on the surface of events. I have a profound appreciation of the power of language, but I cannot live in a world of chattering the way Groucho Marx and some contemporary philosophers appear able to do. I view preoccupation with language, including the famous "linguistic turn," as the folly of academics whose lives are consumed by conversation, glib repartee, and argument. I am too close to the silent people, to the nonverbal nonintellectuals who constitute the bulk of humankind, not to know the places where the stream of words dries up in the sands of feeling or the mountains of action.

The same sense of a vast nonhuman environment makes it impossible for me to accord special metaphysical prerogatives to thought, minds, or persons. Of course, all the information that reaches us about the world is conditioned by our cognitive apparatus. But this equipment consists of earth-bound organs, not transcendental faculties. Accordingly, it must be placed in the context of its biological role of sustaining our bodies and enabling us to find our way in the world.

Santayana taught me that the ultimate issue in philosophy and in every-day life is the health of one's soul. Unfortunately, he never experienced the joy of living in a supportive community and hence did not offer an account of the intricate links between the personal and the social. I learned to think these relationships by reading Royce and Dewey, but full experiential under-standing had to wait until I came to feel that my home was at Vanderbilt and in Nashville.

I was fortunate to begin my teaching at William & Mary. Eight years of attending to undergraduates made it impossible for me to forget that the ultimate purpose of teaching philosophy is to reach a broader audience. Mentoring graduate students who will carry on the task of reflection is a special joy, but in the end even that needs justification in terms of the good it will do future undergraduates and the community at large. Philosophy, unlike molecular biology, cannot be expected to uncover hidden facts. Even if it did, however, this arcane knowledge would demand application and practical results.

By the time I moved from William & Mary to Vanderbilt, I was ready to teach at the graduate level. I got lucky again: I found excellent students who worked hard and needed primarily guidance and encouragement to get on with their projects. Being by nature self-willed, I have great respect for the autonomy of others, which made it easy for me to support generations of graduate students in the pursuit of their ends. My tendency is to let them write on what they wish and derive instruction from how I suggest that they trim their luxuriant growths. The wide variety of their inquiries has broad-ened my interests and has in aggregate taught me much more than I was able to teach any one of them.

At Vanderbilt, I started teaching American philosophy. This led me to read Dewey again. The second time around, I thought he was scintillating and in many particulars clearly right. I expanded my reading and reflec-tion beyond Dewey to Peirce, James, Royce, and Mead, and more recently to Alain Locke, the personalists, Jane Addams, and a host of lesser-known or neglected thinkers. On certain topics, I now agree with the pragmatists, though on others I continue to be at a great distance from them.

I agree, for example, that thought is not an end in itself and that knowledge presupposes purposes. They are also on the right track in refusing to deal with decontextualized problems and in rejecting the separation of values from facts. But I cannot make myself believe that social construction goes all the way down. Somewhere there must be a residuum of things or facts on which the edifice of our thought is built.

This conviction is embodied in the distinction I draw between objective, choice-inclusive, and conventional facts. We enjoy significant leeway in creating order by classification out of the welter of reality that surrounds us. Every item in our experience is saturated with features and relations; the plausibility of our conceptual schemes varies with the similarities and the differences among objects we decide to stress. This means that there is an interplay between things and our choices in the creation of many of the facts we ordinarily, though mistakenly, consider objective elements of the world. Such choice-inclusive facts include those on which we base our social life, our psychological discernments, and our biology.

The interplay is possible only if there are elements of the world independent of our choices. We find these elements in the limits nature sets to our classifications and in the momentous difference between existence and nonexistence. We can characterize human beings, for example, as persons, as animals, and as gravitating bodies, but not as solar systems or two-volume dictionaries. Moreover, in whatever conceptual garb we dress beloved others, their death betokens our impotence; no construction or reconstruction of facts can lead them back to life.

Objective or independent facts provide, therefore, the ground on which or the material out of which we build the edifice of human knowledge. This conception allows for the post-Kantian claim that much of the world bears a human stamp, and yet retains the sanity of supposing that there are externally imposed limits to human creativity. It acknowledges a reconstructive element in much knowing and considerable flexibility in our schemes of classification without abandoning the idea of an independent reality that is at least somewhat determinate. It pays equal heed to Dewey's claim of the social construction of reality and Santayana's sense that we are surrounded by a deep and ancient world.

This approach to the role intelligent agents play in structuring the world has rich implications for our view of human nature. It enables us to distinguish a variety of natures all of which are legitimately human and can thereby serve as the philosophical underpinning of an ethics of toleration. Moreover, it deprives the word "natural" of its moral wallop, providing ample illustrations that widely divergent values and behaviors can be natural and, in their contexts, understandable.

The account of human natures that grows out of my theory of choice-inclusive facts is modestly original. I continue to work out its details and implications, and hope eventually to show its power in a single volume. I have already explored its bearing on issues in psychology, bioethics, and morality, but much more needs to be done to see it in full context and to assess both its social and its explanatory value.

The theory of choice-inclusive facts constitutes a good example of the sort of philosophical idea I value. I am interested in theories that have a close connection to concerns arising in the course of daily life. Ideas of great abstraction or generality hold little fascination for me. Though I think philosophical reflection is intrinsically delightful—it certainly constitutes one of the great pleasures of my life—its ultimate value is closely tied to the contribution it can make to the improvement of the human condition.

Another example of such a theory is my account of mediation, designed to explain the sources of manipulativeness, irresponsibility, and individual powerlessness in industrial societies. A complex condition besets people in the crowded modern world. In spite of the rhetoric of respect for individuals, they feel insignificant and disregarded. Working in large institutions, they view themselves as passive and not in control of their lives. The sense that they fail to author their own deeds makes them reluctant to take responsibility for them. The more tightly integrated their social world becomes, the more they experience their existence as fragmented and lacking in meaning.

The syndrome is well known; social philosophers identified it at least two hundred years ago. But they have not done well in explaining it and in prescribing remedies. They have called it "alienation" and supposed that it results from some social malformation or other. Their descriptions of the condition contained hidden value judgments, and their prescriptions for eliminating it were meant to move us in the direction of their favorite utopias.

My theory of mediation explains the syndrome without reference to any social malfunction. The values it relies on, moreover, are not mine, but belong to the people who live the fragmentation. Improvement must be measured, accordingly, by their reduced frustration and enhanced ability to view their actions as their own.

I believe that alienation is simply the price we pay for corporate existence, the cost of our comfort. Passivity, manipulativeness, and irresponsibility flow naturally from operating in vast mediated chains. In such institutions, the natural unity of actions is shattered: planning, doing, and enjoying/ suffering the consequences no longer reside in single individuals, but are distributed among different people. The condition is not fully curable, but we can improve things by taking steps to counterbalance the fragmentation. Openness within institutional chains, reducing the psychic distance between planners, doers, and sufferers, and giving a full hearing to all interested parties, among other strategies, help individuals understand their situations and accept them as appropriate.

Mediation theory has enabled me to see alienation phenomena with a clarity, and to understand them with a simplicity I have not found in more metaphysical and more tendentious accounts. Whenever I present these ideas to nonprofessionals, they need little effort to recognize their condition and apprehend its causes. Their responses bolster my confidence that the theory is on the right track.

A conviction underlying my views on several subjects is that solutions to problems tend not to be permanent or complete. Moreover, all improvements carry their own costs, which can readily grow into new problems needing solutions. If there are any permanent elements in the human condition, the inability to secure costless benefits is certainly one of them. Religious people call this "fallenness" or "original sin," which seems so pervasive that ironically, as I tried to show in a recent essay, it interferes even with formulating a viable notion of heaven and thus of a particularly desirable afterlife.

Believing in what our fervent hopes promise has, in any case, never much appealed to me. I think, on the contrary, that the dignity due our intelligence requires seeing the world and our prospects in it with unclouded eyes. Religion gets undue support from our desire to escape the pain of loss and the dread of death. Although they do not bring out the best in religion, I have no quarrel with such consolations. But philosophers should not need them. They ought to have the courage to look into the abyss alone and to face sudden tragedy and inevitable decline with equanimity born of joy or at least of understanding. I am prepared to be surprised to learn that we have a supernatural destiny, just as I am prepared to be surprised at seeing my neighbor win the lottery. But I don't consider buying tickets an investment.

Philosophers need courage also to leave the security and comfort of the university and address nonacademic people on issues of personal significance and public policy. As a profession in this country, we have reached a level of irrelevance that renders commercial presses reluctant to publish our work. The in-groupish abstraction of philosophy books makes them the butt of jokes. Yet the public is hungry for thoughtful commentaries on the affairs of life and for guidance on how to deal with its problems. The response to *In*

Love with Life showed me the magnitude of the need people experience for philosophical reflections on what they do and what befalls them. Meeting this need is a project of the greatest importance for philosophers. I continue to contribute to the effort as a writer and promoted it as chair of the Centennial Committee of the American Philosophical Association.

The Centennial Committee was created to celebrate the hundredth anniversary of the founding of the American Philosophical Association by calling attention to the personal value and social usefulness of philosophy. The committee's intention was to create an audience for philosophy and to encourage philosophers to address that audience. Both tasks are difficult, the first because academics have little public relations experience and the second because many colleagues lack the interest, the language, or the temperament to speak about matters beyond their technical specialties. Nevertheless, slow progress is possible, and I have now completed collecting money for a modest endowment so that this work can continue. I am unable to think of anything more important for the future of academic philosophy in this country than for it to become less academic.

Having had more than my share of bad instructors, I sought a job in education as a way to earn a living while I continued my philosophical reflections. I never suspected that I would develop a passion for teaching. Yet conveying to others the benefits I receive from philosophy has become a burning desire and a consuming activity in my life. I do it in a way that seems to some a form of witnessing, showing the immediate pertinence of philosophical ideas to my life.

Immense satisfaction attends my good fortune in having had the opportunity to make a contribution to the lives of thousands of undergraduates. I view this multitude of people as extended family: I keep in touch with as many of them as I can and cheer them on in the pursuit of their purposes. I hope philosophy has made a significant difference in their lives. I have also been fortunate in having launched more than sixty young philosophers on their careers. My relation to them is one of lifelong concern and support; helping them with their problems and careers is of vital importance to me. I think of these activities not as the result of optional commitments on my part, but as the continuing expressions of my philosophical beliefs.

People whose minds are energetic and who are interested in their fields find it easy to teach well. Bored instructors are boring and the self-absorbed fail to place themselves in the shoes of their students to see how what they say is received. Thinking before one's students' eyes—which means, among other things, teaching without notes—demonstrates what one expects them to do. Keeping in mind the interconnectedness of things and especially the relations of what one teaches to the ordinary concerns of students renders instruction vivid and, when things go well, even memorable.

By no means least, good teaching requires deep respect for students. The activity is hallowed because it enables one human being to contribute to the creation of another. Its chance of success is enhanced by embedding it in wider human relations; truly good teachers tend to offer caring companionship as the context of instruction. Perhaps all learning is imitation; if so, there is added reason for teachers to offer themselves as living examples to their students. Knowledge that makes little difference to the instructor's life is, in any case, rightly suspicious and may deserve to be disregarded by students.

The professionalization of the disciplines within the university has made teaching an activity to be minimized or, ideally, avoided. Although some colleges still prize good teaching and universities make a show of appreciating it, rewards in both employing institutions and in the profession closely track publication records. Tenure, promotion, increases in salary, reductions of teaching load, grants, fellowships, positions in professional organizations, and offers of employment depend in significant measure on research productivity. As a result, the primary loyalty of educators is no longer to the local institution and its students, but to the broader profession and peers who can write recommendations.

Philosophers play this game no less than do historians and literary scholars, generating vast quantities of publications of dubious quality. The price of this Niagara of printed words must be calculated in wasted trees, neglected students, and loss of devotion to the culture and values of the local university. The pluralists who revolted against the leadership of the American Philosophical Association in the late 1970s had professionalization as one of their grievances. Rhetorically, the revolt pitted analytic philosophers against Continentalists and pragmatists. But the causes of the conflict were deeper and more numerous than disagreement about philosophical method and style.

The APA was run by a self-perpetuating circle of people largely from elite East Coast graduate schools. They thought distinction gained through publications was evidence of ability to run the affairs of the association. They viewed teaching institutions as useful primarily for placing graduate students and allowed them neither representation nor influence in the inner councils of the APA. Eastern Division elections occurred in the business meeting of the annual convention, effectively disenfranchising those who were not on the program and could thus not have their way paid to distant cities. The revolt was at least as much a reaction against the professionalized exclusiveness of the APA as an attack on the dominance of analytic philosophy.

Santayana is surely right that one's philosophy must be honest in the double sense that one must act on what one believes and that one must not believe what one cannot enact. The demand to act on my principles made me join the pluralist revolt, and it explains my continuing efforts to open up the APA when I was elected to various offices in the organization. My decisions to remain at Vanderbilt also express my commitment to my students and to the university that has become my home. I have an intense loyalty to people near to me, which shows itself in my readiness to go to great lengths to promote their good. This attitude defines my relation to friends, students, and family.

I also believe that although some things matter intensely, many of the things that upset people are of little significance. This conviction has enabled me to live without condemning much and without the desire to run other people's lives. The connected respect for autonomy has been the source of great happiness for me; I attribute my deeply satisfying relations to my children to mutual acceptance built on caring and on love. Love and respect have also served as the foundation of the extraordinary relationship my wife and I enjoy, sharing all the tasks and pleasures of life, and reflecting and writing together on the problems of education.

In graduate school, we are taught to write with footnotes, evoking authority for all questionable claims. Philosophers, like other human beings, find it consoling to run with the crowd and embrace few views that are out of favor. Knowing the fickleness of public opinion, I could never make myself believe that the number of people holding a position has anything to do with its truth. Accordingly, I have learned to write without footnotes, and, when it seemed appropriate, I have embraced wildly unpopular, though not intrinsically outrageous, ideas.

I was for a while committed to epiphenomenalism, and I am one of few people insisting that philosophy imposes special demands on its practitioners. I do not have many companions in trying to do metaphysics as a nominalist, and am in a tiny minority in speaking bluntly on behalf of euthanasia. My recent work on moral progress places me at odds with the vast majority of my colleagues, who find it difficult to affirm the superiority of Western values. I have not hesitated to publicize my view that a particular university administration was corrupt and that its leader should resign. I view plain speaking about matters of significance not as a privilege of the educated but as the obligation of people who enjoy the benefits of tenure and professorship.

Pain and eventual loss appear to me inevitable elements of the human condition. Suffering and disappointment can be reduced by intelligent effort, but they cannot be erased. At the point where we run out of ameliorative strategies, graceful acceptance of whatever fate may throw our way makes for inner peace and better life. Such stoic equanimity has hardened me against disaster from an early age. I am careful, however, not to employ it too soon or as an alternative to energetic assault upon the world, rather than as a final stance after every effort has failed.

The consideration that in the end we die has disturbed my enjoyment of life just as little as the fate of the food I eat interferes with the delight of a good meal. Focusing on the destination makes us forget the pleasures of the road. Should the eventual extinction of the sun send cold shivers down our backs? Surely not; such issues simply do not matter. Untold generations will have basked in the light before the dark descends. Their joy redeems eventual disaster, or at least proves it irrelevant. Sometimes it is best to avert our gaze, for viewing matters in context liberates the mind, but seeing them in their ultimate outcome can paralyze it.

This is one of the many lessons of finitude we tend to forget. Descartes' view that the will is infinite needs to be supplemented by the observation that the mind finds it just as tempting to expand its scope beyond reasonable limits. If it is wise to look a week ahead, we suppose, it must be better to think of what may happen in a year or a decade. Reflecting on what is possible over an unlimited period of time generates foolish theories, baseless hopes, and unending worry. A part of the reason why animals live better than some humans is their freedom from ultimate concerns; they act as if they knew that finite creatures are not designed to deal with totality.

Up to a point, life gets better in proportion to our ability to get absorbed in the immediate. Failure rehearses memories, caution advises planning; future and past squeeze us from two sides until life becomes the hurried conversion of one into the other. Even universities have become beehives that leave little time for leisured reflection or the life-giving moments in which one can simply *be*. Few things are more difficult for our burdened and busy generation than focus and absorption. These are the gifts of immediacy, which is not some unconceptualized given but simply the present in whose movement we can feel at home. Momentary forgetfulness can liberate us from the future and the past and reveal the exhilarating beauty of whatever comes our way. This is transcendence—probably the only sort available to animals.

I am grateful for living at a time when I can contribute to the recovery of American philosophy, a great and greatly neglected national treasure. The founding of the Society for the Advancement of American Philosophy, in which I gladly participated, serves as clear evidence that just a few determined and persevering individuals can have a lasting effect on the future of a profession. We need to continue expanding the canon by adding to it thinkers whose work is excellent but who have, for one reason or another, been neglected over the years. I work on this, as I work on bringing philosophy into contact with a broader public, with the conviction that the energy and vision of a small band of people can make all the difference we need.

The activist element in American philosophy seems to fit well with my temperament. I value the sort of robust engagement with the world that evokes personal activity and aims at social improvement. Scholarly imprisonment in universities strikes me as intellectually narrowing and emotionally impoverishing. It tends to make professors timid and compliant souls. I am interested in ordinary people and their problems because I see myself as no different from them; I simply cannot take claims about aristocracy of any sort seriously.

As a consequence, I love philosophy for the perspectives it offers on human difficulties and the tools it provides for their resolution. Thinking about what I see around me is one of the great pleasures of my life. Acting on what I believe combines the satisfaction of being a whole person with the exhilaration of an experiment. Academics who live only in the mind sadden me. Their truncated existence denies them the robust delights and the sound common sense of those who engage the world on multiple levels. A sense of practical reality is a badly needed balance to excessive cerebration.

Philosophy needs balance no less than do philosophers. Even if it could attain the precision of some of the natural sciences, philosophy would need the literary imagination to complete its task. Its product is not disinterested knowledge but a relationship that changes lives. To establish that relationship, we need to communicate both discursive ideas and visions. The manner of the communication can be as important as its substance; people respond to what is well thought and well said. The magnificence of philosophical ideas and the excellence of their expression are, therefore, integrally connected to their effectiveness. My ideal has always been to write philosophy with the beauty and inventiveness of Mozart's music, though I would also like for my ideas to be true in some sense on which philosophers will never agree. The momentousness of this ideal is measured best by seeing how far I fall short of it.

In the end, I do not want to be absorbed in the technical details of the problems of philosophy. My passion is to deploy philosophy to deal with the important issues that face us as individuals, as a nation, and as members of the human race. There is a large public waiting anxiously for what philosophy can offer—for careful thinking, clear vision, and the intelligent examination of our values. That is where the future of philosophy lies, that is where American philosophy has always pointed us, and that is where I will continue to be.

JOHN LACHS is Centennial Professor of Philosophy at
Vanderbilt University.

LIBRARY
ELIZABETHTOWN COMMUNITY
& TECHNICAL COLLEGE
600 COLLEGE STREET RD
ELIZABETHTOWN, KY 42701

LIBRARY
ELIZABETHTOWN COMMUNITY
& TECHNICAL COLLEGE
600 COLLEGE STREET RD
ELIZABETHTOWN, KY 42701